Bes
in Central Colorado
around Aspen, Marble, Leadville,
Buena Vista and Crested Butte

Diane Greer

Boot Jockey Press

Best Hiking in Central Colorado
around Aspen, Marble, Leadville, Buena Vista and Crested Butte
1st Edition, February 2017

All photos and original maps by the author
Cover photo: Maroon Bells, Buckskin Pass (Hike 1)

Your Safety is Your Responsibility

The author assumes no responsibility for the safety of users of this guide. Outdoor recreational activities involve a certain degree of risk and are by their very nature potentially hazardous. It is not within the scope of this guide to allow for disclosure of all potential hazards and risks involved in outdoor activities. All participants in such activities must assume the responsibility of their own actions and safety.

Furthermore, the author has done her best to make sure the information in this guide is as accurate and useful as possible. However, things can change, trails get rerouted, road conditions change, regulations are modified, etc. Hikers using the information in this guide should make allowances for the possibility that it may not be correct.

Even the best guide and maps can't replace good judgment and common sense. Be prepared and cautious. You will have a safer and more enjoyable trip.

Table of Contents

Introduction

The Basecamps

Locator Map

Aspen Hikes

Marble Hikes

Crested Butte Hikes

Buena Vista Hikes

Leadville Hikes

Appendix Hikes

Best Day Hikes in Central Colorado around the towns of around Aspen, Marble, Leadville, Buena Vista and Crested Butte

An opinionated guide to the best day hikes in one of Colorado's best hiking areas, the Sawatch and Elk Mountains in Central Colorado.

If you're like me you love to hike and want to spend as much of your vacation and time off as possible on the trail. The challenge is weeding through all the online and hardcopy information to find the best hikes -- the trails that take you above timberline to beautiful mountain lakes nestled in dramatic cirques, to passes with see forever views and to glorious alpine meadows filled with wildflowers.

This opinionated guide does the work for you, choosing the best day hikes in one of Colorado's best hiking areas, the Sawatch and Elk Mountains around the towns of Aspen, Buena Vista, Crested Butte, Marble and Leadville. The Sawatch and Elk Mountain ranges offer the quintessential Rocky Mountain hiking experience with glacial valleys leading to vast alpine expanses sprinkled with glistening lakes amid soaring peaks. Three national forests and six wilderness areas protect this amazing landscape. Over 200 peaks rise above 13,000-ft. with 20 of the summits topping 14,000-ft.

The hikes in this guide, best hiked between mid-July and mid-September, appeal to hikers who like to go high and hike 6 to 12 miles a day. Trails gain between 900- to 3,500-ft in elevation. Many of the trails offer great intermediate turnaround points for those seeking shorter hikes. All are reached in less than an hour drive from five great base camps; Aspen, Buena Vista, Crested Butte, Marble and Leadville.

The base camps, each with its own distinct character, are linked by scenic drives traversing beautiful river valleys and crossing the high passes.

- Aspen to Leadville: The Top of the Rockies Byway between Aspen and Leadville, follows the narrow and winding CO-82 southeast through breathtaking scenery over 12,096-ft. Independence Pass to Twin Lakes, where it turns left (north) onto US-24 to Leadville. Along the way the route passing two of Colorado's tallest peaks, Mt Elbert (14,333-ft.) and Mt. Massive (14,421-ft.). Total Distance: 58.5 miles.

- Leadville to Buena Vista: To reach Buena Vista from Leadville, follow US-24 south for 34.5 miles on the Top of the Rockies Byway and Collegiate Peaks Byway. The scenic drive along the Collegiate Peaks Byway features wonderful views of the 14,000-ft. peaks of the Collegiate Peaks Wilderness rising above the valley floor to the west. Total Distance: 34-miles.

- Aspen to Marble and Crested Butte: From Aspen take CO-82 northwest through the scenic Roaring Fork Valley to Carbondale and turn left onto CO-133, which is the start of the West Elk Loop Byway. The route ascends the beautiful Crystal River Valley, passing County Road 3, the turnoff to

1

Marble. Beyond the turnoff the route climbs over McClure Pass (8,755-ft.), travels by the Paonia Reservoir and turns left (east) on the Kebler Pass Road (aka Gunnison County Road 12). The Kebler Pass Road, a good gravel road passable by passenger cars, climbs through beautiful forest to its namesake pass at 10,007-ft. before descending to Crested Butte: Total Distance: 104-miles.

- Crested Butte to Buena Vista: From Crested Butte head south on CO-135 to Almont and turn left (east) onto CO-742 toward the Taylor Park Reservoir. Just past the Reservoir, turn right onto the Cottonwood Pass Road (CO-209 that turns into CO-306). The route climbs over Cottonwood Pass (12,126-ft.) to Buena Vista, along the way enjoying great views of Taylor Park and the Collegiate Peaks. (Part of the Cottonwood Pass Road is a good gravel road passable by passenger cars.) Total Distance: 75.5-miles.

Aspen, Buena Vista, Crested Butte and Leadville offer accommodations, campgrounds, restaurants and bars catering to a wide range of budget levels. Groceries, outdoor stores and laundromats along with bakeries and internet cafes provide the essential services needed by outdoor travelers. Marble is a much smaller town with limited services.

The first section of this guide describes the towns, identifying local services, highlighting nearby attractions and suggesting activities for non-hiking/rainy days. The second section offers detailed trail descriptions with photos, maps and elevation profiles of the recommended hikes.

Extensive photo galleries and interactive maps with GPS tracks of the hikes are available on a companion website – www.hikingwalking.com.

I love feedback and would like to hear your opinion on how to improve the guide and the website. Obviously the selection of the best hikes is subjective, based on my personal opinion. Send an email (editor@hikingwalking.com) or post a comment on the website about the pros and cons of a particular hike or if you believe other hikes should be included in the "best of" list.

About the Ratings

All the hikes in this guide are recommended. That being said I want to make it easier for hikers to differentiate between trails. As such, hikes within a region are rated in relation to other hikes in the area. That does not mean that a hike rated as three stars is not worth doing. It just means if you only have a few days in a given area you might want to consider tackling the higher rated hikes first.

Abbreviations

RT – Round-Trip, NF – National

Aspen, Colorado

Location: On CO-82, 42 miles southeast of Glenwood Springs and 43 miles northwest of US-24 at Twin Lakes.

In the winter Aspen (7,908-ft.), located 41 miles southeast of Glenwood Springs and 200 miles southwest of Denver, is renowned as a world-class ski area and playground for the rich and famous. In the summer the town takes on a decidedly different personality. Fur coats and designer attire give way to hiking boots and tee shirts as scores of regular folks descend upon the town, attracted to the area's great recreational opportunities and amazing scenery.

The town lies nestled at the head of the Roaring Fork Valley, amid the incredible landscape of the Elk and Sawatch Mountain ranges and surrounded by the White River National Forest. Almost half of the adjacent forest is comprised of wilderness areas – the Maroon Bells/Snowmass, the Hunter-Fryingpan and the Collegiate Peaks. The forest is packed with excellent hiking trails leading over the areas high passes, traversing glorious wildflower-filled meadows and wandering past shimmering alpine lakes cradled beneath jagged peaks.

Around Town

Aspen, founded as a mining camp, prospered during the Colorado Silver Boom in the 1880's. By 1887 the town boasted a population of 15,000 and was considered one of the riches silver mining areas in the U.S. The wealth fueled a building boom. Jerome Wheeler built the Wheeler Opera House and the Hotel Jerome. Stately Victorian homes, banks and retail establishments sprung up around town.

The collapse of the silver market in 1893 lead to a half century of decline, reversed in the 1940's with the development of a ski resort on Aspen Mountain. Thankfully during the transformation of the town into a premier ski destination the town planner's decided to preserve its Victorian personality and historic structures.

History buffs will enjoy the Wheeler-Stallard House Museum, the former mansion of Jerome Wheeler that is now a museum displaying exhibits and artifacts from the Roaring Fork Valley. A tour of the Smuggler Mine, located on the slopes of Smuggler Mountain just north of town, is recommended for anyone who wants to learn about silver mining and the area's mining history. The guided tour takes guests into the mine and demonstrates hard rock mining techniques used in the late 19th century. Call (970) 925-2049 for more information.

If you like Victorian architecture take an evening stroll around the town's residential backstreets, north of Main Street, to see restored structures as well as recently built houses in keeping with the town's historic character. Another option is a visit to the Wheeler Opera House, restored to its former Victorian opulence. Today the opera house is a great place to hear music or see a movie after a hard day on the trail.

While you are exploring town be sure to visit the Hallam Lake Nature Center. The 25-acre preserve on the north side of town at 100 Puppy Smith Street features a nice half mile nature trail that winds through wetlands with stops at various observation decks. The Center is a good place to see birds and, in the evening, deer, fox and other mammals.

There are a number of nice walks that begin from town. The Rio Grande Trail, a hiking and biking trail starting behind the Post Office on Puppy Smith Street, is an easy and popular walk following the old Denver and Rio Grande Railroad bed along the Roaring Fork River with good views of the valley. The first 2-miles of the trail are paved.

Hunter Creek is another popular trail that begins north of downtown on Lone Pine Road. The moderate trail paralleling Hunter Creek gains 700-ft in the first mile and provides access to a number of other hiking trails in the area.

Nearby Attractions

The Maroon Bells Scenic Area, located 10 miles from Aspen up the Maroon Creek Road, is the premiere attraction in the area. Here you can explore a beautiful glacial valley surrounded by 14,000-ft. peaks. The center pieces of the valley are the iconic Maroon Bells, two maroon colored 14,000-ft peaks beautifully reflected in the crystalline waters of Maroon Lake.

Several short trails, the Maroon Lake Trail, the Falls Loop Trail, the Maroon Creek Trail and the Crater Lake trail, ranging from 1.0 to 3.6 miles wander around the scenic area's lakes and meadows, providing wonderful views of the surrounding peaks. Two longer trails, Buckskin Pass and West Maroon Pass, along with the popular Four Pass Loop backpacking trail start at the foot of Maroon Lake.

Vehicle access to the Maroon Bells is restricted during the summer to preserve the fragile ecosystem. From 9am-5pm shuttle buses leave from the Rubey Transit Center in downtown Aspen and the Aspen Highlands Village to the Maroon Bells. Check the bus schedule for departure times.

A visit to the ghost town of Ashcroft, located 11 miles south of Aspen on the Castle Creek Road, is another popular diversion on a day off or after a hike to Cathedral Lake or American Lake. The self-guided tour around the former mining town, once larger and more populated than Aspen, visits nine of the original buildings and the sites of several other structures. Plaques explain the history of the buildings and the area.

Another option for a day off is the scenic 20-mile drive to Independence Pass. Head southeast from Aspen on Highway 82, a narrow winding road leading to the pass at 12,096-ft. A paved trail leads from the parking area to a viewing platform at 12,135-ft. with panoramic views of the glacier-sculpted Colorado Rocky Mountain peaks. Along the way stop at the Grottos (8 mile up the road) and take a short hike past interesting rock formation and the ghost town of Independence (15 miles up the road). Independence was one of the first successful gold camps in the area. Today a self-guided tour leads past the few remaining log cabins at the site. Independence Pass can also be done in conjunction with a hike to Lost Man, Midway Pass or New York Creek.

Further afield is a day trip to Redstone in the Crystal River Valley, located 47 from Aspen. The main attraction is Redstone Castle, the 42 room estate of coal and steel baron John Cleveholm Osgood. Tours include the main rooms on the first level and a few of the bedrooms on the upper floors. After the tour take a walk around the quaint little mining village and visiting the antique shops, art galleries and handicraft boutiques.

Food, Lodging and Services

Aspen, its sister ski areas at Buttermilk Mountain, Aspen Highlands and Snowmass, and the fast growing down-valley towns of Basalt and Carbondale, provide a full complement of accommodations, restaurants, retail establishments and services to fit just about every budget.

With a few exceptions accommodation in Aspen, including condos, hotels and bed and breakfasts, are expensive. Better deals can be found in nearby Snowmass Village, Basalt, located 19 miles northwest of Aspen, or Carbondale, located 30 miles northwest of Aspen, which is home to a few of the chain hotels.

If you like to camp there are national forest campgrounds off Highway 82 and along the Maroon Creek Road. Campgrounds along the Maroon Creek Road are very popular. Advance reservations through recreation.gov are highly recommended.

Just about every kind of food imaginable is available in Aspen. Restaurants prices range from inexpensive to the outrageous. For those who prefer to cook for themselves there are two good grocery stores in town, Clark's Market at 300 Puppy Smith St. and City Market at 711 E. Cooper. The best baked goods can be found at Main Street Bakery and Café, 201 E Main Street, which is also a popular spot for breakfast. Satisfy your caffeine cravings at Ink! Coffee at 520 E. Durant and Victoria's Espresso at nearby 510 E Durant.

Hiking and backpacking supplies are available at Ute Mountaineering at 210 S. Galena. There is also a great hardware store, Alpine Ace Hardware, in the basement in the mall housing Clark's Market at 30 Puppy Smith St.

Internet access is available in the local coffee shops and also at the Public Library on Mill Street just north of Main. Explorer Booksellers, at 221 E Main, stocks area hiking books and maps along with a great selection of leisure reading.

The main visitor center in Aspen, open Monday – Friday, is located at 425 Rio Grande Place. The visitor center at the Wheeler Opera House, 320 East Hyman Ave, is open 7 days a week.

Marble, Colorado

Location: On County Road 3, 6 miles east of Colorado Hwy 133, 28 miles south of Carbondale, 58 miles southwest of Aspen and 86 miles northeast of Gunnison, CO.

Marble (7,956-ft.) is an authentic, unpretentious hamlet nestled in the upper Crystal River Valley surrounded by the tall peaks of the Maroon Bells-Snowmass and Raggeds Wilderness areas. The tiny town is a reminder of what Colorado use to be, a place of quiet natural beauty unspoiled by ski and condo developments.

Put away your cell phone before you get to town. It doesn't work here. The only pay phone is located next to the fire station, as is the only mail box. You'll not mind disconnecting from the outside world since you will be well occupied with your favorite outdoor activities; hiking, biking, fishing, four-wheeling and horseback riding – just to name a few.

Around Town

The town, founded in 1899, is famous for the Yule Marble Quarry located at an elevation of 9,500-ft. The quarry, first discovered in the late 1870's, produces a beautiful, flawless white marble that was used to build the Lincoln Memorial in 1916 and the Tomb of the Unknown Solider in 1931.

The quarry, and by extension, the town have seen goods days and bad. A marble fabrication mill, the largest of its kind at the time, was completely destroyed by an avalanche in 1912. After being rebuilt, a large portion of the mill was consumed by a large fire in 1925 resulting in its permanent closure. During World War II the quarry closed and its steel equipment was sold for scrap to support the war effort. With the closure Marble essentially became a ghost town.

Over the intervening years the quarry has gone through a number of owners that have opened and then closed the quarry a few times. RED Graniti, an Italian Company, now owns the quarry which is again producing marble. The quarry is closed to the public but visitors are allowed to explore the remains of the old mill, now the Marble Mill Site Park, located in town about 100 yards south of the fire station.

In the 1960's people began moving back to the area, lured by the natural beauty of the peaceful valley filled with outdoor recreation opportunities. Some of the town's historic buildings still stand and have been restored, such as the Marble School, Haxby House, St. Paul's Church, The William Parry House, the Town Hall and the Marble City Bank building, now the home of the Marble Hub and Coffee Bar. Note the Marble Hub serves as the visitor center and offers public wi-fi access. Take a stroll around town to see the original structures.

Nearby Attractions

The old mining road between Marble and Crystal City through Lead King Basin is now a popular and challenging jeep/ATV road. The 11-mile Lead King Basin loop is only recommended for experienced drivers. The Crystal Mill, a photogenic wood mill built in 1893, the ghost town of Crystal and the beautiful scenery are the main attractions along the route. I recommend allocating time for the beautiful hike to Geneva Lake if you drive the loop.

The Mill and the ghost town are located 6 miles east of Marble and are accessible in the summer via the very rocky one-lane road. You need a high clearance 4WD vehicle to reach the sites. Contact Crystal River Jeeps for a tour. Check on local conditions before setting out on your own. You can also walk to the sites along the road.

The Crystal River, which runs through the town of Marble, supports wild populations of brown, rainbow, cutthroat and brook trout along with mountain whitefish. Locals recommend fishing the stretch of the river above town. There is also public access to the river along CO Highway 133. Beaver Lake, located to the west of town, is stocked with trout and a favorite destination for families. Beautiful Geneva Lake is a beautiful backcountry lake for fishing, although it can be crowded with backpackers on the weekends in the summer.

Redstone, a former coal mining town along the banks of the Crystal River on CO Highway 133, is located eleven miles from Marble. The town has been preserved and restored and is now a delightful village of summer homes, antique shops, art galleries and handicraft boutiques. The main attraction is Redstone Castle, the 42 room estate of coal and steel baron John Cleveholm Osgood. Tours include the main rooms on the first level and a few of the bedrooms on the upper floors. There are some nice B&B's, lodges and cabins in town along with three restaurant and a general store.

Food, Lodging and Services

There is limited lodging in Marble. See the Marble Chamber of Commerce website for the current list of options. Slo Groovin' BBQ, at 101 W 1st Street, is the best and only place to eat, unless you are staying at a lodge offering dining services. Redstone, located 11 miles north from Marble along CO 133, offers a variety of accommodations and three restaurants. The Marble Grocery Store sells some basic items and is only open in the summer. There is also a small general store in Redstone. The nearest full-service grocery stores are in Carbondale, 28 miles north of CO Highway 133, and Paonia, 35 miles south on CO Highway 133.

The National Forest service operates the Bogan Flats Campground, located 1.5 miles up CO 3 (the road to Marble) along the Crystal River. Sites are reservable on recreation.gov. Mari Daes RV Park, at 215 W Park Street in

Marble, offers camping and RV sites with a bath house, electric and water hookups and a dump station.

For those with a high-clearance 4WD, there are Forest Service designated car camping sites along the jeep road to Crystal City.

Leadville, Colorado

Location: On US-24, 38 miles southwest of Vail and 34 miles north of Buena Vista

Leadville (10,152-ft.), a Victorian era mining town, lies in a high valley near the headwaters of the Arkansas River between the Sawatch and Mosquito Ranges, 38 miles southwest of Vail and 34 miles north of Buena Vista. The town is surrounded on three sides by the rugged peaks and glaciated valleys of the San Isabel National Forest. To the southwest of town Colorado's two tallest peaks, Mt Elbert (14,333-ft.) and Mt. Massive (14,421-ft.), fill the skyline.

Around Town

Leadville, a booming mining town during the 1880's Colorado gold rush, was once home to more than 30,000 residents with over 100 saloons, dance halls, gambling houses and brothels. Wealth from the mines fueled the construction of stores, hotels, opulent Victorian mansions and even an opera house.

During its heyday a colorful cast of characters passed through town. Future millionaires that got their start during the boom included Meyer Guggenheim, Marshall Fields and David May. The Tabor Opera House attracted the top talent of the day, featuring shows starring Harry Houdini, John Philip Sousa, Oscar Wilde and Sara Bernhardt. The infamous gunfighter and gambler Doc Holiday drifted to town after the OK Corral incident and was later convicted of attempted murder after unsuccessfully trying to kill Billy Allen in Hyman's Saloon.

Today, thanks to preservation efforts, an amazing amount of the town's rich history is still on display. Seventy square blocks of downtown Leadville have been designated a National Historic Landmark of Victorian architecture.

If you like Victorian era architecture take a walk along Harrison Ave, the town's main street, and the adjoining side street to see historic structures — some restored and other still in need of some TLC. A historic walking tour map is available at the local Chamber of Commerce, at 809 Harrison Street.

Mining enthusiast will want to stop at the National Mining Hall of Fame and Museum on 120 W. 9th Street. This excellent museum includes displays, photographs, artifacts and replicas showcasing American mining. Another interesting spot is the Matchless Mine and Baby Doe's Cabin, located 1.25 miles east on East 7th Street. The small museum tells the rags to riches to rags story of Horace Tabor and his second wife Baby Doe. Tabor struck it rich with the Matchless Silver Mine and became Leadville's first multi-millionaire.

A tour of the Hopemore Mine is well worth the time. The guided tour descends 600 feet down a vertical shaft and then takes an underground walking tour of the hard rock mine. Hopemore is located in Leadville's National Historic Mining District at 2921 County Road 1, reached by turning east on E 5th Street from US-24 (Harrison Ave). Call (719) 486-0301 for more information.

For a view of what life was like during the boom era visit the Healy House Museum and Dexter Cabin at 912 Harrison Street. Healy House, an 1878 Greek Revival clapboard house, features lavish Victorian furnishing collected in Leadville. The neighboring Dexter Cabin, built in 1879, is a surprising plush log cabin owned by a wealthy local.

Tour the Tabor Opera House, at 308 Harrison Street, and Horace Tabor's first Leadville home, located at 116 E. 5th Street, for different views of life during the mining boom. Victorian furniture along with relics from the mining era are also on display at the Heritage Museum on 102 E 9th Street.

Nearby Attractions

If you need a day off from hiking there is plenty to do around the Leadville area. The Turquoise Lake Recreation Area and the Twin Lakes Reservoir offer opportunities for fishing, boating, biking and picnicking. Take some time to wander the town's back streets to see the historic buildings. You can also take a boat trip or hike to Interlaken, an historic site preserving an old resort. To reach Turquoise Lake follow US-24 to the south end of town, turn west on County Road 4/McWethy Drive and then follow the signs to the lake. The Twin Lakes Reservoir is located south of Leadville at the intersection of US-24 and CO-82, the road to Independence Pass.

Extend the trip to Twin Lakes with a drive to Independence Pass at 12,095-ft, one of the highest paved passes in the United States. The drive features wonderful views of the surrounding peaks and forests. At the pass a paved trail leads from the parking area to a viewing platform at 12,135-ft. with panoramic views of the glacier-sculpted Colorado Rocky Mountain peaks. The pass is located on CO-82, 23.5 miles west of the intersection with US-24 and 38 miles from Leadville.

Seventeen miles north on US-24 are the remnants of Camp Hale, home of the 10th Mountain Division where troops were trained in Alpine and Nordic skiing and winter survival techniques during World War II. Historic plaques explaining the history of the camp and its construction are located throughout the site.

Just south of town is the Leadville National Fish Hatchery, the second oldest fish hatchery in existence. Visitors can tour the hatchery, feed the fish and learn about the fish production process. The Hatchery includes nature trails, a picnic area and playground. Reach the hatchery by driving south on

US-24 for about three miles beyond downtown and then turning west on CO-300. Follow CO-300 for 2.2 miles to the hatchery.

If you are interested in railroad history hike the easy Colorado Midland trail. The trail follows sections of the railroad bed of the first standard narrow gauge line to cross the Continental Divide and ends at the Hagerman Tunnel at 11,528-ft. Along the way the trail traverses pretty meadows, visits two small lakes and passes the remains of trestles, snow sheds, cuts through solid rock and the ruins of Douglass City, which housed immigrants that built the line.

Food, Lodging and Services

For a small town of just 2,600 people Leadville has a pretty good selection of lodging, restaurants and bars and retail shops. Accommodations range from small hotels and B&B's in historic buildings to more modern motels. There is also a reasonable selection of vacation rentals, cabins and condos around town.

If you prefer to camp there are large developed campgrounds at the Turquoise Lake Recreation Area and Twin Lakes Reservoir. The surrounding national forest also has plenty of established camping areas along with opportunities for dispersed camping.

The main tourist information center is located at 809 Harrison Ave. The Safeway at 1900 N Poplar St at the north end of town is well stocked with the basics for making a good meal. If you need reading material or a map check out the Book Mine at 522 Harrison Ave. The store specialized in books on local interest and history, recreation, geology and nature along with best seller and children's materials. Sawatch Backcountry, at 460 Harrison, stocks a wide range of outdoor gear and is staffed by friendly, enthusiastic people.

For a caffeine fix, baked goods and internet access check out City on a Hill at 508 Harrison. They also make breakfast and sandwiches for lunch.

Mountain Laundry, on 1707 N Poplar St, provides basic laundry facility and showers.

Buena Vista, Colorado

Location: *On US Highway 24, 34 miles south of Leadville, 24 miles north of Salida, 93 miles west of Colorado Springs and 122 miles southwest of Denver*

Buena Vista (7,954-ft.), which means beautiful view, truly lives up to its name. The town, between Leadville and Salida in the Upper Arkansas River valley, is surrounded by the high peaks of the San Isabel National Forest. The area boasts the highest concentration of summits over 14,000-ft. in Colorado and is home to the Arkansas River -- one of state's most popular whitewater rivers, making the town a magnet for outdoor enthusiasts.

From May through Labor Day rafters and kayakers descend on the town, floating the Arkansas River on outings ranging from exciting family rafting trips to hair-raising adventures through challenging rapids. By mid-summer hordes of peak baggers come to scale the area's 14,000-ft. summits. Hikers with less lofty goals discover glorious scenery along trails ascending beautiful valleys to shimmering alpine lakes and high passes surrounded by towering peaks in the Collegiate Peaks and Mt. Massive Wilderness areas.

Around Town

Buena Vista, pronounced "BEW-na Vista" by the local denizens, is a friendly, laid-back town of about 2,700-people. The town developed in the 1870's as a supply center for miners in the Upper Arkansas Valley and ranchers that had settled along the Arkansas River. By the 1880's construction of an ore sampling plant and smelter drew laborers to the town. Three railroads, the Denver, South Park & Pacific, the Denver & Rio Grande and the Midland ran through town, servicing mining communities to the north. Freight wagons lumbered along the town's streets carrying ore from the nearby mining town of St. Elmo. The influx of people created a boom and for a period the town was known for its raucous saloons, gambling halls and brothels.

As with other Colorado mining communities, the demise of the mining industry resulted in a downturn. For a time in the early 1900's the area was renowned for producing head lettuce. The lettuce boom lasted until 1948 when refrigerated railroad cars allowed West Coast lettuce growers to compete in the local markets. Today tourism, farming and ranching are the town's mainstays.

East Main Street, to the east of U.S. Highway 24, is the heart of town. Many of the buildings dating back to the late 1800's still stand and are now restaurants, coffee shops, boutiques and other businesses. At the east end of East Main Street, next to the Arkansas River, is River Park. The park includes a playground, dog park, skate park and disc golf course. A bridge across the Arkansas River provides access to mountain biking, hiking and horseback trails along the of the Midland Trail system.

The Barbara Whipple trail, actually several interconnecting trails on the east side of the Arkansas River, is a popular place for a short walk. The trail system is accessed from the bridge cross the Arkansas River in River Park. A 1.3 miles loop travels through pinon pines along a section of the Old Midland Railroad grade. Overlooks along the trail offer terrific views of the Collegiate Peaks to the west. Kiosks along the trail offer information about the area's history. The hike can be extended by combining segments of trail system. A map of the trail system is available at River Park.

Buena Vista's new downtown area, called South Main, was developed in conjunction with a world-class whitewater park for kayakers along the Arkansas River. The walkable, pedestrian friendly community incorporates residential, shopping, lodging and restaurants in a compact area adjacent to the park. Kayakers can literally suit up at home, shoulder their kayaks and walk to the park.

The growing area, which features live music during the summer weekends, is becoming quite popular with visitors. A trail runs north along the Whitewater Park to the town's River Park, creating a lovely place to watch kayaker and take a stroll in the evenings. From River Park it is an easy walk along East Main Street to the restaurants and shops in the older section of downtown. After wandering around downtown, pick a side street to loop back to South Main.

An interesting stop in town is the Buena Vista Heritage Museum, located in the old Court House at 506 East Main Street. The museum includes historic relics and exhibits explaining the town's history along with a large model train display.

Hikers looking for a day off will find plenty of companies specializing in rafting and kayaking trips along the Arkansas River. There are also lots of opportunities to learn Stand Up Paddle boarding. If you are already a veteran of the sport, Cottonwood Lake, along CO 306 to the east of town, is a great place to paddle and enjoy the beautiful scenery. SUP veterans looking for thrills will have fun paddling through the water features in the Whitewater Park.

If you are looking for something different to do in the evening, check out what is playing at the Comanche Drive-In Theatre. While waiting for the movie to start enjoy the great views of the Collegiate Peaks. Bring cash, no credit or debit cards accepted. The drive-in is located three miles west of Buena Vista along CO 306.

Nearby Attractions

In addition to whitewater sports, there are plenty of things to do if you want to take a day off from hiking. A nice day can be spent combining a trip to Twin Lakes and Independence Pass (12,095-ft.) on the Continental Divide, one of the highest passes in the U.S. To reach Twin Lakes drive north on U.S. 24 for 19.2 miles and and turn left (west) on CO 82 W, aka the "Top of the Rockies Scenic Byway." Follow CO 82 west for 6.3 miles along the north shore of Twin Lakes to the town of Twin Lakes, located on the north side of the highway beneath Mt. Elbert, Colorado's highest peak. Take some time to wander the town's back streets to see the historic buildings. You can also take a boat trip or hike to Interlaken, an historic site preserving an old resort.

When you are done visiting Twin Lakes, continue west on CO 82 to Independence Pass (23.5 miles west of the intersection with US 24). The drive features views of the surrounding mountains and forests. At the pass a short paved trail leads to an overlook with incredible panoramic views of the surrounding peaks.

Another nice destination is Cottonwood Pass (12,126-ft.). From the traffic light on East Main Street and CO 306, head west on CO 306 for 18 miles to the pass with great views of the Sawatch Range, the Collegiate Peaks and Taylor Park Reservoir. The trip can be combined with a half day hike to Ptarmigan Lake.

If you like ghost towns take a scenic drive up Chalk Creek Canyon to St. Elmo, once home to over 1,000 people during the area's mining boom. Stroll around the site to see many of the town's original building, which have been preserved. To reach St. Elmo drive south on US 24 for 8 miles and turn right (west) on scenic County Road 162/Chalk Creek Road at Northrop. The paved road eventually turns to gravel, reaching the town in 15.8 miles.

The ghost towns of Vicksburg and Winfield are located 9 miles and 12 miles (respectively) up the scenic Clear Creek Reservoir Road/County Road 390. At its peak in the 1880's, the mining community of Vicksburg housed 700 people and had 40 buildings including two saloons, two billiard halls, two hotels, a boarding house and a blacksmith shop. Some of the original cabins are still occupied in the summer. Winfield in 1890 boasted a population of 1,500. Both towns, maintained by the Chaffee County Historic Society, include nicely preserved structures and are listed on the National Register of Historic Places.

Fishermen and boaters might want to stop at the Clear Creek Reservoir on the way to Vicksburg and Winfield. The lake offer excellent fishing for rainbow, cutthroat and brown trout along with tiger muskies and kokanee salmon. Twin Lakes Reservoir is another great place to catch trout. The Gold Medal Waters along the Arkansas River offers great fishing for brown and rainbow trout. Cottonwood Creek along CR 306 is another favorite of local fishermen.

A trip to Salida is a good option for a rainy day. The small town, 24 miles south of Buena Vista along US 285, is home to a thriving artist community. Artist-galleries, along with restaurants and other retail venues, line the streets in the town's historic district.

A visit to Leadville is another great choice for a rainy day. The town includes an interesting mining museum, historic houses and mine tours. See the Leadville section of this guide for more information.

Food, Lodging and Services

Buena Vista offers a good selection of accommodations, a nice variety of restaurants and the basic services required by outdoor recreationalists. You might want to start at the Buena Vista Visitor Center at 343 US Highway 24 (east side of the highway and south of E Main Street) to pick up maps and other local information.

Lodging includes hotels, motels, B&B's, vacation rentals, cabins, RV parks and campgrounds. There are two large campgrounds in the San Isabel National Forest: the Collegiate Peaks campground, with sites reserved through recreation.gov, and the Cottonwood Lake Campground (first come, first served). Both campgrounds are located along CO 306.

Other campgrounds include sites at Chalk Creek Canyon, Chalk Creek Lake and Winfield. Nice dispersed campsites are located along the Clear

Creek Reservoir Road / CR 390. See the Salida Ranger District Camping page on the San Isabel National Forest website for more information.

Restaurants, cafes and coffee shops vary from fast food joints along US Highway 24 to great local spots like the Simple Eatery at 402 E Main, Rock House Kitchen at 421 E Main and the Eddyline at 926 S Main. For a caffeine fix and breakfast I recommend the Buena Vista Roastery at 409 E Main. A nice grocery store, City Market, is located at 438 US Highway 24, on the west side of the highway south of E Main Street.

Hiking and backpacking supplies are available at The Trailhead at 402 E Main. Colorado Kayaks at 327 E Main sells and rents paddleboards, kayaks, rafts and all the accessories you need for a whitewater adventure. Fishermen in need of supplies and advice should stop at ArkAnglers at 517 South Highway 24.

Crested Butte, Colorado

Location: On CO 135, 28 miles north of Gunnison and 92 miles northeast of Montrose

Crested Butte (8,885-ft.), located 28 miles north of Gunnison, is renowned for skiing in the winter and mountain biking in the summer. What many people don't realize is the town is also a great basecamp for hikers with plenty of scenic trails in the surrounding Elk Mountains, home to the West Elk, Raggeds and Maroon Bells-Snowmass Wilderness areas. As an added bonus, during the height of the summer the alpine meadows of the high country are awash in an amazing display of wildflowers, considered by many to be the best in the state.

Around Town

Crested Butte got its start in the 1880's as a supply center for nearby silver mines but soon found it was sitting atop extensive coal deposits. At the turn of the century when other Colorado mining towns were in decline, the town survived thanks to coal and coke production. Coal kept the economy going until the early 50's when the mines started to close.

The town experienced a reversal of fortunes when a ski resort was constructed on the slopes of town's namesake mountain, Crested Butte (12,162-ft.), in 1961. Developers moved in, building modern hotels and condos, eventually turning the area around the base of the mountain into a world class ski resort. The community centered around the resort incorporated as a separate town called Mt. Crested Butte in 1974.

That same year a large portion of the town of Crested Butte was listed on the National Register of Historic Places, leading to the preservation and restoration of the town's Victorian-era buildings. New buildings in the district are constructed in keeping with the historic architectural style.

With the ski resort development concentrated in Mt. Crested Butte, the town of Crested Butte has retained its small town western atmosphere accented with a young, laid-back vibe. Shops, restaurants and bars now occupy the colorful Victorian buildings along Elk Ave, the town's main drag, and the adjacent side streets. Studios of artists drawn to the town are found throughout the area.

The historic district is a great place to take a stroll and admire the Victorian architecture while browsing the town's eclectic collection of retail establishments. Benches positioned throughout the downtown provide perches for relaxing and watching the local scene.

While strolling around town stop by the Crest Butte Visitor's center at 601 Elk Ave (at the corner of 6th Street) to pick-up maps and other useful information. Visit the Crested Butte Mountain Heritage Museum, at 331 Elk Avenue (at the corner of 4th Street), to learn about the area's history.

For a bird's-eye view of the area ride the Silver Queen lift from the base area at the ski resort to the top station at 11,340-ft. From there a very steep 2.6 mile round-trip hike leads to the summit of Crested Butte (12,162-ft.). Panoramic views from the top encompass the Elk Mountains, the surrounding valleys and the town. The ski resort is reached by driving 4 miles north on 6th Street, which turns into the Gothic Road.

Diehards can walk all the way to the top of the mountain on various trails. Get a map at the ski area to see the routes, such as the Westside and Columbine trails, that ascend to the top station for the Red Lady chairlift, and then follow the road to the summit.

Crested Butte, dubbed the Wildflower Capitol of Colorado, is ablaze with wildflowers throughout much of the summer. Where to see the best flowers changes as the summer progresses, moving from the lower valleys near town to the high country. Some of my favorite trails for seeing wildflowers are; Beckwith Pass, Rustler Gulch, Oh Be Joyful, the East Fork valley along the Frigid Air Pass and West Maroon Pass trails, North Pole Basin and Brush Creek (described below). The timing of the wildflower displays will vary by year. Check at the visitor to center to find the best places to see wildflowers while you are visiting the area.

Wildflower enthusiasts should check out the annual Crested Butte Wildflower Festival, typically scheduled in early to mid-July. The celebration of blossoms includes tours, workshops and hikes all geared to viewing and learning about wildflowers.

Try the Brush Creek/East River trail if you are looking for an easy walk near town with great wildflowers. The 4.5 miles round-trip hike travels up the East River Valley on an old road with terrific views of the East River and White Rock Mountain. From downtown drive 2 miles south on Colorado 135 and turn left (northeast) on the Brush Creek Road/County Road 738. Follow the road to the end of the pavement, about 1.9 miles, and park at the trailhead on the left (north) side of the road.

Mountain bikers will want to head to the Evolution Bike Park at the ski area. The park offers a variety of trails for all skill levels. During the summer the Red Lady and Silver Queen lifts whisks bikers up to the top stations where several single track trails descend the mountain. Overall Crested Butte and the surrounding area offer over 700 miles of single track trails. Stop by the visitor center or one of the bike shops in town for maps and more information.

During the summer it seems as if there are more bikes than cars in Crested Butte. In addition to the Bike Park and single track trails, you will see bikers on the dirt roads that crisscross the area's backcountry. Be considerate and share the road. Get a map at the Chamber of Commerce so you know which trails bikers frequent. To avoid bikes on the trail, stick with the trails in wilderness areas where bikes are not permitted.

Nearby Attractions

A trip to Gunnison, 27 miles south of Crested Butte on CO 135, is a good option for a rainy day. The western town features the Gunnison Pioneer Museum. The five acre property includes 16 historic buildings, a train exhibit with a depot and a Denver & Rio Grande Narrow Gauge train and an excellent collection of antique cars.

Curecanti National Recreation Area is another good rainy day option. To reach the area drive south on CO 135 for 27 miles to Gunnison and then turn left (west) on US 50 W for 9 miles to the beginning of the Blue Mesa Reservoir. Continue west on US 50 along the shore of the reservoir to the Elk Visitor Center (16 miles from Gunnison). Here you can pick-up literature on short hikes, fishing and other activities. Note: Boat tours on the reservoir need to be scheduled in advance. See the website for more information.

Continuing along Highway 50 will lead to the turnoff to the Black Canyon of the Gunnison National Park. To reach the Park from the Elk Creek Visitor Center in Curecanti, drive west on US 50 for 41.3 miles and turn right (north) on CO 347 N. Follow CO 347 north for 7.0 miles to the South Rim of the canyon.

The Kebler Pass Road is a popular scenic drive in the area, especially in the fall when the aspen are turning. The 31-mile drive over Kebler Pass (10,007-ft.) offers great views of the West Elk Mountains and the Ruby Range. In Crested Butte, head west on Elk Ave and turn left (south) on 1st Street. Follow 1st Street for two blocks and then turn right (west) on Whiterock Avenue, which turns into the Kebler Pass Road/CO 12. The road ends at Highway 133, just south of the Paonia Reservoir. At the highway, simply turn around and return to Crested Butte. I recommend combining the drive with a hike to Beckwith Pass.

Alternatively, drive over Kebler Pass and turn right (north) on CO 133 N, following the road for 26 miles to Redstone in the Crystal River Valley. The main attraction is Redstone Castle, the 42 room estate of coal and steel baron John Cleveholm Osgood. Tours include the main rooms on the first level and a few of the bedrooms on the upper floors. After the tour take a walk around the quaint little mining village and visit the antique shops, art galleries and handicraft boutiques.

Food, Lodging and Services

Crested Butte and Mt. Crested Butte offer a variety of accommodations, restaurants and retail establishments to fit a range of budgets. There are a number of small lodges, inns and B&B's in Crested Butte. A larger selection of hotels and vacation rentals are available at the ski resort. See the local Chamber of Commerce website for a complete listing of options.

If you would like to camp in the nearby Gunnison National Forest, check out the Gothic Campground located 9 miles up the Gothic Road (6th Street). There is a main campground and then a number of individual sites to the north off the Gothic Road. Sites are first come-first serve. Another nice option is the Lake Irwin Campground, reservable on recreation.gov. Drive west on the Kebler Pass Road for 5 miles and then turn right (north) on Forest Road 826. The campground is 2 miles up the road. Further afield are the National Forest campgrounds along the Taylor Canyon road.

At large camping is allowed along the Slate River Road, two to three miles up the road. Avoid areas marked as private property along the road. Car camping sites are also located along the Brush Creek Road. Check at the visitor center for more options. If you have an RV, the Crested Butte RV Resort is the only game in town if you want hook-ups.

The town of Crested Butte offers the best selection of restaurants. Most are located along Elk Avenue and the adjacent side streets. There are some restaurants around the ski resort, not all are open during the summer. Be sure to check. For a coffee fix I recommend Camp 4 Coffee, on 4th Street to the south of Elk Ave, and First Ascent Coffee Roaster, at 21 Elk Ave (west end of the town). For groceries visit Clark's Market on 5th Street at Bellview Ave.

List of Hikes and Locator Maps
Hikes with distances and difficulty rating

Map Codes: WLM - Western Locator Map, NELM - Northeastern Locator Map and SELM - Southeastern Locator Map

Aspen Hikes
1. Buckskin Pass: 3.4 - 9.2 miles (RT), strenuous,WLM
2. Electric Pass: 9.2 miles (RT), very strenuous, WLM
3. Cathedral Lake: 5.6 miles (RT), strenuous, WLM
4. Four Pass Loop: 26.4 miles (loop), strenuous, WLM
5. Capitol Lake: 12.8 miles (RT), strenuous, WLM
6. West Maroon Pass: 3.4 - 13.0 miles (RT), strenuous, WLM
7. Lost Man: 9.6 (RT) or 8.8 miles (one way), moderate, NELM
8. Lyle and Mormon Lakes: 5.8 miles (RT), moderate, NELM
9. Midway Pass: 7.8 miles (RT), moderately-strenuous, NELM
10. West Snowmass Pass: 12.4 miles (RT), strenuous, WLM
11. New York Creek: 8.2 miles (RT), moderately-strenuous, NELM
12. Willow Pass and Lake: 9.4 - 12.2 miles (RT), strenuous, WLM
13. Hell Roaring:5.4 miles (RT), moderate, WLM
14. American Lake: 6.4 miles (RT), moderately-strenuous, WLM
15. Thomas Lakes: 8.2 miles (RT), moderate, WLM
16. Josephine Lake: 7.7 - 8.0 miles (RT), moderately-strenuous, NELM

Marble Hikes
17. Geneva Lake: 4.2 miles (RT), moderate, WLM
18. Avalanche Pass: 7.4 miles (RT), strenuous, WLM
19. Anthracite Pass: 2.5 - 6.8 miles (RT), moderate, WLM
20. Raspberry Creek Loop: 9.4 miles (RT), strenuous, WLM

Crested Butte Hikes
21. Frigid Air Pass: 9.6 miles (RT), moderately-strenuous, WLM
22. North Pole Basin: 7.0 miles (RT), moderately-strenuous, WLM
23. West Maroon Pass from Crested Butte: 7.8 miles (RT), moderately-strenuous, WLM
24. Oh Be Joyful and Blue Lake: 13.2 miles (RT), moderately-strenuous, WLM
25. Yule Pass: 4.9 miles (RT), easy-moderate, WLM
26. Rustler Gulch: 7.4 - 9.2 miles (RT), moderate, WLM
27. Frigid Air and Hasley Pass: 7.8 - 9.6 miles (Loop), moderately-strenuous, WLM
28. Beckwith Pass via Cliff Creek: 4.7 - 9.4 miles (RT), moderate, WLM

Buena Vista Hikes

29. Browns Pass via Denny Creek: 7.6 - 10.2 miles (RT), moderately-strenuous, SELM

30. Lake Ann: 6.6 - 12.0 miles (RT), moderate, SELM

31. Bear Lake: 11.0 miles (RT), moderately-strenuous, SELM

32. Missouri Gulch/Elkhead Pass: 9.0 miles (RT), strenuous, SELM

33. Ptarmigan Lake: 6.2 - 6.8 miles (RT), moderate, SELM

34. North Fork Lake Creek: 8.1 miles (RT), moderately-strenuous, NELM

35. Browns Lake: 5.8 - 12.0 miles (RT), moderately-strenuous, SELM

36. Interlaken: 4.7 miles (RT), easy, NELM

37. The 14ers, SELM
    a. Huron Peak: 6.5 - 10.5 miles (RT), very strenuous
    b. Mt. Belford: 8.0 miles (RT), very strenuous
    c. Mt. Yale: 8.9 miles (RT), very strenuous
    d. Mt. Harvard: 13.6 miles (RT), very strenuous

Leadville Hikes

38. Fancy Pass - Missouri Pass: 8.1 miles (RT), moderately-strenuous, NELM

39. Missouri Lakes and Pass: 7.1 miles (RT), moderately-strenuous, NELM

40. Native Lake/Highline Trail: 4.6 - 11.2 miles, moderately-strenuous, NELM

41. Windsor Lake: 2.2 miles (RT), strenuous, NELM

42. Colorado Midland: 6.0 - 7.0 miles (RT), easy-moderate, NELM

Abbreviation: RT - round trip

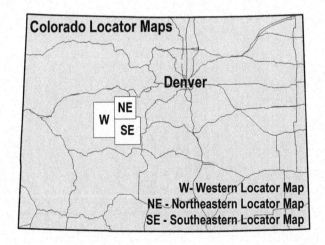

Western Locator Map

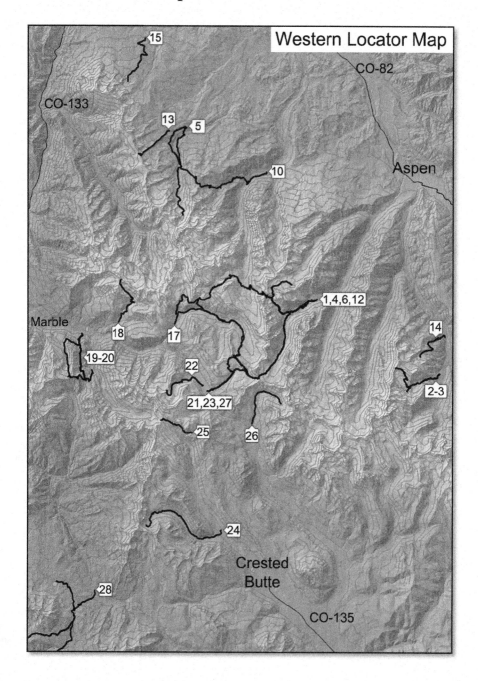

Northeastern Locator Map

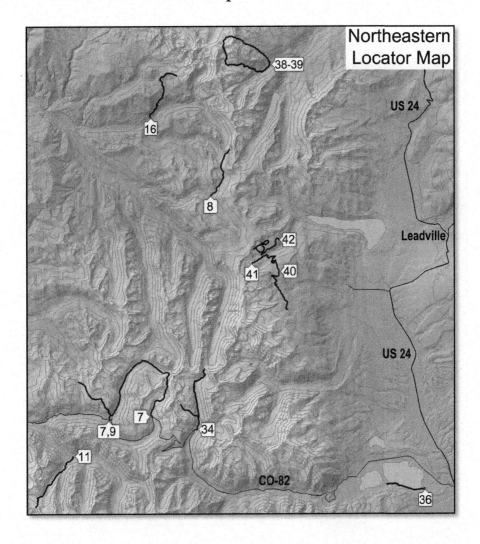

Southeastern Locator Map

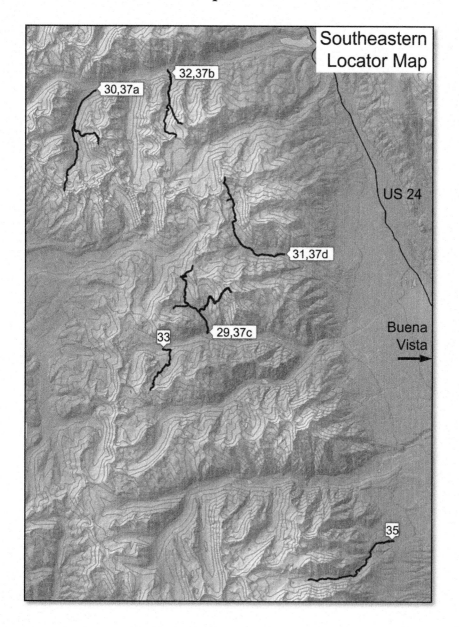

1. Buckskin Pass ★★★★★

Distance: 3.4 - 9.2 miles (RT)

This popular trail climbs to a 12,462-ft. pass with panoramic views of the 14,000-ft. peaks towering above the heart of the Maroon Bells-Snowmass Wilderness. Visual delights along the trail include lofty peaks, two stunning alpine lakes and beautiful alpine meadows.

Distance: 3.4 miles (RT) Crater Lake
9.2 miles (RT) Buckskin Pass
Elevation: 9,580-ft. at Trailhead
10,076-ft. Crater Lake
12,462-ft. Buckskin Pass
Elevation Gain: 496-ft. Crater Lake
2,882-ft. Buckskin Pass
Difficulty: strenuous

Basecamp: Aspen
Area: Maroon-Snowmass Wilderness, White River NF
Best Season: July - September
USGS Map(s): Maroon Bells

Why Hike Buckskin Pass

If I only had time for one hike in the Aspen area I'd choose Buckskin Pass. The hike features spectacular views of the Maroon Bell and Pyramid Peak, wanders by two beautiful lakes, traverses gorgeous alpine meadows and ends at a dramatic pass.

From the pass stunning views extend west to a sea of granite pinnacles. Hagerman Peak and Snowmass Mountain (14,092-ft.) tower above Snowmass Lake. Rugged Capitol Peak (14,130-ft.) and Mount Daly rise to the northwest of Snowmass Mountain. Pyramid Peak (14,018-ft.) and a jagged ridgeline of 13,000-ft. peaks dominate the skyline to the east while the Sleeping Sexton and Maroon Bells rise above the ridge to the south.

Be forewarned you will not be alone on this popular hike. My advice is to get an early start so you can enjoy a degree of solitude at the pass, have plenty of time to soak in the scenery and then descend before the onset of afternoon thunderstorm, a common occurrence in the Rockies.

Trailhead to Crater Lake/West Maroon Junction

Trailhead to Crater Lake/West Maroon Junction
Distance from Trailhead: 3.4 miles (RT)
Ending/Highest Elevation: 10,076-ft.
Elevation Gain: 496-ft.

Few trails can surpass the stunning views from the start of the Buckskin Pass hike at the foot of Maroon Lake. Mirrored in the lake's waters are the iconic Maroon Bells (14,156-ft. and 14,014-ft.), towering above the head of the valley. Pyramid Peak's (14,018-ft.) jagged crags rise to the south while the

crimson spires of the Sievers Mountains form the backdrop for beautiful aspen groves to the north.

Follow the Maroon-Snowmass trail along Maroon Lake's north (right) shore to a junction at the "Deadly Bell's Kiosk" near the head of the lake. Progress will be slow along this section of the trail as the gorgeous scenery invites frequent stops.

At the junction the Scenic Loop Trail branches left. We turn right to stay on the Maroon-Snowmass trail, which ascends a wide rocky path through Aspen and spruce trees along the northwest side of the valley. Openings in the trees offer views of rugged Pyramid Peak rising to the south. About a mile from the start the moderately steep trail climbs an ancient rock slide forming a natural dam that created Crater Lake. As you reach the top of the slide enjoy wonderful views of the Maroon Bells and the Sleeping Sexton, located on the ridge extending north from North Maroon Peak.

From the top of the slide the trail descends gently toward Crater Lake. Slightly before reaching Crater Lake arrive at a junction at 1.7 miles. Take the right fork, signed for Maroon-Snowmass trail. The West Maroon trail, heading straight ahead, leads to Crater Lake and West Maroon Pass.

Junction to Buckskin Pass

Segment Stats: 2.9 miles (one-way) with a 2,386-ft. elevation gain
Distance from Trailhead: 9.2 miles (RT)
Ending/Highest Elevation: 12,462-ft.
Elevation Gain: 2,882-ft.

The Maroon-Snowmass trail ascends steeply through aspen and spruce forest for 0.6 miles to Minnehaha Gulch. Breaks in the trees along the lower section of the climb provide nice views of the Maroon Bells, Crater Lake and the West Maroon Valley. As you gain elevation the trees thin and great views open to the west across Minnehaha Gulch to the Sleeping Sexton and North Maroon Peak.

The initial ascent is along the northeast side of the the the gulch, a deep ravine channeling a stream. At 2.9 miles the path rock hops across the stream to the southwest side of the gulch. Beyond the crossing the trail climbs a hillside through pretty meadows and downed trees, toppled by avalanche activity. The meadows offer wonderful panoramas of North Maroon Peak to the southwest and Pyramid Peak to the southeast.

At the end of the gulch the trail climbs a steep gully beside a small stream festoon with wildflowers and emerges onto a beautiful basin clad in alpine meadows. Buckskin Pass, the saddle looming above the head of the steep valley, is now in sight.

Ascend the meadows on a series of switchbacks with wonderful views of North Maroon Peak and the Sleeping Sexton. Pyramid Peak dominates the skyline to the southeast. At 3.75 miles reach a trail junction. Turn left toward Buckskin pass. The trail to the right heads to Willow Pass. (The hike to Willow is nice but the views from the pass pale when compared to the panorama from Buckskin.)

Beyond the junction the trail heads west and crests a small rise. Ahead the trail is seen zigzagging steeply up to the pass. The final section of the trail climbs 480-ft in just over 0.5 miles. The amazing scenery and hillsides sprinkled with wildflowers invite frequent rest stops and help divert your attention from the stiff ascent.

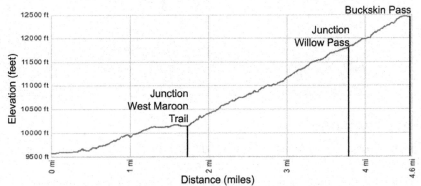

As you crest Buckskin Pass at 4.6 miles a stunning panorama springs into view. To the west Snowmass Peak, Hagerman Peak and Snowmass Mountain (14,092-ft.) tower above Snowmass Lake. Rugged Capitol Peak (14,130-ft.) and Mount Daly rises to the northwest of Snowmass Mountain. Pyramid Peak (14,018-ft.) and a jagged ridgeline of 13,000-ft. peaks dominate the skyline to the east while the Sleeping Sexton and Maroon Bells rise above the ridge to the south.

On the west side of the pass the trail can be seen winding its way downhill toward Snowmass Lake. See the information on the Four Pass Loop backpacking trip for information on the trail beyond Buckskin pass.

After soaking in the view return the way you came, enjoying the wonderful views as you descend.

Buckskin Pass is a very popular hike. My advice is to get an early start so you enjoy a degree of solitude at the pass, have plenty of time to soak in the scenery and then descend before the onset of afternoon thunderstorm, a common occurrence in the Rockies.

Note: Backpackers will find a variety of nice campsite in designated sites in the trees along the western shore of Crater Lake. There are also many nice campsites in Minnehaha Gulch. Camping is not allowed in the alpine meadows before Buckskin Pass.

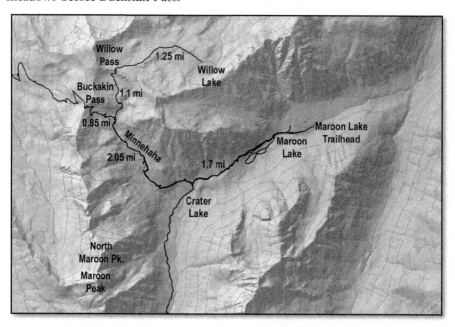

Driving Directions

From Aspen: The Maroon Bells has limited accessibility by car. From mid-June through Labor Day the Maroon Creek Road is restricted to vehicles from 8:00 a.m. to 5:00 p.m. beyond the T-Lazy 7 Ranch, unless you have campground reservations or you are overnight backpacking. Travel is also restricted from 8:00 a.m. to 5:00 p.m. on Friday, Saturday and Sunday from Labor Day to September 30th.

A shuttle bus, which leaves every 20-30 minutes, departs from the Aspen Highlands ski area. There is paid parking at Aspen Highlands or you can take the free Castle Maroon Bus from the Rubey Park Transit Center in downtown Aspen to Aspen Highlands. Dogs are allowed on the bus. Bus tickets that cover the bus and admission to the Maroon Bells Scenic area are sold at Four-Mountain Sports in Aspen Highlands.

Please note the Maroon Bells Scenic Area is a recreation fee area. The Interagency, Senior & Golden Access Passes are honored. Fees apply at all times. Self-pay stations are available during off hours.

If you are driving to the Maroon Bells Scenic Area or Aspen Highlands for the shuttle bus from downtown Aspen, follow Hwy 82 heading west to the roundabout just outside of town. Exit the roundabout at the Maroon Creek Road. In approximately one mile reach Aspen Highlands, turn left here for the shuttle.

If arriving during non-bus hours or heading to the backpacker's overnight parking area, continue another 4 miles to the Maroon Bells Scenic Area Welcome Station. The use fee will be collected here, or in the fee tube immediately behind the station if unmanned. Continue another 5 miles to the parking lot at Maroon Lake. Parking is VERY limited in both the day use and overnight lots.

2. Electric Pass ★★★★★
Distance: 9.2 miles (RT)

A strenuous hike to the highest trail pass in Colorado featuring spectacular panoramic views of the high peaks and ridges of the Elk Mountains, including Castle and Cathedral Peaks to the southwest and the Maroon Bells, Snowmass Mountain, Pyramid Peak and Capital Peak to the northwest.

Distance: 2.3 miles (one-way) Junction
9.2 miles (RT) Electric Pass
Elevation: 9,880-ft. Trailhead
11,790-ft. Junction
13,500-ft. Electric Pass
Elevation Gain: 1,910-ft. Junction
3,620-ft. Electric Pass

Difficulty: strenuous-difficult
Basecamp: Aspen
Area: Maroon Bells-Snowmass Wilderness, White River NF
Best Season: July - September
USGS Map(s): Hayden Peak

Why Hike Electric Pass

If you are looking for a challenge and incredible panoramic views, hike the trail to Electric Pass. This strenuous hike, gaining over 3,600-ft. in 4.7-miles, climbs to a spectacular viewpoint on a high ridge running between Cathedral Peak and Peak 13635. From the pass awe inspiring vistas stretch southwest to the high peaks and ridges surrounding Cathedral Lake and ringing the head of the Castle Creek Valley. To the northwest a quintet of 14ers, North and South Maroon Peak, Snowmass Mountain, Pyramid Peak and Capital Peak, pierce the skyline amid a sea of ridges and summits.

On the return from the pass be sure to stop at beautiful Cathedral Lake, an alpine jewel cradled in a dramatic cirque beneath the rugged pinnacles and crags of Cathedral and Malamute Peaks.

It is essential to get an early start. The aptly names Electric Pass is a lightening magnet. Hikers should be off the pass and below the saddle leading to the pass before noon to avoid electric storms that frequently hit the pass in the early afternoon. The trail is not recommended for anyone with a fear of heights or hikers uncomfortable on narrow, exposed trails.

Trailhead to the Junction with Electric Pass

Distance from Trailhead: 2.3 miles (one way) / 4.6 miles (RT)
Ending/Highest Elevation: 11,790-ft.
Elevation Gain: 1,910-ft.

The trail to Cathedral Lake and Electric Pass wastes no time gaining altitude. From the parking area (see driving directions below) the trail immediately starts climbing through beautiful groves of mature aspen. Soon the trail curves to the west and enters the Pine Creek Valley at an overlook with scenic views of the upper Castle Creek valley.

Once in the Pine Creek drainage the ascent steepens as the trail climbs above the northwest side of Pine Creek through aspen groves that give way to spruce/fir forest. Pine Creek rushes down the ever deepening gorge beside the trail. At 0.7 miles the trail passes a pretty waterfall along the creek.

Past the falls the trail curves left (southwest), continuing its ascent on steep grades. Meadows and openings in the trees offer fine views of the rugged ridge rimming the south side of the valley. Be sure to turn around for nice views across the Castle Creek Valley.

The grade abates at 1.5 miles as the trail crosses a boulder field created by rock slides cascading from the steep slopes to the north of the trail. The boulder field provides the first views of the peaks at the head of the valley.

Beyond the boulder field the trail traverses a stand of trees and then follows gentle grades as it curves to the right (northwest) above a boggy willow-choked meadow at 1.6 miles. The open meadow offers fine views of Malamute Peak (13,348-ft.) and several unnamed peaks rising above the head of the valley.

Past the meadow the trail turns left (west) and climbs through scrub brush and trees, crossing a small rockslide beneath the south facing slopes of Leahy Peak (13,322-ft.) at 1.7 miles. The grade steepens at 2.0 miles as the path crosses a large talus field and then ascends steep switchbacks up the basin's headwall.

Crest the top of the headwall at 2.2 miles. The grade now moderates as the trail heads south and soon reaches a junction at 2.3 miles. Here the trail to Electric Pass turns right (west). The trail straight ahead leads to Cathedral Lake.

Junction to Electric Pass

Segment Stats: 2.3 miles (one-way) with a 1,710-ft. elevation gain
Distance from Trailhead: 9.2 miles (RT)
Ending/Highest Elevation: 13,500-ft.
Elevation Gain: 3,620-ft.

The hike to Electric Pass, turn right at the junction and follow the trail as it climbs a hillside though willows and scattered trees to a second intersection at 2.5 miles with an unmarked trail heading left to Cathedral Lake. Bear right at the second junction to stay on the trail to the pass. (The trail to the left will be used on the return leg of the hike to visit the lake.)

As you head toward the pass turn around and look south to see Cathedral Lake nestled in a rocky bowl beneath Malamute Peak. To the west the spires along Cathedral Peak's north ridge are now in view. Peak 13635 towers above the valley to the north while Leahy Peak rises to the east. The trail to Electric Pass will ascend to the saddle on the ridge between the two peaks.

Beyond the junction the path begins a steep ascent through willow thickets and pretty alpine meadows, skirting the east side of the huge talus field beneath Cathedral Peak's north ridge. At 3.0 miles the trail turns right (east and then southeast) as it climbs steeply up meadows sprinkled with wildflowers beneath the west facing slopes of Leahy Peak.

At 3.25 miles the trail turns left (northwest), continuing the steep climb up switchbacks toward the saddle between Peak 13635 and Leahy Peak. As you climb enjoy the ever improving panorama of summits, including Malamute Peak, Cathedral Peak (13,943-ft.) and Castle Peak (14,265-ft.), to the southwest.

Reach the saddle on the ridge at 4.1 miles where views stretch east/northeast to a sea of peaks and ridges in the Collegiate Peaks and Hunter-Fryingpan Wilderness areas. To the southwest are grand views of Cathedral Lake, Cathedral Peak, Castle Peak and the summits towering above the head of the Castle Creek Valley.

The trail now climbs a series of steep switchback up the ridge to the northwest of the saddle. At 4.25 miles the trail turns left (west), following a narrow, exposed trail ascending along steep scree slopes beneath Peak 13635. Exercise extreme caution along this section of the trail. The footing is not great in areas where the trail crosses minor rockslides. Not everyone is comfortable on this section of the trail. If in doubt, turn around.

Reach Electric Pass (13,500-ft.) at 4.6 miles. The pass, situated on the ridge running between Cathedral Peak and Peak 13635, is located well above the low point on the ridge and just 135-ft. below Peak 13635. You only need to look at the steep cliffs below the low point on the ridge to understand the routing of the trail.

From the pass stunning panoramic views extend west/northwest to the high peak of the Maroon Bells-Snowmass Wilderness. On a clear day you can see a quintet of 14ers; Maroon Peak (14,156-ft.), North Maroon Peak (14,014-ft.), Pyramid Peak (14,018-ft.), Snowmass Mountain (14,092-ft.) and Capitol Peak (14,130-ft.). Cathedral Peak soars above the ridge to the southwest. To the south the peaks towering above the head of the Castle Creek Valley form the backdrop for Cathedral Lake, nestled in a rocky bowl beneath Malamute Peak. Distant views of the Collegiate Peaks fill the skyline to the east.

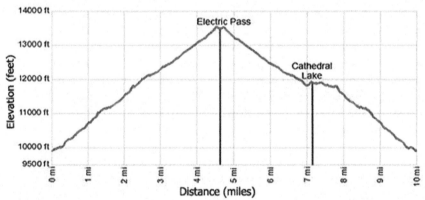

When you are done enjoying the views, carefully work your way back to the saddle and then descend the alpine meadows to the junction with a use trail dropping down to Cathedral Lake at 6.6 miles. If time, energy and the weather permit, I strongly recommend a side trip to visit Cathedral Lake. The side trip adds about 1.0 mile to the hike, making the to the pass and the lake 9.9 miles (RT).

Please note that the trail to Electric Pass is not recommended for anyone with a fear of heights or hikers uncomfortable on narrow, exposed trails.

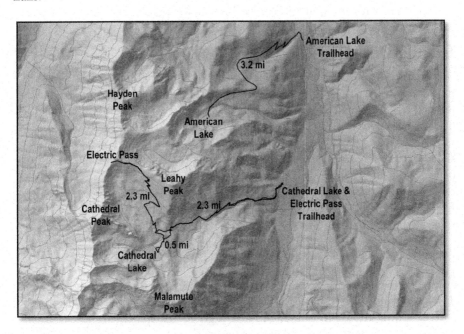

Side Trip to Cathedral Lake

Segment Stats: 1.0 mile
Distance to Pass and Lake from Trailhead: 9.9 miles (RT)
Elevation at the Lake: 11,866-ft.
Elevation Loss to the Lake: 11,634-ft.

To visit the lake, turn right (south) at the junction and follow the trail as it curves to the southeast and drops steeply down to a junction at 6.9 miles near Cathedral Lake's outlet stream. The path to the left (east/northeast) descends to the trailhead. Cross the outlet stream and turn right (south/southwest), joining the main trail to Cathedral Lake. The trail now ascends on moderate grades through meadows and willow thickets to the shelf cradling Cathedral Lake at 7.1 miles.

Cathedral Lake (11,866-ft.) is an alpine jewel surrounded by jagged peaks, crags and rugged cliffs. Cathedral Peak towers above the lake to the west while Malamute Peak rises to the southwest. From the south end of the lake fine views extend north toward Electric Pass.

The lake is a popular destination, so do not expect solitude. Thankfully the eastern shoreline is long enough to allow parties to spread out and enjoy the lovely setting.

31

When you are done lazing around the lake, follow the trail back to the outlet stream. Cross the creek and turn right (east/northeast) at the junction on the other side of the creek. The trail now descends on easy grades to the first junction with the trail to Electric Pass at 7.6 miles. From here retrace your steps to the trailhead for a 9.9 mile hike.

Driving Directions

From Aspen: Drive 0.5 miles west of Aspen on CO 82 to the roundabout. Go around the roundabout and turn right at the Castle Creek Road. (The Castle Creek Road is the third exit on the roundabout when heading west on CO 82.) Drive 12.2 miles on the Castle Creek Road and turn right onto a gravel road signed for the Cathedral Lake trail. The turn is shortly after Ashcroft, a restored ghost town open to the public. Continue 0.5 miles up the rough gravel/dirt road, passable by passenger cars if driven carefully, to the trailhead parking area. This is a popular trailhead and the lot fills early during the summer. If the lot is filled, additional parking can be found along the access road.

3. Cathedral Lake ★★★★★
Distance: 5.6 miles (RT)

This popular hike steeply ascends Pine Creek canyon, traveling through forests and meadows, to Cathedral Lake, a gorgeous alpine gem nestled in a dramatic cirque beneath rugged granite peaks.

Distance: 5.6 miles (RT) to Cathedral Lake
Elevation: 9,880-ft. at Trailhead 11,866-ft. at Cathedral Lake
Elevation Gain: 1,986-ft. to Cathedral Lake
Difficulty: strenuous

Basecamp: Aspen
Area: Maroon Bells-Snowmass Wilderness, White River NF
Best Season: July - September
USGS Map(s): Hayden Peak
See Page 31 for map

Why Hike Cathedral Lake

Cathedral Lake is deservedly one of the most popular day hikes in the Aspen area. The stiff climb, ascending 2,000-ft. up beautiful Pine Creek canyon, traverses aspen groves, spruce-fir forests and pretty meadows on its way to Cathedral Lake, an alpine jewel cradled in a stunning cirque of jagged granite summits and rugged ridges, anchored by Cathedral Peak (13,943-ft.).

Hikers with the time and energy will want to extend the hike by climbing the challenging and steep trail to Electric Pass, a spectacular viewpoint on a high ridge running between Cathedral Peak and Peak 13635.

Trailhead to Cathedral Lake

The trail to Cathedral Lake and Electric Pass wastes no time gaining altitude. From the parking area (see driving directions below) the trail immediately starts climbing through beautiful groves of mature aspen. Soon the trail curves to the west and enters the Pine Creek Valley at an overlook with scenic views of the upper Castle Creek valley.

Once in the Pine Creek drainage the ascent steepens as the trail climbs above the northwest side of Pine Creek through aspen groves that give way to spruce/fir forest. Pine Creek rushes down the ever deepening gorge beside the trail. At 0.7 miles the trail passes a pretty waterfall along the creek.

Past the falls the trail curves left (southwest), continuing its ascent on steep grades. Meadows and openings in the trees offer fine views of the rugged ridge rimming the south side of the valley. Be sure to turn around for nice views across the Castle Creek Valley.

The grade abates at 1.5 miles as the trail crosses a boulder field created by rock slides cascading from the steep slopes to the north of the trail. The boulder field provides the first views of the peaks at the head of the valley.

Beyond the boulder field the trail traverses a stand of trees and then follows gentle grades as it curves to the right (northwest) above a boggy willow-choked meadow at 1.6 miles. The open meadow offers fine views of Malamute Peak (13,348-ft.) and several unnamed peaks rising above the head of the valley.

Past the meadow the trail turns left (west) and climbs through scrub brush and trees, crossing a small rockslide beneath the south facing slopes of Leahy Peak (13,322-ft.) at 1.7 miles. The grade steepens at 2.0 miles as the path crosses a large talus field and then ascends steep switchbacks up the basin's headwall.

Crest the top of the headwall at 2.2 miles. The grade now moderates as the trail heads south and soon reaches a junction at 2.3 miles. Here the trail to Electric Pass turns right (west). We continue straight ahead toward Cathedral Lake.

Past the junction the trail ascends through fields of willows with scattered stands of trees as it climbs a bench to the lake basin. Along the way the path goes by a second junction with a side trail that branches right and connects with the trail to Electric Pass. Shortly after the second junction the trail crosses Cathedral Lake's outlet stream with the aid of a few logs and well placed rocks.

The final ascent to the lake features even improving views of the rocky crags and spires rising above the head of the basin. To the northwest views open to Peak 13635.

After cresting a small hill stunning Cathedral Lake springs into view. The trail now descends gently to the lake at 2.9 miles. Cathedral Lake is an alpine jewel surrounded by jagged granite peaks and crags. Cathedral Peak towers above the lake to the west while Malamute Peak anchors the ridge to the south. Look to the northwest to see the trail to Electric Pass climbing the stark talus ridge to the left of Leahy Peak.

Hikers with the time and energy will want to extend the hike by climbing the challenging and steep trail to Electric Pass, a spectacular viewpoint on a high ridge running between Cathedral Peak and Peak 13635. I recommend hiking to the pass first and then visiting the lake. The aptly names Electric Pass is a lightening magnet. Hikers should be off the pass and below the saddle leading to the pass before noon to avoid electric storms that frequently hit the area in the early afternoon.

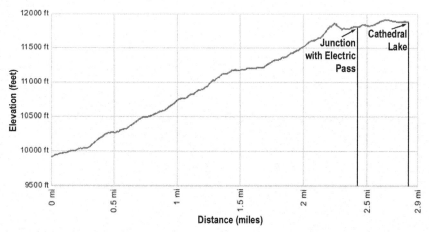

Driving Directions

From Aspen: Drive 0.5 miles west of Aspen on CO 82 to the roundabout. Go around the roundabout and turn right at the Castle Creek Road. (The Castle Creek Road is the third exit on the roundabout when heading west on CO 82.) Drive 12.2 miles on the Castle Creek Road and turn right onto a gravel road signed for the Cathedral Lake trail. The turn is shortly after Ashcroft, a restored ghost town open to the public. Continue 0.5 miles up the rough gravel/dirt road, passable by passenger cars if driven carefully, to the trailhead parking area. This is a popular trailhead and the lot fills early during the summer. If the lot is filled, additional parking can be found along the access road.

4. Four Pass Loop ⭐⭐⭐⭐⭐
Distance: 26.6 miles (RT)

This popular 3-4 day backpacking loop around the stunningly beautiful Maroon Bells climbs over four 12,000-ft. passes and traverses some of the most amazing scenery in the Maroon Bells-Snowmass Wilderness area.

Distance: 26.6 miles (loop)
Elevation: 9,580-ft. at Trailhead
Maximum elevation: 12,500-ft.
Elevation Gain/Loss (approx):
+2,920-ft., -787-ft, +687-ft.,
-2,130-ft., +2,150-ft., -1,440-ft.,
+1,692-ft., -2,882-ft.
Difficulty: strenuous

Basecamp: Aspen and Crested Butte
Area: Maroon Bells-Snowmass Wilderness, White River NF
Best Season: mid-July – mid-September
USGS Map(s): Maroon Bells, Snowmass Mountain

Why Hike the Four Pass Loop

This classic 26.6-mile backpacking circuit around the spectacular Maroon Bells climbs over four 12,000-ft. passes (West Maroon - 12,500 ft.; Frigid Air - 12,415 ft.; Trail Rider - 12,420 ft.; Buckskin - 12,500 ft.) and travels through some of the finest scenery in the Maroon Bells-Snowmass Wilderness. Along the way the popular route through the rugged high peaks of the Elk Mountains traverses gorgeous meadows decorated with wildflowers, visits beautiful alpine lakes and wanders through scenic forest.

Typically it takes three to four days to complete the challenging loop. The trip can be extended with side trips to Geneva Lake and Willow Pass or done at a more leisurely pace to allow time for exploration and relaxation amid the breathtaking scenery.

I recommend walking the loop in a clockwise direction. The trail up the West Maroon Valley is not as steep and therefore easier when carrying a full pack compared to the trail ascending Buckskin Pass. In my view this direction also saves the very best scenery last. This point can certainly be argued since the entire backpack is really quite spectacular.

It is best to wait until mid-summer to attempt the trip. Early summer trips must contend with swift running rivers swollen with snowmelt and deep snow on the high passes. To avoid the crowds plan your trip for mid-week or in the early fall.

Overnight hikers in the Maroon Bells-Snowmass Wilderness are now required to use IGBC approved bear proof food storage containers. For more information on the new food storage rules along with other regulations covering overnight trips in the wilderness see the Maroon Bells-Snowmass Wilderness Regulations at the bottom of the trail description.

35

Trailhead to West Maroon Pass

Distance: 6.5 miles (one-way) to West Maroon Pass (12,500-ft.)
Elevation gain/loss: 2,920-ft.

Few trails can surpass the stunning views from the start of the Four Pass Loop at the foot of Maroon Lake. Mirrored in the lake's waters are the iconic Maroon Bells (14,156-ft. and 14,014-ft.), towering above the head of the valley. Pyramid Peak's (14,018-ft.) jagged crags rise to the south while the crimson spires of the Sievers Mountains form the backdrop for beautiful aspen groves to the north.

Follow the Maroon-Snowmass trail along Maroon Lake's north (right) shore to a junction at the "Deadly Bell's Kiosk" near the head of the lake. Progress will be slow along this section of the trail as the gorgeous scenery invites frequent stops.

At the junction the Scenic Loop Trail branches left. We turn right to stay on the Maroon-Snowmass trail, which ascends a wide rocky path through Aspen and spruce trees along the northwest side of the valley. Openings in the trees offer views of rugged Pyramid Peak rising to the south.

About a mile from the start the moderately steep trail climbs an ancient rock slide forming a natural dam that created Crater Lake. As you reach the top of the slide enjoy wonderful views of the Maroon Bells and the Sleeping Sexton, located on the ridge extending north from North Maroon Peak. From the top of the slide the trail descends gently to Crater Lake.

Slightly before reaching Crater Lake arrive at a junction at 1.7 miles. Continue straight ahead (south) on the West Maroon trail toward Crater Lake and West Maroon Pass. The Maroon-Snowmass trail to the right (west) leads to Buckskin Pass.

After descending to the foot of Crater Lake the trail traverses the lake's right (western) shoreline. Along the way enjoy wonderful views of the Maroon Bells. (Backpackers will find designated campsites among the trees on the western side of the lake.)

At the head of the lake vistas open up the valley. Watch for waterfalls cascading down the western valley wall along this section of the trail.

The trail now follows a gentle grade through meadows, willow thickets and trees and then climbs steeply over a rockslide spilling from the eastern flanks of Maroon Peak. Be sure to turn around at the top of the slide and enjoy great views down valley.

Beyond the slide the trail negotiates a narrow corridor between the creek and talus fields, passing through willows tickets and conifer stands. As the corridor constricts, the trail crosses a few talus fields before being forced to cross to the east side of the creek at 3.6 miles. Early in the season you will need to wade the creek. As the snow runoff subsides, you should be able to rock hop across the braided channel without getting your feet wet.

On the east side of the creek the ascent steepens as the path bashes its way through a large thicket of willows and then continues climbing through a landscape of scrub growth interspersed with conifer stands, some of which harbor nice campsites. Depending on the time of year you might see waterfalls spilling down the eastern wall of the valley along this segment of the trail.

At 4.5-miles the trail crosses back to the western side of the creek and continues its ascent. Soon the last of the trees give way to thickets of scrub willows and the grade steepens as you approach the head of the valley, a large basin rimmed with maroon cliffs and clad in emerald green meadows sprinkled with wildflowers. Be sure to turn around as you climb and take in the wonderful views of the Pyramid massif towering above the eastern side of the valley.

The trail through the basin's meadows veers right (west) as it negotiates the rolling landscape. Near the head of the basin the path crests a rise and heads southwest toward a low point on the ridge. As you near the ridge the way to the pass becomes apparent. The final slog through meadows and stiff ascent of the pass gains 800-ft. in 0.7 miles.

From the top of the pass views extend west to Treasure Mountain. Below are the vast meadows of Purity Basin. To the northeast the Maroon Bells and Pyramid massifs fill the skyline. Belleview Mountain rises along the rugged ridge extending northwest from the pass.

Note that beyond the designated camping sites a Crater Lake, camping came be found in the conifer stands along the West Maroon Valley. It is best to camp before West Maroon Pass or after Frigid Air Pass. Camping spots are very difficult to find between the two passes.

West Maroon Pass to Trail Rider Pass

West Maroon Pass (12,500-ft.) to Frigid Air (12,400-ft.)
Distance: 2.4 miles (one way)
Elevation gain/loss: +687-ft./-787-ft.

Frigid Air (12,400-ft.) to Trail Rider Pass (12,420-ft.)
Distance: 7.1 miles (one way)
Elevation gain/loss: +2,150-ft./-2,130-ft.

From the top of West Maroon Pass the trail descend steeply on switchbacks through scree covered slopes and meadows to Purity Basin, renowned for its amazing displays of wildflowers. After descending 0.75 miles from the pass and losing 800-ft the trail reaches the junction of the Frigid Air Pass Trail, heading right. The trail to the left leads down the East Fork valley to Schofield Park.

Follow the undulating trails as it ascends northwest through lovely meadows. To the west/southwest are gorgeous views of Galena Mountain, Treasure Mountain, Mount Baldy, Cinnamon Mountain and, in the distance, Purple Mountain and the other peaks of the Ruby Range. Peak 12648, a red pyramid-shaped mountain, towers above the valley to the northwest.

Reach a junction near a small pond beneath Peak 12648. Turn right (north) on the signed trail to Frigid Air Pass. The trail to the pass skirts the left (west) side of the pond and climbs very steep switchbacks to Frigid Air Pass (12,415-ft.), gaining 365-ft in 0.3 miles.

As you crest the pass stunning views open to the Maroon Bells towering above the emerald green meadows of the Fravert Basin. The white granite of Snowmass Mountain (14,092-ft.) and Hagerman Peak (13,841-ft.), dominating the view to the northwest, stand in sharp contrast to the crimson-brown mudstone of the Maroon Bells massif. Bellview Mountain (13,233-ft.) rises along the ridge at the head of Fravert Basin. Behind you, to the west/southwest, Mt Baldy, Treasure Mountain and Purple Mountain fill the skyline.

Descend from the pass via a series of steep switchback into the Fravert Basin through wildflowers and alpine scrub. This section of the trail provides glorious views of the Maroon Peak as well as the red rock ridges lining the north and eastern sides of the basin.

As you lose altitude the grade abates a bit. About 1.3 miles from the pass, the trail travels through a spruce forest and then skirts the edge of the woods, paralleling the course of the North Fork of the Crystal River, which is really just a stream at this point. Along the way you will pass a few campsites.

At 2.75 miles from Frigid Air Pass the trail enters the woods and then drops down a steep headwall to the lower basin alongside cascades and small waterfalls on the North Fork. As the descent steepens, the river becomes a magnificent waterfall spilling down a rocky gorge gouged out of the headwall. At the base of the headwall the path enters a large meadow that affords wonderful views of the falls and a nice campsite sheltered in a copse of trees.

Beyond the meadow follow the trail through spruce forest and meadows to a crossing of the North Fork of the Crystal River. Just before the crossing reach a trail junction. The path heading left leads to camping areas. Stay right and cross to the river. (Signs in the area point toward Lead King Basin.)

On the other side of the river the trail passes through meadows and a few stands of spruce trees, staying above the marshy valley floor. Just under 0.9 miles from the river crossing reach a second junction signed for Geneva Lake, heading left, and Trail Rider Pass, to the right. Turn right and climb a series of steep switchbacks ascending through meadows and aspen groves. Great views of the Maroon Bells to the southeast and Lead King Basin to the west help divert your attention from the stiff climb.

When the trail reaches a deep drainage it turns north and continues to switchback uphill beside the creek to second junction with a trail leading to Geneva Lake. This section of the trail, from the first junction with the Geneva Lake trail to the second junction, gains 1,130-ft in a mile.

At the second trail junction the path to the left (west) crosses the creek and heads to Geneva Lake. Our trail turns right (northeast) and continues ascending the drainage, crossing the creek twice before turning right (east) and climbing steeply to the top of a ridge with the help of a few switchbacks.

From the top of the broad ridge views to the southwest extend to the Treasure Mountain massif and the peaks around Lead King Basin. To the northeast Snowmass and Hagerman Peaks rise above the beautiful basin beneath Trail Rider Pass, the saddle on the ridge at the head of the basin.

Follow the trail as it drops gently into the basin, passes to the right of a small lake and then wanders northeast through beautiful meadows. Rock outcroppings and small clusters of trees scattered about the basin harbor great, albeit exposed, campsites.

The trail arcs left (north) near the head of the basin and climbs through flower-speckled meadows toward the pass. The expansive panorama to the southwest along with the ever improving views of Hagerman and Snowmass Peaks serve as distractions from the stiff climb to the pass that gains 700-ft. in 0.6 miles.

As you crest the pass views unfold to Snowmass Lake, cradled in a granite cirque to the northeast. The jagged crags of Snowmass and Hagerman Peaks rise along the ridge extending northwest of the pass. Treasure Mountain dominates the skyline to the southwest.

39

Trail Rider Pass to Buckskin Pass

Trail Rider Pass (12,420-ft.) to Snowmass Lake (10,980-ft.)
Distance: 2.2 miles (one way)
Elevation gain/loss: -1,440-ft.

Snowmass Lake (10,980-ft.) to Buckskin Pass (12,462-ft.)
Distance: 3.8 miles (one-way)
Elevation gain/loss: +1,692-ft./-210-ft.

On the eastern side of Trail Rider pass the trail descends on switchbacks through alpine meadows and then follows a descending traverse along a steep hillside high above the southeast side of Snowmass Lake. The grade steepens as the rocky trail skirts a talus field. Past the talus field the path crosses a large meadow and then enters the trees. After losing 1,400-ft. in just under 2.0 miles from the pass the trail reaches a signed junction with a path heading left to Snowmass Lake. The short trail to Snowmass Lake leads to a large camping area at the southeast end of the lake.

The views from the vantage points at the end of the Snowmass Lake are sublime. Massive Snowmass Mountain (14,092-ft.) towers above the head of the lake. Hagerman and Snowmass Peaks rise along the ridge extending south from Snowmass Mountain while a jagged line of granite peaks rims the northwestern side of the lake.

To continue on the Four Pass Loop return to the signed junction with Snowmass Lake. Take the path pointing in the direction of the Maroon-Snowmass Trail (essentially straight ahead), cross a small stream and come to a second junction in 0.1-miles with the Maroon-Snowmass Trail, with a sign pointing right (southeast) toward Buckskin Pass. Turn right and follow the trail as it ascends gentle grades through forest to cross a minor ridge and then drops down to a large marshy meadow. The trail skirts the north side of the meadow and crosses Snowmass Creek on two logs. Views from the meadows extend southeast up the Lost Remuda Basin to the west face of the Maroon Bells.

At the end of the meadows, about 1.4 miles from the junction with Snowmass Lake, the trail starts a steep climb on switchbacks up a wooded ridge, gaining over 700-ft in 0.9 miles. At the top of the ridge trees give way to meadows and the grade abates as the path crosses two small streams. Good campsites can be found in the area around the stream crossing. Ahead Buckskin Pass is clearly visible on the ridge to the left of the rocky crag.

Beyond the stream crossing the trail ascends steeply through alpine meadows to the pass, gaining 900-ft. in 1.2 miles. As you crest the pass a stunning panorama springs into view. To the east Pyramid Peak (14,018) and its jagged ridgeline of 13,000-ft. peaks dominate the skyline. The iconic Maroon Bells anchor the rugged ridge to the south of the pass. To the west Snowmass Peak, Hagerman Peak and Snowmass Mountain (14,092-ft.) tower above Snowmass Lake. Rugged Capitol Peak (14,130-ft.) and Mount Daly rises along the ridge extending northwest from Snowmass Mountain.

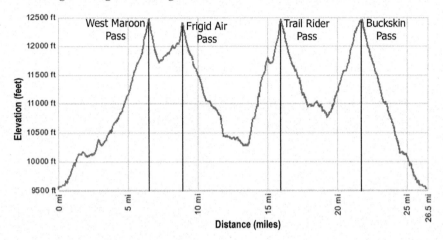

Buckskin Pass to the Trailhead

Buckskin Pass (12,462-ft.) to Trailhead (9,580-ft.)
Distance: 4.6 miles (one-way) to Trailhead
Elevation gain/loss: -2,882-ft.

Descend the east side of Buckskin pass on steep switchbacks through meadows sprinkled with wildflowers. Along the way enjoy wonderful views of North Maroon Peak, the Sleeping Sexton and Pyramid Peak. The initial descent to the junction with the trail to Willow Pass loses over 700-ft. in 0.7 miles. At the junction continue following the switchbacks downhill to the right. The trail ascending to the left leads to Willow Pass.

At the foot of the basin the trail descends a steep gully beside a small stream festoon with wildflowers and enters Minnehaha Gulch. Initially the trail stays on the right (southwest side) of the gulch as it drops through hillsides clad in pretty meadows and down trees, toppled by avalanche activity. About 1.5 miles from the pass the trail crosses the northeast side of the stream and continues its descent through trees and meadows. Good campsites are scattered throughout Minnehaha Gulch.

At 2.3 miles from the pass the path swings northeast away from the gulch and descends steeply through aspen and spruce forest to a trail junction just beyond the north end of Crater Lake, 1.7 miles from the trailhead. Backpackers looking for a nice place for a break might want to take a short detour to visit the pretty lake nestled beneath the photogenic Maroon Bells.

After admiring Crater Lake return to the junction and head left, ascending an ancient rockslide that forms a natural dam holding Crater Lake. As you reach the top of the slide be sure to turn around and enjoy wonderful vistas of the Maroon Bells and the Sleeping Sexton.

Descend from the rockslide on a moderately steep grade. At the foot of the slide, about 1.0 mile from the Maroon Lake trailhead, the rocky trail widens and continues its descent along the northwest side of the valley to a trail junction near the head of Maroon Lake. At the junction follow the trail traversing along the lake's north shore to the trailhead, along the way enjoying the stunning views of the Maroon Bells, Pyramid Peak and the Sievers Mountains.

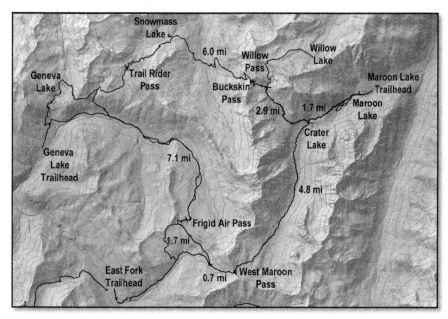

Driving Directions

From Aspen: The Maroon Bells has limited accessibility by car. From mid-June through Labor Day the Maroon Creek Road is restricted to vehicles from 8:00 a.m. to 5:00 p.m. beyond the T-Lazy 7 Ranch, unless you have campground reservations or you are overnight backpacking. Travel is also restricted from 8:00 a.m. to 5:00 p.m. on Friday, Saturday and Sunday from Labor Day to September 30th.

A shuttle bus, which leaves every 20-30 minutes, departs from the Aspen Highlands ski area. There is paid parking at Aspen Highlands or you can take the free Castle Maroon Bus from the Rubey Park Transit Center in downtown Aspen to Aspen Highlands. Dogs are allowed on the bus. Bus tickets that cover the bus and admission to the Maroon Bells Scenic area are sold at Four-Mountain Sports in Aspen Highlands.

Please note the Maroon Bells Scenic Area is a recreation fee area. The Interagency, Senior & Golden Access Passes are honored. Fees apply at all times. Self-pay stations are available during off hours.

If you are driving to the Maroon Bells Scenic Area or Aspen Highlands for the shuttle bus from downtown Aspen, follow Hwy 82 heading west to the roundabout just outside of town. Exit the roundabout at the Maroon Creek Road. In approximately one mile reach Aspen Highlands, turn left here for the shuttle.

If arriving during non-bus hours or heading to the backpacker's overnight parking area, continue another 4 miles to the Maroon Bells Scenic Area Welcome Station. The use fee will be collected here, or in the fee tube immediately behind the station if unmanned. Continue another 5 miles to the parking lot at Maroon Lake. Parking is VERY limited in both the day use and overnight lots.

From Crested Butte: The Four Pass Loop can also be started from the East Fork trailhead near Schofield Park. Follow the trail to the Frigid Air/West Maroon junction and then start the loop from there. (The one-way distance to the junction is 3.1 miles.)

From the intersection of Elk Avenue (main street) and 6th Street in Crested Butte, head north on 6th Street, which turns into the Gothic Road (sometimes referred to as the Schofield Pass Road). Follow the Gothic Road (CO 317) for 13.2 miles to Schofield Pass, passing the ski area and the research facilities at Gothic along the way. The dirt road is suitable for 2WD cars up to the town of Gothic at 7.9 miles. Beyond Gothic the road become rougher and a high clearance/4WD vehicle is recommended. (AWD/4WD is necessary if the road is wet.)

Continue over Schofield pass, descending the north side of the pass on switchbacks and then through meadows for 0.8 miles and turn right (east) into the signed East Fork trailhead. The turn is right before you hit Schofield Park, a large open park at the foot of the switchbacks. As you enter the trailhead, bear right into the parking area. The road branching to the left is for horse trailers.

Maroon Bells-Snowmass Wilderness Regulations

Before leaving on your backpack, please check the White River Forest website Wilderness Regulations page for current regulations to insure that there are not any temporary closures or other restrictions not listed below. The website address is http://www.fs.usda.gov/detail/whiteriver/specialplaces/?cid=stelprd38258 63 .

Food Storage -- NEW!!!:

a) **Bear proof food storage is now required in the Maroon Bells-Snowmass Wilderness**. All food, garbage and attractant must be stored in hard-sided bear-resistant containers. The Maroon Bells-Snowmass Wilderness is in bear country and due to an increase in use, increase in bear activity and a focus on safety the Forest Service has instituted new regulations that requires overnight hikers to use IGBC (Interagency Grizzly Bear Committee Courtesy) approved bear proof food storage containers. Approved bear cannisters can now be rented or purchased in Aspen at Aspen Expeditions and Ute Mountaineering and in Carbondale at Ragged Mountain Sports. Many outdoor stores sell the containers. If you intend to rent a container, check ahead of time to determine availability.

b) As a reminder of proper use of the containers; all food (including alcohol), trash, and toiletries must fit in the container.

Permits: Each party overnighting in the Maroon Bells-Snowmass Wilderness is required to self-register at the trailhead and to carry a copy of the registration with them during their visit. There is no fee charged and no limit to the number of permits issued. There are free self-registration Wilderness Use Permits available at the trailhead, one at the parking lot and one at the wilderness boundary on the way to Crater Lake. The Forest Service now requires people to include their camping locations for each night. This greatly helps the Forest Service to document the highest used camping areas.

Camping:

a) Is not allowed within one hundred (100) feet of any lake, stream or National Forest System Trail;

b) Is not allowed within 1/4 mile of Conundrum Hot Springs, Copper Lake, Crater Lake, Geneva Lake, Capitol Lake, and Thomas Lakes, except at designated campsites.

Campfires:

a) Are not allowed within one hundred (100) feet of any lake, stream or National Forest System Trail;

b) Are not allowed within ¼ mile of Crater Lake;

c) Are not allowed above 10,800 ft. elevation

Group Size: No more than 10 persons per group, and a maximum of 15 pack or saddle animals. Note: see current regulations regarding hitching, hobbling, tethering and livestock feed for pack animals on the White River National Forest Wilderness Regulations page: (url:http://www.fs.usda.gov/detail/whiteriver/specialplaces/?cid=stelprd38 25863).

Dogs:

a) All dog must be under physical restraint of a leash not to exceed six (6) feet in length.

b) Dogs are not allowed within the Conundrum Creek Valley from Silver Dollar Pond (2.25 miles North of Conundrum Hot Springs) to Triangle Pass (1.5 miles Southwest of Conundrum Hot Springs), including Conundrum Hot Springs.

Switchbacks: Please don't cut switchbacks. "Short-cutting" switchbacks causes soil erosion! When you cut a trail you kill vegetation and loosen soil creating a new trail that channels water from storms and snowmelt, causing erosion and trail damage.

Leave No Trace: Always practice Leave No Trace principles when backpacking.

5. Capitol Lake ★★★★★
Distance: 12.8 miles (RT)

This long hike ascends a pretty valley through aspen groves and spruce-fir forest interspersed with meadows to Capitol Lake, an alpine jewel nestled beneath the massive west face of Capital Peak (14,130-ft.).

Distance: 12.8 miles (RT)	**Basecamp:** Aspen
Elevation: 9,475-ft. at Trailhead	**Area:** Maroon Bells-Snowmass
11,580-ft. at Capitol Lake	Wilderness, White River NF
Elevation Gain: 2,105-ft.	**Best Season:** July –September
Difficulty: strenuous	**USGS Map(s):** Capitol Peak

Why Hike to Capitol Lake

From the Capitol Creek trailhead views stretch south to majestic Capitol Peak (14,130-ft.), a massive sentinel towering over the Capitol Creek Valley. This hike traverses the valley's aspen groves, spruce-fir forests and meadows to visit scenic Capital Lake, an azure jewel cradled beneath the Peak's monumental west face. Beyond the lake the trail crosses Capitol Pass (12,060-ft.) and connects with the Avalanche Creek trail.

Capitol Lake makes a great, albeit long, day hike. The route is popular with day hikers as well as backpackers accessing the West Snowmass and Avalanche Creek trails and climbers seeking to summit Mt. Daly or Capital Peak, one of Colorado's most difficult fourteeners to climb.

Trailhead to Capitol Lake

The Capital Creek trailhead (see driving directions below) is located on a ridge overlooking the Capital Valley with wonderful views of massive Capital Peak (14,130-ft.) towering above the head of the valley. Two trails depart from the ridge and lead up the valley, Capital Creek Trail #1961 and Upper Capitol Creek Trail #1963 (aka the Ditch).

Capital Creek Trail #1961 drops off the ridge, heading downhill on switchbacks through sage brush and scrub oak to the valley floor, losing 425-ft in 0.7 miles. On the valley floor the trail hops over an irrigation ditch and then traverses a large meadow to the opposite side of the valley where it crosses a wooden bridge spanning Capital Creek.

On the other side of the bridge is a junction with the Nelson Creek trail, which turns left (east). We follow the Capital Creek trail to the right (southwest) as it ascends the east side of the valley on moderate grades through pretty aspen groves.

At 1.9 miles the trail passes through a meadow with nice views of Capitol Peak and Mount Daly, rising to the east (left) of Capitol Peak. For the next mile the path continues its journey up valley through mixed conifer stands and small meadows sprinkled with wildflowers.

At 2.9 miles the trail curves west to circumvent a ridge. En route the path tunnels through a tall thicket of willows, crosses a creek draining the western flank of Haystack Mountain and then ascends a large meadow. At the end of the meadow the path veers south and reenters the trees, arriving at the junction with the Capital Ditch trail (see description below) at 3.3 miles.

Beyond the junction the trail wanders past a few ponds and then traverses a large meadow providing nice views of Capitol Peak and the red sandstone ridge rimming the western side of the valley. Soon the path arrives at the junction with the West Snowmass trail, descending the hillside from

the east, at 3.8 miles.

Our path now passes through thick stands of conifers interrupted by a series of meadows cleared by avalanches tumbling down the steep slopes to the east and west of the trail. From the meadows Capitol Peak and a few lesser granite crags loom above the head of the valley.

Up to this point you may have run into cows grazing in the meadows. At 4.3 miles reach a wooden fence marking the boundary for the grazing allotment in a large copse of mixed conifers. Be sure to close the gate to insure the cows do not wander any further up valley.

Past the fence the grade steepens as the trail passes through trees and meadows offering intermittent views of the rugged cliffs and craggy peaks lining the valley. At 5.1 miles the path emerges from the trees and crosses a large meadow formed by avalanches spilling down the slopes of Mt Daly. At the end of the meadow the trail switchbacks steeply up a wooded headwall. Openings in the forest provide nice views down valley.

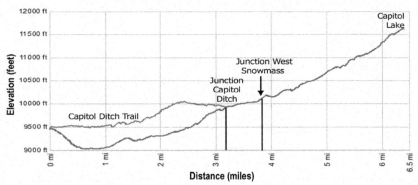

At the top of the headwall the path crosses Capitol Creek on a log at 5.4 miles. The trail, now on the west side of the stream, follows the winding course of the stream along the edge of a meadow, skirting a talus field. The meadow offers great views of Mt. Daly rising above the eastern side of the valley.

At 5.7 miles the trail crosses back to the east side of the creek and resumes its steep ascent, heading southeast through beautiful meadows with thigh-high wildflowers. Backpackers will find nice campsites in the trees to the east (left) of the trail shortly after the creek crossing.

From this point to Capitol Lake the trail gains 550-ft in 0.7 miles. Wonderful views of Capital Peak towering over the head of the valley and the interesting jagged peaks and craggy ridges rising to the west help divert your attention from the climb.

Follow the trail as it ascends the eastern side of the valley to skirt a rocky knoll at the head of the basin. At 6 miles (11,375-ft.) pass a sign prohibiting wood fires and requiring camping in designated sites.

The trail crosses the creek one last time before the final stiff climb through meadows to the lake. Just before reaching the lake the path meets two unmarked trail junctions. At the first junction a faint climbers trail heads left (east), ascending to the northeast ridge of Capitol Peak. Another faint trail goes right (west) to designated campsites on a rocky knoll.

Just a few feet beyond the first junction the trail splits at the second unmarked junction. The right fork traverses talus slopes along the west (right) side of the lake and then climbs over a saddle, referred to as Capitol Pass (12,060-ft.) on some maps, to connect with the Avalanche Creek trail.

The left fork leads to the north end of the Capitol Lake, an azure jewel cradled beneath the steep west face of Capitol Peak. On calm days the lake provides beautiful reflections of the peak's massive west face, towering 1,800-ft. above the south end of the lake.

After relaxing at the lake retrace your steps to the trailhead. For variety consider taking the Capital Ditch trail (see below) on the return leg.

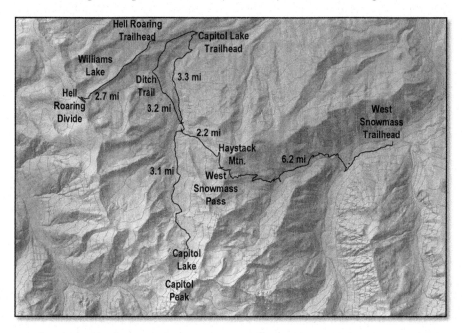

Alternative Start: Capitol Ditch Trail

Distance from Trailhead: 3.2 miles (one way)

The Capital Ditch trail leaves from the western end of the trailhead parking area and travels alongside an irrigation ditch beneath the ridge defining the western side of the valley. The trail and the ditch follow the arc of the valley as it curves south toward Capitol Peak. At 1.4-miles leave the irrigation ditch behind and ascend the hillside through aspen and conifer stands, gaining about 500-ft. in 1.0 mile. As you climb, the trees give way to meadows with wonderful views of Capital Peak.

After 2.4 miles the trail tops out and descends to Capitol Creek at a wide ford at 3.2-miles. Don't cross the creek here, instead follow the trail about 150-ft up the creek to a bridge crossing the creek. On the other side of the creek reach the junction with the Capitol Creek Trail #1961.

There are a number of good camping spots around the trail junction on the western side creek.

Driving Directions

From Aspen: Drive 14 miles west of Aspen on Highway 82 to Old Snowmass and turn left on Snowmass Creek Road (just past to the Conoco Gas station on the south side of the highway). Continue 2 miles to a "T" intersection and turn right. Drive 5 miles to the end of the pavement and then continue on the dirt road for another 3 miles to the trailhead. The last mile is on a rough 4WD road. If you don't have a 4WD, park in the BLM meadow on the right approximately 2.25 miles below the trailhead. Note: The road continues past the Capitol Creek Trailhead and climbs very steeply to the Hell Roaring Trailhead. The road is slick when wet.

6. West Maroon Pass ★★★★★
Distance: 3.4 - 13.0 miles (RT)

Imposing peaks, pretty waterfalls, stunning lakes, a huge alpine basin and panoramic views from a 12,500-ft. pass encompassing the Maroon Bells, Pyramid Peak and Treasure Mountain are the scenic rewards on this 13-mile (RT) hike to West Maroon Pass.

Distance: 3.4 miles (RT) Crater Lake
13.0 miles (RT) to West Maroon Pass
Elevation: 9,580-ft. at Trailhead
10,076-ft. at Crater Lake
12,500-ft. at West Maroon Pass
Elevation Gain: 496-ft. Crater Lake
2,920-ft. to West Maroon Pass

Difficulty: strenuous
Basecamp: Aspen
Area: Maroon Bells-Snowmass Wilderness, White River NF
Best Season: July –September
USGS Map(s): Maroon Bells
See Page 42 for Map

Why Hike to West Maroon Pass

Wonderful views of the Maroon Bells and Pyramid Peak, pretty waterfalls, two stunning lakes and a scenic alpine basin await hikers on this popular 13-mile (RT) hike to West Maroon Pass. The journey follows the Maroon-Snowmass trail to Crater Lake the climbs the long, narrow West Maroon valley beneath the towering crags of the Maroon Bells and Pyramid massifs.

The pass is located on a ridge at the head of the valley above a huge basin rimmed with maroon cliffs and clad in emerald meadows sprinkled with wildflower. Views from the pass extend west to Treasure Mountain. To the east the Maroon Bells and the Pyramid Peaks fill the skyline.

The popular hike is part of the famous 26-mile Four Pass Loop, a backpacking trip climbing four pass over 12,000-ft. in the Maroon-Snowmass Wilderness. With proper planning the route is part of a longer day hike to Crested Butte or a the first segment of a two day trip covering the West and East Maroon trails with overnight accommodations in Crested Butte.

Trailhead to Crater Lake

Distance from Trailhead: 3.4 miles (RT)
Ending/Highest Elevation: 10,076-ft.
Elevation Gain: 496-ft.

Few trails can surpass the stunning views from the start of the West Maroon Pass hike at the foot of Maroon Lake. Mirrored in the lake's waters are the iconic Maroon Bells (14,156-ft. and 14,014-ft.), towering above the head of the valley. Pyramid Peak's (14,018-ft.) jagged crags rise to the south while the crimson spires of the Sievers Mountains form the backdrop for beautiful aspen groves to the north.

Follow the Maroon-Snowmass trail along Maroon Lake's north (right) shore to a junction at the "Deadly Bell's Kiosk" near the head of the lake. Progress will be slow along this section of the trail as the gorgeous scenery invites frequent stops.

At the junction the Scenic Loop Trail branches left. We turn right to stay on the Maroon-Snowmass trail, which ascends a wide rocky path through Aspen and spruce trees along the northwest side of the valley. Openings in the trees offer views of rugged Pyramid Peak rising to the south. About a mile from the start the moderately steep trail climbs an ancient rock slide forming a natural dam that created Crater Lake. As you reach the top of the slide enjoy wonderful views of the Maroon Bells and the Sleeping Sexton, located on the ridge extending north from North Maroon Peak.

From the top of the slide the trail descends gently toward Crater Lake. Slightly before reaching Crater Lake arrive at a junction at 1.7 miles. Continue straight ahead (south) on the West Maroon trail toward Crater Lake and West Maroon Pass. The Maroon-Snowmass trail to the right (west) leads to Buckskin Pass.

Crater Lake to West Maroon Pass

Segment Stats: 4.8 miles (one-way) with a 2,424-ft. elevation gain
Distance from Trailhead: 13.0 miles (RT)
Ending/Highest Elevation: 12,500-ft.
Elevation Gain from Trailhead: 2,920-ft.

After descending to the foot of Crater Lake the trail traverses the lake's right (western) shoreline. Along the way enjoy wonderful views of the Maroon Bells. (Backpackers will find designated campsites among the trees on the western side of the lake.)

At the head of the lake vistas open up the valley. Watch for waterfalls cascading down the western valley wall along this section of the trail.

The trail now follows a gentle grade through meadows, willow thickets and trees and then climbs steeply over a rockslide spilling from the eastern flanks of Maroon Peak. Be sure to turn around at the top of the slide and enjoy great views down valley.

Beyond the slide the trail negotiates a narrow corridor between the creek and talus fields, passing through willows tickets and conifer stands. As the corridor constricts, the trail crosses a few talus fields before being forced to cross to the east side of the creek at 3.6 miles. Early in the season you will need to wade across the creek. As the snow runoff subsides, you should be able to rock hop across the braided channel without getting your feet wet.

On the east side of the creek the ascent steepens as the path bashes its way through a large thicket of willows and then continues climbing through a landscape of scrub growth interspersed with conifer stands, some of which harbor nice campsites. Depending on the time of year you might see waterfalls spilling down the eastern wall of the valley along this segment of the trail.

At 4.5-miles the trail crosses back to the western side of the creek and continues its ascent. Soon the last of the trees give way to thickets of scrub willows and the grade steepens as you approach the head of the valley, a large basin rimmed with maroon cliffs and clad in emerald green meadows sprinkled with wildflowers. Be sure to turn around as you climb and take in the wonderful views of the Pyramid massif towering above the eastern side of the valley.

The trail through the basin's meadows veers right (west) as it negotiates the rolling landscape. Near the head of the basin the path crests a rise and heads southwest toward a low point on the ridge. As you near the ridge the way to the pass becomes apparent. The final slog through meadows and stiff ascent of the pass gains 800-ft. in 0.7 miles.

From the top of the pass views extend west to Treasure Mountain. Below are the vast meadows of Purity Basin. To the northeast the Maroon Bells and Pyramid massifs fill the skyline. Belleview Mountain rises along the rugged ridge extending northwest from the pass.

The pass is the turnaround point for most day hikers. Backpackers use the trail as either the first or last leg of the popular 26-mile Four Pass Loop, a 3-5 day backpacking trip climbing four passes over 12,000-ft. in the Maroon-Snowmass Wilderness.

Note to Backpackers: Beyond the designated camping sites a Crater Lake, camping came be found in the conifer stands along the east and west side of the West Maroon Valley. If you are doing the Four Pass Loop it is best to camp before West Maroon Pass or after Frigid Air Pass. Camping is very difficult in the Purity Basin between the two passes.

With proper planning it is possible to cross West Maroon Pass on a day hike and end up at the East Fork trailhead in Schofield Park, 14 miles from Crested Butte. (From more information see the West Maroon Pass from Crested Butte trail description.) You need to spot a car at the Schofield Park trailhead, arrange a ride (taxi: (970) 349-2620 or (970) 948-9893) or try to hitch your way back to Crested Butte (not recommended on the infrequently traveled road).

Some folks make this into a two day trip by staying in Crested Butte overnight and then arranging transportation to the East Maroon trailhead for a 16-mile one-way hike back to the East Maroon Trailhead. You then need to either walk up valley to Maroon Lake or take the shuttle bus back to Aspen.

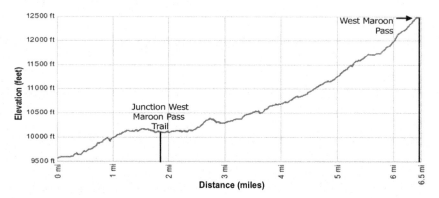

Driving Directions

From Aspen: The Maroon Bells has limited accessibility by car. From mid-June through Labor Day the Maroon Creek Road is restricted to vehicles from 8:00 a.m. to 5:00 p.m. beyond the T-Lazy 7 Ranch, unless you have campground reservations or you are overnight backpacking. Travel is also restricted from 8:00 a.m. to 5:00 p.m. on Friday, Saturday and Sunday from Labor Day to September 30th.

A shuttle bus, which leaves every 20-30 minutes, departs from the Aspen Highlands ski area. There is paid parking at Aspen Highlands or you can take the free Castle Maroon Bus from the Rubey Park Transit Center in downtown Aspen to Aspen Highlands. Dogs are allowed on the bus. Bus tickets that cover the bus and admission to the Maroon Bells Scenic area are sold at Four-Mountain Sports in Aspen Highlands.

Please note the Maroon Bells Scenic Area is a recreation fee area. The Interagency, Senior & Golden Access Passes are honored. Fees apply at all times. Self pay stations are available during off hours.

If you are driving to the Maroon Bells Scenic Area or Aspen Highlands for the shuttle bus from downtown Aspen, follow Hwy 82 heading west to the roundabout just outside of town. Exit the roundabout at the Maroon Creek Road. In approximately one mile reach Aspen Highlands, turn left here for the shuttle.

If arriving during non-bus hours or heading to the backpacker's overnight parking area, continue another 4 miles to the Maroon Bells Scenic Area Welcome Station. The use fee will be collected here, or in the fee tube immediately behind the station if unmanned. Continue another 5 miles to the parking lot at Maroon Lake. Parking is VERY limited in both the day use and overnight lots.

7. Lost Man ★★★★☆
Distance: 4.6 - 8.8 miles (RT)

This hike traverses two scenic valleys with pretty lakes separated by a panoramic pass. From the pass wonderful views extend to the peaks and ridges along Continental Divide and in the Hunter-Fryingpan and the Collegiate Peaks Wilderness areas.

Distance: 4.6 miles (RT) to Lost Man Pass
8.8 miles (semi-loop) to Lower Lost Man Trailhead
Elevation: 11,520-ft. at Trailhead
12,810-ft. at Lost Man Pass
10,540-ft. Lower Lost Man Trailhead
Elevation Gain: 1,290-ft. to Pass
-2,270-ft. Lower Lost Man Trailhead

Difficulty: moderate
Basecamp: Aspen
Area: Hunter-Fryingpan Wilderness, White River NF
Best Season: July –September
USGS Map(s): Independence Pass, Mt. Champion

Why Hike Lost Man

The Lost Man trail provides instant gratification to anyone who loves traversing high alpine terrain with see forever views. Starting at 11,500-ft. off Highway 82 just below Independence Pass (12,095-ft.), the trail features some of the easiest access to an alpine wonderland of meadows and lakes anywhere in the area.

The trail begins with a moderate ascent along the nascent Roaring Fork River, passing pretty Independence Lake before topping out at panoramic Lost Man Pass (12,815-ft.). Beyond the pass the trail drops to picturesque Lost Man Lake then descends through beautiful meadows with great views of the Williams Mountains to Lost Man Reservoir and the lower trailhead on Highway 82, located 4-miles west of your starting point.

The hike can be done as an out and back or, with a car shuttle, a semi-loop. Please note that walking along Highway 82 to return to your car at the upper trailhead parking area at Linkins Lake is not recommended. Highway 82 is a very narrow road with little or no shoulder.

Trailhead to Lost Man Pass

Distance from Trailhead: 4.6 miles (RT)
Ending/Highest Elevation: 12,810-ft.
Elevation Gain: 1,290-ft.

The Linkins Lake/Upper Lost Man trailhead starts just below timberline to the west of where the Roaring Fork River, really just a creek at this point, drops through a culvert channeling the river beneath Highway 82 near Independence Pass (12,095-ft.). (See driving directions below.)

Follow the trail as it ascends on moderate grades through scrub willows up the left (west) side of the Roaring Fork, passing the last few pockets of spruce trees along the way. In less than 0.2 miles come to the junction with the Linkins Lake trail heading left (northwest). Stay right. Just beyond the junction enter the Hunter-Fryingpan Wilderness.

At 0.5 miles cross to the east side of the river on a log bridge. Soon you leave the last of the willows behind as the trail continues its steady ascent through emerald green meadows sprinkled with wildflowers. The Geissler Mountains rise above the basin to the northwest while Twining Peak dominates the ridge to the east.

As you climb be sure to turn around and enjoy ever improving views of Independence Mountain (12,703-ft.) and a sea of jagged ridges and summits in the Collegiate Peaks Wilderness to the south.

After walking just over a mile the grade steepens as the trail curves east away from the Roaring Fork and climbs to a bench, circumventing boggy meadows around the river. Once on the bench the trail again heads north, crossing rivulets fed by snowfields from the slopes to the east.

Just before arriving at the southwest end of Independence Lake the trail crosses the lake's outlet stream. Reach the lake, set amid wildflower-filled meadows at the base of a ridge anchored to the southeast by Twining Peak, at 1.75 miles. Follow the trail as it climbs through meadows along the left (west) side of the lake and heads towards Lost Man Pass, the obvious saddle on the ridge to the north.

Beyond the lake ascend rock strewn meadows on a moderately steep trail to the top of the pass (12,815-ft.) at 2.3 miles. Lost Man is a good example of why hiking to pass is so enjoyable. As you crest the ridge the view to the north unfolds all at once. Lost Man Lake lies cradled in a rocky bowl edged with talus slopes and meadows. Panoramic views extend north to the craggy peaks and ridges of the Continental Divide and Hunter-Fryingpan Wilderness.

To the south, the emerald green expanse of the Roaring Fork drainage is rimmed by the Geissler Mountains and Twining Peak. Across the highway views extend south to a sea of summits in the Collegiate Peaks Wilderness.

Lost Man Pass to Junction with South Fork Pass

Segment Stats: 2.6 miles (one-way) with a 1,200-ft. elevation loss
Distance from Trailhead: 9.8 miles (RT)
Ending/Highest Elevation: 11,610-ft.
Elevation Gain: -1,200-ft.

If you are looking for a short hike the pass is a good turnaround point. Otherwise to complete the semi-loop or do a longer out-and-back day hike, descend the north side of the pass on steep switchbacks through a boulder field to the head of Lost Man Lake, losing 330-ft. in 0.3 miles. At the base of the pass follow the trail as it traverses the right (east) side of the lakeshore through rocky meadows dotted with wildflowers.

At the foot of the lake the path starts its decent of the Lost Man drainage, making a wide arc to the north and then west, through a large meadow with scenic views of the Williams Mountains rising to the west. The trail briefly crosses to the west side of Lost Man Creek as it drops through a boggy area filled with wildflowers and small pockets of scrub willows.

As you lose elevation the scrub growth thickens. Soon the trail crosses back to the west side of the creek and plots a course slightly above the valley floor, skirting the marshy areas along the creek. Trees start to appear on the southwest side of the valley as you drop below the timberline.

At 4.6 miles the trail ascends a small knoll and reaches the South Fork Pass junction at 4.9 miles. If you have the time and energy a side trip to the pass, gaining 140-ft. in 0.3 miles, is a pleasant diversion. Be forewarned that the views, while nice, are hardly panoramic. The junction is a good point to turn around if you are doing a long out-and-back hike from the upper trailhead.

South Fork Junction to Lower Lost Man Trailhead

Segment Stats: 3.9 miles (one-way) with a 1,070-ft. elevation loss
Distance from Trailhead: 8.8 miles (semi-loop)
Ending/Highest Elevation: 10,540-ft.
Elevation Gain/Loss from the Trailhead: 1,290-ft./-2,270-ft.

From the South Fork junction the path follows the arc of the valley as it curves to the south, descending along the west side of the creek. Along the way the path travels through meadows and scrub growth, skirting the edge of spruce-fir forest growing on the slopes above trail. At 7.5 miles the trail enters a large meadow with nice views down valley.

Reach the head of Lost Man Reservoir at 8.2 miles. The path now wanders along the lake's western shore to a junction with an old jeep road heading left (east) at the foot of the lake. To reach the lower Lost Man trailhead stay right. The path climbs about 70-feet up a hillside to meet the Midway Pass trail, which switchbacks steeply up the hillside to the right (northwest). Bear left, following the trail as it loses 130-ft in 0.3 miles as it drops to a wooden bridge crossing the creek. The parking area by Highway 82 is located a short distance beyond the bridge.

Please note that walking along the highway to return to your car at the upper trailhead parking area is NOT recommended. Highway 82 is a very narrow road with little or no shoulder.

Optional Side Trip to Linkins Lake

Distance from Trailhead: 1.2 miles (RT)
Ending/Highest Elevation: 12,008-ft.
Elevation Gain: 488-ft.

From the Linkins Lake / Upper Lost Man trailhead, follow the trail for 0.2 miles to a signed junction and turn left (northwest) toward Linkins Lake. (The trail to the right leads to Independence Lake and Lost Man Pass.) Follow the trail as it ascends steeply up the hillside to the glacial cirque holding Linkins Lake (12,008-ft.) at 0.6 miles. From the lake enjoy magnificent views of the high alpine meadows and summits surrounding the Continental Divide.

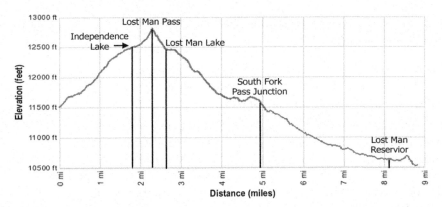

Driving Directions

From Aspen: There are 2 ways to access the Lost Man Trail:

1) Linkins Lake / Upper Lost Man trailhead: Drive 18.5 miles east of Aspen on Highway 82 to the parking lot on the left (north) side of the road at the last switchback before Independence Pass. The trailhead is on the left (north) side of the road just to the left of where the Roaring Fork River drops through a culvert channeling the river beneath Highway 82.

2) Lower Lost Man / Midway Pass trailhead: Drive 14 miles east of Aspen on Highway 82 to a large trailhead parking lot on the left (north) side of the road, directly across from Lost Man Campground.

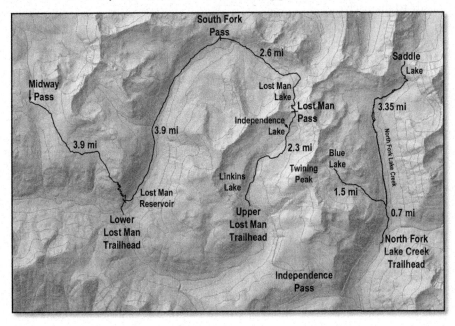

8. Lyle and Mormon Lakes ★★★★☆
Distance: 5.8 miles (RT)

One of the most scenic hikes in the Hunter Fryingpan area starts at 10,730-ft. and climbs at a moderate pace through acres of meadows with stunning wildflowers displays to two beautiful lakes.

Distance: 5.8 miles (RT)
Elevation: 10,730-ft. at trailhead
 11,665-ft. at the high point on the
trail
Elevation Gain: 935-ft.
Difficulty: moderate

Basecamp: Aspen
Area: Holy Cross Wilderness,
White River NF
Best Season: July –September
USGS Map(s): Nast

Why Hike to Lyle and Mormon Lakes

If you are looking for a little solitude and a great destination take a hike to Lyle and Mormon Lakes. This scenic hike, one of the best in the Hunter-Fryingpan area, traverses gorgeous wildflower-filled meadows with nice views of the nearby peaks on its way to two beautiful lakes.

Be forewarned that you will spend as much time driving to the trailhead, located on the Hagerman Pass Road in the upper reaches of the Fryingpan Valley, as you will hiking. But do not let the long ride deter you. The drive is quite scenic and those that invest the driving time will find they have the trail mostly to themselves.

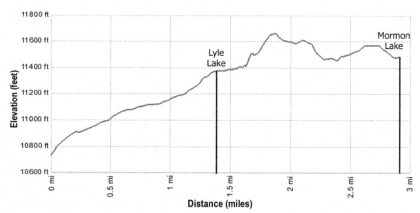

Trailhead to Mormon Lake

From the parking area (see driving directions below) the trail heads northeast, ascending on moderate grades up a broad valley clad in wildflower-filled meadows sprinkled with trees. Just over a mile from the start the grade steepens as the trail curves left (north) and climbs a grassy draw to Lyle Lake (11,390-ft) at 1.4 miles. Pretty Lyle Lake is set in a granite bowl amid meadows scattered with trees.

To reach Mormon Lake cross Lyle's outlet stream and follow the trail around the right (east) side of the lake where is crosses a small boulder field and then climbs to a saddle on the ridge at the north end of the lake. The climb, the steepest on this hike, gains 160-ft. in just under 0.3 miles. From the saddle views extend south to Mount Massive and a panorama of high peaks in the Mount Massive and Hunter-Fryingpan Wilderness Areas.

At the top of the ridge the trail traverses rocky meadows along the western slope of an unnamed 12,367-ft. peak and then dips into and out of a bowl at the head of a small valley. The trail, now heading northeast, exits the bowl by ascending to a bench clad in alpine meadows. Cross the bench, passing to the left of a small tarn and then follow the trail as it descends 80-ft. to Mormon Lake.

Beautiful Mormon Lake is nestled in a rocky basin beneath a steep granite ridge. Views extend northwest to the high peaks of the Holy Cross Wilderness. After taking a break, retrace your steps, enjoying the views and wildflowers on the return trip to the trailhead.

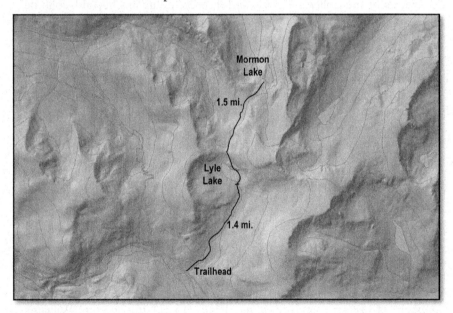

Driving Directions

From Aspen: From the corner of Mill Street and Main Street in Aspen, drive west on West Main Street/CO 82 W for 17.5 miles and turn right on 2 Rivers Road in Basalt. Travel on 2 Rivers Road for 0.8 miles to a stop light and turn right onto Midland Ave, which turns into the Fryingpan Road.

Drive 33 miles along the Fryingpan Road until the pavement ends. Bear left and go 10 more miles until you come to a sign pointing to Hagerman Pass. Turn left onto road #105 for 100 feet. Park by the bulletin board. The rough road can be driven by passenger cars but a 4WD vehicle is recommended. If you are in a passenger car it is best to check with the Forest Service on current road conditions.

From Carbondale: From Carbondale travel east on Hwy 82 for 10 miles and turn left on 2 Rivers Road in Basalt. Travel on 2 Rivers Road for 0.8 miles to a stop light and turn right onto Midland Ave, which turns into the Fryingpan Road.

Drive 33 miles along the Fryingpan Road until the pavement ends. Bear left and go 10 more miles until you come to a sign pointing to Hagerman Pass. Turn left onto road #105 for 100 feet. Park by the bulletin board. The rough road can be driven by passenger cars but a 4WD vehicle is recommended. If you are in a passenger car it is best to check with the Forest Service on current road conditions.

9. Midway Pass ★★★★☆
Distance: 7.8 miles (RT)

Great views of the Collegiate Peaks and the Elk Mountains beyond, solitude and a good workout are your rewards for hiking this lesser used trail to a pass high in the Williams Mountains.

Distance: 7.8 miles (RT)
Elevation: 10,530-ft. at trailhead
12,140-ft. at high point on the trail
Elevation Gain: 1,620-ft.
Difficulty: moderate
Basecamp: Aspen

Area: Hunter-Fryingpan
Wilderness, White River NF
Best Season: July –September
USGS Map(s): Independence
Pass, Mt. Champion, Thimble
Rock
See Page 57 for Map

Why Hike to Midway Pass

This lightly traveled trail climbs steeply through forest up the west side of the Lost Man Valley before heading northwest through meadows and then alpine tundra along the east side of the Coleman Creek drainage. Once above the timberline the trail enjoys fine views of Green Mountain (12,791-ft.), Independence Mountain (12,703-ft.) and the summits of the Collegiate Peaks Wilderness rising to the south of the Roaring Fork Valley. Geissler Mountain (13,186-ft.) and Twining Peak (13,711-ft.) in the Williams Mountains dominate the view to the east. To the southwest are distant views of the high peaks in the Elk Mountains in the Maroon Bells-Snowmass Wilderness.

From the high point on the trail at 3.0 miles the path drops down to Midway Pass, a saddle on a low ridge separating the Coleman Creek and Midway Creek drainages, at 3.9 miles. The pass is pleasant but hardly the highlight of the trip. The steep valley walls on either side of the saddle limit the views. Green Mountain towers above the Roaring Fork Valley to the south while unnamed peaks in the Hunter-Fryingpan Wilderness fill the skyline to the north.

The pass is the turnaround point for day hikers. On the north side of the pass the Midway trail descends the Midway valley and connects with the Hunter Creek and Woody Creek trails, offering opportunities for overnight trips in the Hunter-Fryingpan Wilderness.

Trailhead to Midway Pass

The trail to Midway Pass starts at the Lost Man trailhead (see driving directions below) and follows the Lost Man trail as it heads west, quickly crossing a wood bridge over Lost Man Creek. Beyond the crossing the trail curves to the right (northeast) and ascends on easy grades to a junction at 0.4 miles. Turn left (northwest) at the junction on the trail toward Midway Pass. The Lost Man trail continues straight ahead toward the Lost Man Reservoir.

The path now climbs steeply up a forested hillside on 18 switchbacks. Openings in the trees offer nice views of Green Mountain (12,791-ft.), Independence Peak (12,703-ft.) and other nearby summits towering above the south side of the Roaring Fork valley. The Geissler Mountains rise to the east across the Lost Man Valley.

Reach the top of the switchbacks and the boundary for the Hunter Fryingpan Wilderness at 1.4 miles. The trial now continues its ascents on moderate grades through spruce-fir forest. Soon the grade abates as the trail travels along a wooded bench.

At 2.0 miles the trees give way to wet meadows and dense willow patches. After a short climb the trail curves left (west), crosses a braided stream and then ascends on easy grades. Depending on the time of year you may cross a few more small streams trickling down the slopes above the trail.

Once above timberline the trail enjoys fine views of Green Mountain, Independence Peak and the summits of the Collegiate peaks wilderness to the south of the Roaring Fork Valley. To the southwest are distant views of the high peaks in the Maroon Bells-Snowmass Wilderness. On a clear day you should be able to pick out Castle Peak (14,265-ft.) and Cathedral Peak (13,943-ft.). Peak 13033 towers above the trail to the north.

The climb resumes on moderate grades at 2.4 miles. Follow the trail as it skirts the right (north) side of a small, photogenic tarn at 2.7 miles and turns to the right (northwest). The trail now ascends through alpine tundra to a bench beneath the west side of Peak 13033 at 3.0 miles. This is a high point of the hike at 12,140-ft. From the bench views open to the peaks rising along the west side of Midway pass.

After a brief stint traveling along the bench, the trail drops on easy grades through alpine tundra along the right (east) side of the Coleman Creek drainage. At 3.5 miles the descent steepens as the trail gradually swings left (northwest), crosses a small stream and then drops to the saddle dividing the Coleman Creek and Midway Creek drainages. This is Midway Pass (11,840-ft.) at 3.9 miles.

The pass is pleasant but hardly the highlight of the trip. The steep valley walls on either side of the saddle limit the views. Green Mountain towers above the Roaring Fork valley to the south. View stretch north into the Hunter-Fryingpan Wilderness. Nearer at hand a small tarn lies nestled in a boggy meadow beneath unnamed 12,000-ft. peaks.

For day hikers the pass is a good turn around point. On the north side of the pass the Midway Trail descends the Midway Valley and connects with the Hunter Creek Trail at 8.6 miles and the Woody Creek Trail at 10.6 miles, providing opportunities for overnight trips into the Hunter Fryingpan Wilderness.

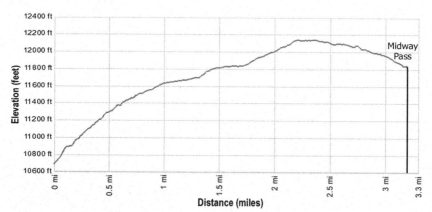

Driving Directions

From Aspen: Drive 14 miles east of Aspen on Highway 82 to the Lost Man trailhead parking area on the left (north) side of the road. The parking lot is directly across from the Lost Man Campground. The trail begins on the left (north) side of the parking area and initially follows the Lost Man trail.

10. West Snowmass Pass ★★★★☆
Distance: 12.4 miles (RT)

Solitude, a good workout and nice views, along with a chance to see wildlife, are the rewards for hikers of this lightly used trail ascending steeply to the saddle separating the Snowmass and Capitol Creek Valleys.

Distance: 12.4 miles (RT)
Elevation: 8,400-ft. at trailhead
 11,780-ft. at the Saddle
Elevation Gain: 3,380-ft.
Difficulty: strenuous
Difficulty: moderate

Basecamp: Aspen
Area: Maroon Bells-Snowmass,
White River NF
Best Season: July –September
USGS Map(s): Capitol Peak
See Page 48 for Map

Why Hike to West Snowmass Pass

The West Snowmass trail is a good option for hikers looking for a little solitude, a good workout and some nice views. The lightly used trail climbs to a saddle at the top of a ridge separating the Snowmass and Capitol Valleys. Views from the saddle extend southeast to the high peaks of the Maroon Bells-Snowmass Wilderness. To the west, the red rock peaks lining the Capitol Creek drainage extend north to Mt. Sopris.

The trail offers good opportunities to spotting deer, elk and other wildlife. On two separate occasions I have seen small black bears loping through the woods near the creek.

From the top of the ridge the trail drops steeply to Capitol Creek where it links with the Capitol Creek trail, offering backpackers options for an extended loop trips. Keep in mind that after crossing Snowmass Creek the West Snowmass Trail gains 3,000-ft. in 4.5 miles. Not an easy trail if carrying a full pack.

Trailhead to the Saddle

Distance from Trailhead: 12.4 miles (RT)
Ending/Highest Elevation: 11,780-ft.
Elevation Gain: 3,380-ft.

The trail to West Snowmass Pass initially follows the Maroon-Snowmass trail. From the trailhead (see driving directions below) the Maroon-Snowmass Trail ascends on moderate grades through aspen and mixed conifers, following the arc of the Snowmass Creek drainage as it heads southwest. Openings in the trees provide views of Snowmass Creek meandering along the valley floor to the west of the trail.

After gaining 200-ft. in 0.5-miles the grade levels for the next mile. Reach the junction with the West Snowmass trail at 1.5-miles. At the junction the West Snowmass trail turns right and drops down to Snowmass Creek on a long switchback. Depending on the time of year the cold and

swift creek varies in depth from knee to ankle deep. Sandals are recommended to protect your feet while negotiating the large slippery rocks in the creek bed.

Across the creek the trail ascends on moderate grades through a large meadow and then enters the forest of aspen and mixed conifers. Soon after entering the trees the trail comes to a gated fence marking the beginning of National Forest land. Beyond the fence the trail climbs switchbacks up the hillside high above the north side of West Snowmass Creek.

At 2.6 miles the path drops to cross a minor drainage then resumes its ascent. The grade abates a bit at 3.0 miles as the trail nears the creek, traveling through forest interspersed with pretty meadows.

At 4.0 miles reach an unmarked junction at a large meadow with wonderful views of Clark Peak and Mt. Daly (13,300-ft.). The prominent trail to the left (south) descends through the meadow to nice campsites along West Snowmass Creek. We bear right (west) on a trail that ascends steeply through forest and meadows up the hillside beneath Haystack Mountain (12,206-ft.). As you climb the trees thin yielding ever improving views of the surrounding peaks.

Reach at trail junction at 5.0 miles. Here the Nickelson Creek trail heads right. We bear left at the junction, continuing the climb up the steep hillside. Good views of Mt. Daly and the peaks to the south and southeast distract you from the stiff ascent.

At 5.6 miles the trail enters a large grassy basin on the south flank of Haystack Mountain. Follow the trail as it climbs steeply, swings right (north) and then left (west) to reach the saddle at the top of the ridge between Haystack Mountain and Mt. Daly at 6.2 miles.

From the saddle views extend southeast to the high peaks of the Maroon Bells-Snowmass Wilderness. To the west, the red rock peaks lining the Capitol Creek drainage extend north to Mt. Sopris (12,953-ft.).

The pass is a good turnaround point for day hikers. After taking in the view retrace your steps to the trailhead.

Saddle to Junction with the Capitol Creek Trail

Segment Stats: 2.2 miles (one-way) with a 1,730-ft. elevation loss
Distance from Trailhead: 8.4 miles (one way)
Ending/Highest Elevation: 10,050-ft.
Elevation Gain: -1,730-ft.

Beyond the saddle the trail drops off the ridge and makes a steep descent through seldom visited meadows and forest to the junction with the Capitol Creek trail at 8.4 miles, providing options for extended overnight loop trips combining the Snowmass and Capitol Creek valleys.

Backpackers should keep in mind that after crossing Snowmass Creek the West Snowmass Trail climbs 3,000-ft. in 4.5 miles to the saddle and then loses 1,750-ft. in 2.2 miles. This is not an easy trail when carrying a full pack.

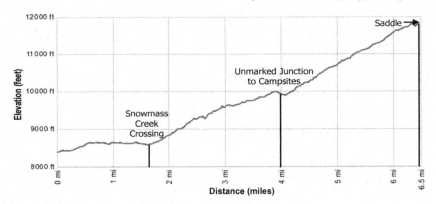

Driving Directions

From Aspen:

Option 1 (Rough, steep and narrow road for part of the drive): Drive 6 miles west of Aspen on Highway 82 and turn left on the Brush Creek Road (the main road to Snowmass Village). Continue on Brush Creek Road for 5.5 miles through Snowmass Village and then turn right on Divide Road.

Divide Road turns into a gravel road and passes the Krabloonik Restaurant and Kennels. The rough road descends steeply to the bottom of the Snowmass Creek valley where it forks. Take the left fork. Pass the East Snowmass trailhead on the left. Continue another 0.2 miles to the Maroon-Snowmass Trailhead, which is also the starting point for the West Snowmass

Trail, at the end of the road. When parking, please do not block the gate leading to the ranch at the west end of the parking lot.

Note: there is limited parking at the trailhead. The trailhead, popular with backpackers traveling to Snowmass Lake, can get quite crowded on the weekends.

Option 2 (Better option for 2WD vehicles): Drive 14 miles west of Aspen on Highway 82 to Old Snowmass and turn left on the Capitol Creek/Snowmass Creek Road (next to the Conoco Gas station on the south side of the highway). Continue 2 miles to a "T" intersection. Turn left and follow Snowmass Creek Road (CO Rd. 11) for 5.8 miles to a fork in the road. Take the left fork, staying on Snowmass Creek Road (CO Rd. 11) for 3.4 miles to a "T" intersection. Take a right. Soon you will pass the East Snowmass trailhead on the left. Continue another 0.2 miles to the Maroon-Snowmass Trailhead, which is also the starting point for the West Snowmass Trail, at the end of the road. When parking, please do not block the gate leading to the ranch at the west end of the parking lot.

Note: there is limited parking at the trailhead. The trailhead, popular with backpackers traveling to Snowmass Lake, can get quite crowded on the weekends.

11. New York Creek ★★★★☆
Distance: 8.2 miles (RT)

This nice hike climbs to a 12,290-ft. saddle on the divide separating the Bowman Creek and New York Creek Valleys. At the divide enjoy great views of American Flag and Italian Mountains and nearby peaks in the Collegiate Peaks and Hunter-Fryingpan Wilderness areas.

Distance: 8.2 miles (RT) to Saddle
Elevation: 10,070-ft. at Trailhead
12,290-ft. at Saddle
Elevation Gain: 2,220-ft. to Saddle
Difficulty: moderate-strenuous

Basecamp: Aspen
Area: Collegiate Peaks
Wilderness, White River NF
Best Season: July –September
USGS Map(s): New York Peak

Why Hike New York Creek

This pleasant, lightly used trail ascends through spruce-fir forests and pretty meadows to a high saddle on the ridge separating the Bowman and New York Creek valleys. From the saddle fine views stretch south to American Flag Mountain (12,713-ft.) and Italian Mountain (13,378-ft.) rising above the Taylor River valley. Difficult Mountain (12,934-ft.), Green Mountain, the Williams Mountains and a sea of peaks in the Collegiate Peaks Wilderness fill the skyline to the north/northeast.

Note that a half mile section of the hike travels along the access road for the aqueduct system that diverts water from New York and Brooklyn drainages to Grizzly Reservoir. From the reservoir a tunnel carries the water under the Continental Divide to the Twin Lakes Reservoir.

Certainly the road and the diversion intakes detract from the scenic value of the hike. That being said, it is a nice hike up a lovely valley where you are likely to run into few other hikers. The trail is a good option if you have done many of the other hikes around the Aspen area and are looking for new territory to explore.

Trailhead to Saddle between Bowman and New York Creek Valleys

From the New York Creek parking area (see driving directions below) the trail heads south and crosses Lincoln Creek. Depending on the time of year the wide crossing can be knee or ankle deep. Use care when crossing the river early in the season.

Beyond the crossing a boot beaten path traverses gravel flats with scattered willows to a second crossing of a smaller tributary stream. On the other side of the stream the trail passes between tall willows and then curves to the southwest as it ascends gradually along an old jeep road through spruce-fir forest and then scrubby meadows. From the meadows enjoy views of Peak 12450 rising to the west.

At 0.25 miles the trail plunges back into the trees. Soon the grade steepens as the trail climbs a few switchbacks. At 0.75 miles the trail starts ascending through a second meadow on steep switchbacks. As you climb, enjoy every improving views of Peak 12450 to the west and Green Mountain (12,791-ft.) to north.

Reach a junction with the aqueduct access road, an ugly scar in the valley, at 1.0 mile. The aqueduct system diverts water from the New York and Brooklyn Creek drainages to the Grizzly Reservoir. From the reservoir a tunnel carries the water under the Continental Divide to the Twin Lakes Reservoir.

At the junction a trail sign points right (southwest). Make note of this intersection so you do not miss the turn on the return trip to the trailhead.

Turn right and follow the level aqueduct road for 0.5 miles. At 1.3 miles the road reaches the cement intake tunnel for the Brooklyn Gulch Creek Diversion where the road curves to the right and then left before continuing its southwest traverse. Soon the cement intake tunnel for the New York Creek Diversion and the end of the road come into view.

Watch for a trail branching left off the road and entering the forest at 1.5 miles. A small sign off the road marks the turnoff, which is easy to miss. If you miss the turn and reach the end of the road, turn around and walk about 50 yards back on the road until you see the trail on the right.

The trail now ascends through forest on easy grades along the east side of the valley, paralleling New York Creek to the right (west). Pass the sign marking the boundary for the Collegiate Peak Wilderness along the way.

At 2.2 miles the trail curves to the right (west) and crosses to the west side of New York Creek through meadows scattered with willow thickets. Here we get the first views of the peaks rimming the head of the valley.

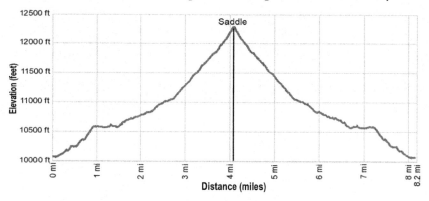

Soon the trail curves left (southwest) and climbs along the west side of the valley on moderate grades though forest and meadows cleared by avalanches spilling down the steep slopes between Difficult Peak (12934-ft.) and New York Peak (12,811-ft.). A few small streams trickle down the hillside.

From the meadows enjoy nice views of Green Mountain to the north/northeast. As the trail gains elevation the rugged peaks rising along the east side of the valley join the scene.

At 2.7 miles the grade steepens as the trail climbs through a pretty meadow and then reenters the forest. The trail crosses a creek at 3.25 miles and a short distance beyond turns sharply left (south), continuing the stiff ascent through scattered trees.

Soon the trees gives way to meadows as the trail reaches the timberline. From this vantage point the Williams Mountains in the Hunter Fryingpan Wilderness form a nice backdrop for Green Mountain to the northeast. Difficult Peaks towers above the east side of the New York Creek Valley.

For the last half mile the trail, marked by rock cairns and wooden posts, climbs steeply through alpine tundra to a 12,290-ft. saddle on the ridge separating the New York Creek and Bowman Creek valleys. As you climb views open to the high peaks lining the east side of Brooklyn Gulch, the valley to the east of New York Creek.

From the divide views extend north to Difficult Peak. Green Mountain, the Williams Mountains and a sea of peaks in the Collegiate Peaks Wilderness fill the skyline to the northeast. American Flag Mountain (12,713-ft.) and Italian Mountain (13,378-ft.) in the Taylor River Valley dominate the view to the south. Grizzly Peak (13,988-ft.) rises above the unnamed summits to the west.

Hikers looking for a longer walk may want to climb along the ridge to the west of the saddle to the top of Peak 12613 for more great views. Another option, only recommended for experienced off-trail warriors, is to follow a seldom used route to Ptarmigan Lake on the south side of the divide at the head of the Tellurium Valley. From the lake the route climbs over the divide and then descends Brooklyn Gulch to the aqueduct road. This option requires good route finding skills. The descent of Brooklyn Gulch is steep with plenty of downed trees and other obstacles. A map marking the old route and a compass are essential.

My recommendation is to take in the views at the New York Creek saddle and then retrace your steps to the trailhead.

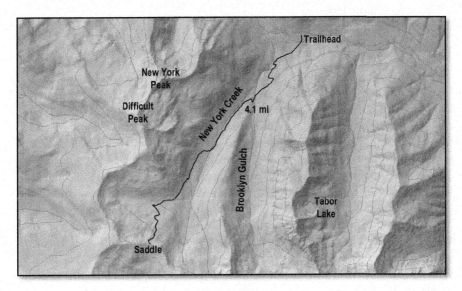

Driving Directions

Driving Directions from Aspen: Drive 10 miles east of Aspen on Highway 82 and turn right on the Lincoln Creek Road. Drive 3.2 miles on Lincoln Creek Road to the New York Creek Trail turnoff on the right. Follow the short access road to the trailhead parking area.

Although a 4WD vehicle is not always necessary, high clearance is a must on the Lincoln Creek Road. Check with the White River Ranger Station in Aspen about current road conditions.

12. Willow Pass and Lake ★★★★☆
Distance: 9.4 - 12.2 miles (RT)

This lightly traveled trail features great views of the Maroon Bells and Pyramid Peak, traverses pretty meadows and ends at a scenic pass with sweeping views of the colorful cirque surrounding the Willow Lake basin.

Distance: 3.4 miles (RT) to Crater Lake
9.7 miles (RT) to Willow Pass
12.2 miles (RT) to Willow Lake
Elevation: 9,580-ft. at Trailhead
10,140-ft. at Crater Lake
12,578-ft. at Willow Pass
11,795-ft. at Willow Lake
Elevation Gain: 560-ft. to Crater Lake
2,998-ft. to Willow Pass
3,781-ft. to Willow Lake

Difficulty: strenuous
Basecamp: Aspen
Area: Maroon Bells-Snowmass Wilderness, White River NF
Best Season: July –September
USGS Map(s): Maroon Bells
See Page 26 for Map

Why Hike to Willow Pass and Lake

The hikes to Willow Pass and Buckskin Pass travel the same trail for the first 3.75 miles before splitting and climbing to the two respective passes, just 0.7 miles apart as the crow flies. If you have limited time and it's your first trip to the Maroon Bells hike to Buckskin Pass first. The stunning views from Buckskin Pass are far superior to the views from Willow Pass. Of course everything is relative in the Maroon Bells. The whole area is amazing.

So why hike to Willow Pass? On a beautiful day extending the hike to Buckskin with a visit to Willow Pass is a great option. Combining the two hikes adds 1.9 miles and 800-ft of elevation gain for an 11.3 mile hike.

Beyond the trail split with Buckskin Pass, the lightly trafficked trail to Willow Pass travels through a pretty basin and then climbs to the high pass with fine views of the colorful cirque surrounding the Willow Lake Basin. Willow Lake, along with a handful of small ponds, lie nestled in the alpine meadows beneath the serrated profile of the Sievers Mountains. Colorful

70

Peak 13336 towers above the valley to the north. To the southeast are great views of the Maroon Bells and a slice of the Pyramid Peak massif.

The second reason to hike to Willow Pass is to visit Willow Lake and the secluded Willow Lake basin. Relatively few people hike and/or camp in this basin, so you are likely to experience a level of solitude not found around other lakes in the Maroon Bells Wilderness. The basin is a fun place to explore, fishing in the lake is good and so are the views, especially if you climb to ridge to the south of the lake.

So if you have the time or are looking for someplace different to visit in the Aspen area, take a hike to Willow Pass and Willow Lake. With a car drop or second vehicle the hike to Willow Pass can be combined with the East Snowmass trail to create a good, off-the-beaten-path overnight backpack.

Another option is a 3-day loop backpack that starts by hiking up Snowmass Creek to Snowmass Lake. On the second day, hike over Buckskin and Willow Passes to Willow Lake. On the final day climb over East Snowmass Pass and then descend the East Snowmass Valley. At the East Snowmass trailhead a short walk along a dirt road leads back to the Snowmass Creek trailhead.

Trailhead to Crater Lake/West Maroon Junction

Distance from Trailhead: 3.4 miles (RT)
Ending/Highest Elevation: 10,140-ft.
Elevation Gain: 560-ft.

Few hikes can top the stunning views from the start of the Willow Pass trail, beginning at the foot of Maroon Lake. Mirrored in the lake's waters are the iconic Maroon Bells (14,156-ft. and 14,014-ft.), towering above the head of the valley. Pyramid Peak's (14,018-ft.) jagged crags rise to the south while the crimson spires of the Sievers Mountains form the backdrop for beautiful aspen groves to the north.

The trail to Willow Pass initially follows the Maroon-Snowmass Trail. The trail starts at a kiosk at the southwest end of the trailhead parking area. If arriving on the shuttle bus, walk down the Maroon Lake Trail to the north shore of Maroon Lake and turn right on the Maroon-Snowmass Trail. The mileage in this description assumes you are starting from the trailhead kiosk.

From the kiosk, follow the Maroon-Snowmass trail along Maroon Lake's north (right) shore to a junction at the "Deadly Bell's Kiosk" near the head of the lake. Progress will be slow along this section of the trail as the gorgeous scenery invites frequent stops.

At the junction the Scenic Loop Trail branches left. We turn right to stay on the Maroon-Snowmass trail, which ascends a wide rocky path through Aspen and spruce trees along the northwest side of the valley. Openings in the trees offer views of rugged Pyramid Peak rising to the south.

About a mile from the start the moderately steep trail climbs an ancient rock slide forming a natural dam that created Crater Lake. As you reach the top of the slide enjoy wonderful views of the Maroon Bells and the Sleeping Sexton, located on the ridge extending north from North Maroon Peak.

From the top of the slide the trail descends gently toward Crater Lake. Slightly before reaching Crater Lake arrive at a junction at 1.7 miles. Take the right fork, signed for Maroon-Snowmass trail. The West Maroon trail, heading straight ahead, leads to Crater Lake and West Maroon Pass.

Junction to Willow Pass

Segment Stats: 3.15 miles (one-way) with a 2,438-ft. elevation gain
Distance from Trailhead: 9.7 miles (RT)
Ending/Highest Elevation: 12,578-ft.
Elevation Gain from Trailhead: 2,998-ft.

The Maroon-Snowmass trail ascends steeply through aspen and spruce forest for 0.6 miles to Minnehaha Gulch. Breaks in the trees along the lower section of the climb provide nice views of the Maroon Bells, Crater Lake and the West Maroon Valley. As you gain elevation the trees thin and great views open to the west across Minnehaha Gulch to the Sleeping Sexton and North Maroon Peak.

The initial ascent is along the northeast side of the the gulch, a deep ravine channeling a stream. At 2.9 miles the path rock hops across the stream to the southwest side of the gulch. Beyond the crossing the trail climbs a hillside through pretty meadows and downed trees, toppled by avalanche activity. The meadows offer wonderful panoramas of North Maroon Peak to the southwest and Pyramid Peak to the southeast.

At the end of the gulch the trail climbs a steep gully beside a small stream festoon with wildflowers and emerges onto a beautiful basin clad in alpine meadows. Buckskin Pass, the saddle looming above the head of the steep valley, is now in sight.

Ascend the meadows on a series of switchbacks with fine views of Maroon Bells and the Sleeping Sexton. Pyramid Peak dominates the skyline to the southeast.

Reach a junction at 3.75 miles. The trail to the left (northwest) leads to Buckskin Pass. We turn right (north) on the trail to Willow Pass and continue the steady climb through pretty meadows. Soon the trail curve around the end of a ridge and then swings to the left (west), climbing steeply up a series of tight switchbacks. Along the way enjoy more great views of the Bells and the Pyramid Peak massif.

At 4.1 miles the grade abates as the trail crests a rise and enters a pretty basin, surrounded by a colorful cirque anchored by Buckskin Peak (13,370-ft.) to the northwest. The trail to Willow Pass is now in sight, climbing to the saddle on the ridge to the north. Follow the trail as it crosses a small stream and then resumes its ascent on moderately steep grades, heading northwest through meadows.

Arrive at the base of the ridge at 4.5 miles. Here the trail starts a short, extremely steep climb up switchbacks etched into the ridge's red and gray talus slopes. Great views to the southeast provide a welcome distraction from the stiff climb.

Willow Pass (12,580-ft.) is reached at 4.7 miles. From the pass great views extend north across the rolling alpine meadows of the Willow Lake basin to the rugged ridge running between Buckskin Peak and Peak 13336. Willow Lake (11,795-ft.) and a few smaller ponds lie nestled in a pretty basin beneath the serrated ridge of the Sievers Mountains. To the southeast are more terrific views of the Maroon Bells and Pyramid Peak massif.

Many hikers will turn around at this point and retrace their steps to the trailhead. If the weather is good and time/energy permit, consider extending the hike with a side trip to Willow Lake. This option will add 2.8 miles (RT) to the hike with an elevation gain/loss of about 790-ft.

From Willow Pass to Willow Lake

Segment Stats: 1.25 miles (one-way) with a -783-ft. elevation loss to the lake
Distance from Trailhead: 12.2 miles (RT)
Ending/Highest Elevation: 11,795-ft.
Elevation Gain from Trailhead: 3,781-ft.

The trail to Willow Lake initially descends steeply through alpine meadows on the north side of Willow Pass before turning right (northeast) and continuing the descent on more moderate grades.

At 5.3 miles the trail curves to the right (east) and the grade abates. To the south are a few small ponds. Pass a junction at 5.5 miles with a faint trail heading northwest toward East Snowmass Pass. Our trail now curves to the right (southeast), traveling through meadows and stunted confers to the north shore of Willow Lake (11,795-ft.) at 6.1 miles. The trail fades as it approaches the lake but the way is obvious.

From the lake enjoy beautiful views of Peak 13336 towering above the valley to the north. The Sievers Mountains fill the skyline to the northeast. The basin is fun to explore. Fishermen will want to try their luck catching some of the lake's brook trout. Backpackers will find nice campsites in the stunted conifers and rock outcroppings around the lake basin.

Return to the Maroon Lake trailhead when you are done exploring the Willow Lake basin. Alternatively turn the hike into an overnight backpack by spending a night in the lake basin. From Willow Lake hikers with a second car positioned at the East Snowmass trailhead can climb the steep trail to East Snowmass Pass and then descend the East Snowmass Trail to the East Snowmass trailhead, located to the west of Snowmass Village, for a 13.6 mile hike or backpack. Note: The trail climbing to East Snowmass Pass is very steep and travels through a boulder field. Portions of the trail are faint where it crosses the lake basin's meadows.

Another option is a 3-day loop backpack that starts by hiking up Snowmass Creek to Snowmass Lake. On the second day, hike over Buckskin Pass and Willow Pass to Willow Lake. On the final day climb to over East Snowmass Pass and drop down the East Snowmass trail to the East Snowmass trailhead. From the trailhead a short walk along a dirt road leads back to the Snowmass Creek trailhead. Note: Bear Canisters are now required for overnight travel in the Maroon Bells Wilderness area. See the Four Pass Loop hike for more information on overnight food storage regulations.

I strongly advise getting an early start when day hiking to Willow Pass and Willow Lake so you can enjoy the pass and the lake before the onset of afternoon thunderstorm, a common occurrence in the Rockies.

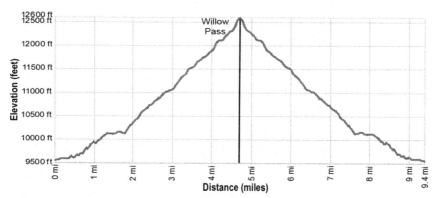

Driving Directions

From Aspen: The Maroon Bells has limited accessibility by car. From mid-June through Labor Day the Maroon Creek Road is restricted to vehicles from 8:00 a.m. to 5:00 p.m. beyond the T-Lazy 7 Ranch, unless you have campground reservations or you are overnight backpacking. Travel is also restricted from 8:00 a.m. to 5:00 p.m. on Friday, Saturday and Sunday from Labor Day to September 30th.

A shuttle bus, which leaves every 20-30 minutes, departs from the Aspen Highlands ski area. There is paid parking at Aspen Highlands or you can take the free Castle Maroon Bus from the Rubey Park Transit Center in downtown Aspen to Aspen Highlands. Dogs are allowed on the bus. Bus tickets that cover the bus and admission to the Maroon Bells Scenic area are sold at Four-Mountain Sports in Aspen Highlands.

Please note the Maroon Bells Scenic Area is a recreation fee area. The Interagency, Senior & Golden Access Passes are honored. Fees apply at all times. Self-pay stations are available during off hours.

If you are driving to the Maroon Bells Scenic Area or Aspen Highlands for the shuttle bus from downtown Aspen, follow Hwy 82 heading west to the roundabout just outside of town. Exit the roundabout at the Maroon

Creek Road. In approximately one mile reach Aspen Highlands, turn left here for the shuttle.

If arriving during non-bus hours or heading to the backpacker's overnight parking area, continue another 4 miles to the Maroon Bells Scenic Area Welcome Station. The use fee will be collected here, or in the fee tube immediately behind the station if unmanned. Continue another 5 miles to the parking lot at Maroon Lake. Parking is VERY limited in both the day use and overnight lots.

13. Hell Roaring ★★★★☆
Distance: 5.4 miles (RT)

This lightly used trail ascends a ridge with nice views of Mount Daly and Capitol Peak then climbs through pretty alpine meadows to Hell Roaring Divide, where views encompass the peaks and ridges of the Avalanche Creek drainage and beyond.

Distance: 5.4 miles (RT)
Elevation: 9,970-ft. at Trailhead
Maximum elevation: 12,080-ft.
Elevation Gain: 2,110-ft.
Difficulty: moderate
Basecamp: Aspen

Area: Maroon Bells-Snowmass Wilderness, White River NF
Best Season: July –September
USGS Map(s): Capitol Peak and Redstone
See Page 48 for Map

Trailhead to the Hell Roaring Divide

From the Hell Roaring Trailhead go through the green gate and follow the trail as it ascends to the top of the ridge on a moderate grade through spruce-fir forest. In 0.2 miles the trail reaches a trail junction. The path to the right leads to Hardscrabble Lake in 0.25 miles. The Hell Roaring trail continues straight.

As the trail climbs along the top of the ridge periodic openings in the trees provide nice views of Mount Daly and Capitol Peak (14,130) rising above the head of the Capitol Creek valley to the south.

Three quarters of a mile from the trailhead the path dips into and out of a small saddle on the ridge. Just as the trail begins climbing out of the saddle reach the junction with the trail to Williams Lake, heading right. The side trip to Williams Lake adds 1.5 miles (RT) to the hike.

Beyond the junction the grade steepens as the trail continues ascending the ridge. Intermittent clearing offer views extending south toward to Capitol Peak and north to timber lined shores of Williams Lake.

At 2.0 miles the trees give way to pretty alpine meadows and the grade moderates as the path climbs switchbacks to the top of the ridge, reaching Hell Roaring Divide at 2.7 miles. From the divide enjoy views of Mt. Sopris to the north and the peaks and ridges lining the Avalanche Creek drainage to the west.

This is the turnaround point for the day hike. The Hell Roaring trail continues over the divide and intersects the Avalanche Creek Trail, losing over 3,700-ft. ft in 4.3 miles (7.0 miles from the trailhead).

A 4WD vehicle is required to reach the trailhead. Hikers driving passenger cars need to add 4.5 miles (RT) to the hiking distances.

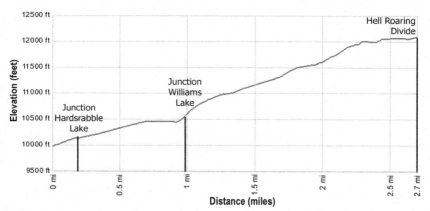

Driving Directions

From Aspen: Drive 14 miles west of Aspen on Highway 82 to Old Snowmass and turn left onto Snowmass Creek Road (just past to the Conoco Gas station on the south side of the highway). Continue 2 miles to the "T" intersection, take a right and travel 7.5 miles until the pavement ends. Follow the dirt road about 3 miles to the trailhead. The last 2.25 miles is on a 4WD road. Hikers without a 4WD need to park in the BLM meadow on the right approximately 2.25 miles below the trailhead. The road is slick when wet.

14. American Lake ★★★★☆
Distance: 6.4 miles (RT)

This short trail climbs steeply through aspen groves, forests and meadows to a high mountain lake just below the timberline, offering hikers a good workout and a great way to acclimate for some of the Aspen area's more challenging trails.

Distance: 6.4 miles (RT)
Elevation: 9,400-ft. at Trailhead
Maximum elevation: 11,390-ft.
Elevation Gain: 1,990-ft.
Difficulty: moderate-strenuous

Basecamp: Aspen
Area: Maroon Bells-Snowmass Wilderness, White River NF
Best Season: July –September
USGS Map(s): Hayden Peak
See Page 31 for Map

Trailhead to American Lake

The American Lake trail ascends steep switchbacks through aspen groves along the north side of a gulch for 1.5 miles before reaching spruce-fir forests where it turns south. From this point the trail alternates between level sections and periodic climbs on easy to moderate grades through forest and wildflower-filled meadows with limited views of the surrounding peaks.

A little over 2.0 miles from the trailhead the path crosses a small ridge and heads west. Approximately 0.5 miles before the lake the trail emerges into a wildflower oasis, surrounded by scree. It then briefly reenters the forest before crossing another large scree field with sounds of a waterfall just ahead and to the left. American Lake, a small emerald green expanse set amid trees with a granite ridge rising above the north shore, is just beyond.

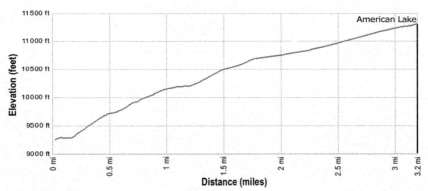

Driving Directions

Driving Directions from Aspen: Drive 0.5 miles west of Aspen on Highway 82 to the Roundabout. Go around the roundabout and turn right on Castle Creek Road. Drive 10 miles to the Elk Mountain Lodge and turn right into the American lake parking lot, located across from the lodge on the west side of the road.

15. Thomas Lakes ★★★★★
Distance: 8.2 miles (RT)

A nice hike to two pretty lakes cradled beneath the twin-summits of Mt. Sopris. Beyond the lakes the trail climbs steeply to the eastern summit of Mt. Sopris.

Distance: 8.2 miles (RT)
Elevation: 8,656-ft. at Trailhead
10,288-ft. at Thomas Lakes
Elevation Gain: 1,632-ft.
Difficulty: moderate

Basecamp: Aspen, Carbondale
Area: Maroon Bells-Snowmass Wilderness, White River NF
Best Season: July –September
USGS Map(s): Mt Sopris, Basalt

Why Hike to Thomas Lakes

Mt Sopris stands alone at the northwest end of the Elk Range, rising almost 6,400-ft above the valleys to the south of Carbondale and west of Aspen. This pleasant hike climbs to the timber lined shores of the Thomas Lakes, nestled beneath the mountain's rugged northeast face.

The trail starts with a moderate climb up an old jeep road and then follows a trail ascending through meadows and forest to the two lakes. Along the way views extend over wooded hills to the high peaks of the Elk Range rising to the east and the Roaring Fork Valley to the north.

The trail is popular with hikers looking for a relatively easy day hike and backpacker seeking to summit Mt. Sopris. Many people backpack to the Thomas Lakes and spend the night before climbing to the summit on the second day. The trail is also a good option for people wishing to acclimatize or if bad weather precludes hiking the higher trails to the east.

Trailhead to Thomas Lakes

Note: This trail is open to mountain bikes up to the Hay Park junction.

The Thomas Lakes/Mt. Sopris trail is located on the south side of the Dinkle Lake Road across from the trailhead parking area. (See driving directions below.) Follow the trail as it heads south through a meadow on easy grades. Soon the trail curves to the right (southwest) and ascends an old Jeep road on moderate grades through a forest of oak and aspens. At 0.7 miles the trail switchbacks to the left (east) as it continues its steady climb.

At 1.1 miles the road curves south and soon reaches an open area where views extend over hills, clad in aspen and evergreens, to the high peaks of the Elk Mountains to the east. Beyond this point the grade eases as the road ends at a metal gate. Pass through the metal gate and follow the trail as it travels through low shrubs and gambel oaks.

At 1.4 miles the trail curves to the left (southeast), ascending through pastures with nice views of the peaks rising to the east and the Roaring Fork Valley to the north. The trail curves to the right (south/southwest) and reaches a "Y" intersection at 1.75 miles. Here the Hay Pass trail branches to the left (south). We turn right (west) toward Mt. Sopris, passing a sign indicating that no bikes are permitted beyond this point.

The trail now climbs on moderate grades through pastures. To the southwest, the twin summits of the Mount Sopris (12,953-ft.) are now visible above the trees.

At 2.1 miles the trail crests a hill and curves to the left (south) in a large open meadow with stunning views of the Mount Sopris massif to the southwest. After a short, steep climb the path curves right (southwest), ascending on easy grades through groves of aspens and evergreens intersperse with small meadows. The meadows and openings in the trees offer partially obstructed views of Mt. Sopris and the valleys to the north. Along the way the trail gets noticeably rockier.

After crossing a creek at 3.2 miles the trail climbs steeply for a short distance. Soon the grade abates and the trail passes a small pond on the right (west). Another pond lies hidden in the trees to the left (east). Beyond the ponds the trail crosses another small stream.

Reach a trail junction at 3.75 miles and the boundary of the Maroon Bells-Snowmass Wilderness. The trail branching left leads to designated campsites. Straight ahead is the main trail towards the upper lake and Mt Sopris. To the right (west), Mt. Sopris towers above the lower (western) Thomas Lake (10,206-ft.).

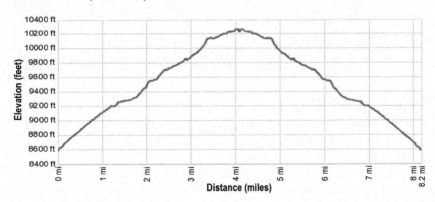

Take a short detour to the timbered eastern shore of the lower lake. Here views extend across the lake to the steep cliffs and rugged talus slopes along the northeast face of the Mt. Sopris massif. Moraines and rocky slopes, marking the path of ancient glaciers, spill down the slopes of the massif.

To continue to the upper lake, return to the junction and take the broad, rocky trail straight ahead (south) toward the Mt Sopris summit. The trail ascends on easy grades through trees, passing designated campsites along the way. Reach the western shore of the upper (eastern) Thomas Lake (10,284-ft.) at 4.0 miles and the south end of the lake at 4.1 miles. The upper lake is surrounded by trees.

Beyond the upper lake the trail starts its steep climb to the top of Mt. Sopris. With an early start fit, well-conditioned hikers can make the climb in one day. A better option is to camp at one of the designated campsites at the lake and climb the remaining four miles to the summit on the second day. If you backpack into the Thomas Lake please make sure you fill out a free registration form at the trailhead. No camping or fires are only allowed within a quarter miles of the Thomas Lakes except at one of the 12 designated campsites.

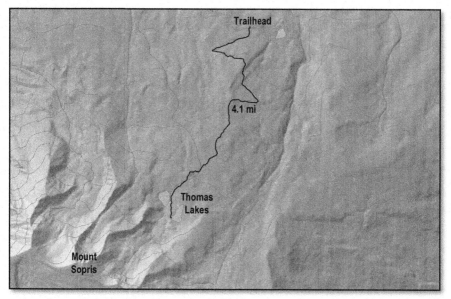

Driving Directions

Driving Directions from Aspen: From the corner of Mill Street and Main Street in Aspen, drive west on West Main Street/CO 82 W for 25 miles and turn left (south) on Emma Road. In 0.1 miles reach a "T" intersection and turn left (east) to stay on Emma Road. Follow Emma Road as it turns right (south) and become Sopris Creek Road. Drive 1.0 mile to a "T" Intersection and turn right (west) on West Sopris Road. Follow West Sopris Road for 5.6 miles and turn left (south) on Dinkle Lake Road. Drive 2.0 miles on Dinkle Lake Road to the Thomas Lakes trailhead on the left (north) side of the road. The trailhead is across the road, on the right (south) side of the Dinkle Lake Road.

Driving Directions from Carbondale: From the intersection of CO 133 and Main Street in Carbondale, travel south on CO 133 S for approximately 1.7 miles and turn left (southeast) on Prince Creek Road (CR 111). Drive 6.3 miles and turn right (south) on Dinkle Lake Road. Drive 2.0 miles on Dinkle Lake Road to the Thomas Lakes trailhead on the left (north) side of the road. The trailhead is across the road, on the right (south) side of the Dinkle Lake Road.

16. Josephine Lake ★★★★★
Distance: 7.7 - 8.0 miles (RT)

The lightly used trail to Josephine Lake wanders through forest, passes two large parks and then travels along a ridge with fine views of the Elk Mountain Range and nearby 12,000-ft. peaks.

Distance: 8.0 miles (RT) to Josephine Lake
Elevation: 9,240-ft. at Trailhead 9,240-ft. at Josephine Lake
Elevation Gain: 11,550-ft. to Josephine Lake
Difficulty: moderate-strenuous

Basecamp: Aspen and Basalt
Area: Holy Cross Wilderness, White River NF
Best Season: July –September
USGS Map(s): Nast, Mount Jackson

Why Hike to Josephine Lake

The off-the-beaten-path hike to Josephine Lake is a good option if you are looking for solitude, good views and the chance to see some wildlife. The lake, located in the Holy Cross Wilderness, is nestled beneath 12,000-ft. peaks in the Sawatch Range. Trailhead access is via a long, scenic car ride up the Hunter Fryingpan Road out of Basalt.

The hike starts with a steep climb through aspen and then spruce-pine forest, passing two large meadows, Henderson Park and Coffeepot Park. Beyond Coffeepot the trail climbs to and then travels along a high ridge to a trail dropping down to Josephine Lake.

As you attain the ridge the trees give way to meadows and views open to a panorama stretching across the rolling hills of the Hunter Fryingpan Wilderness to the Elk Mountain Range in the south. On clear day you should be able to pick out Mt Sopris, Capitol Peak, Snowmass Mountain, the Maroon Bells and Pyramid Peak. Near at hand are the unnamed 12,000-ft peaks filling the skyline to the north.

An optional off-trail side trip continues up the ridge to the top of Peak 12191 with great views of the nearby peaks and lakes.

Trailhead to Josephine Lake

The trail to Josephine Lake starts on the left (northwest) side of Road 501 at the Henderson Park Trailhead. (See driving directions below.) The rocky trail initially heads northwest, climbing steeply up grassy slopes through scattered conifers and aspens. Pass the sign for the Holy Cross Wilderness in 0.1 miles. Soon the trail curves to the right (northeast) and continues its steep ascent. Here views open to the wooded hills to the east.

After hiking 0.4 miles the grade abates. The respite is brief and soon the climb resumes, now on moderately steep grades through aspen groves growing amid ferns, corn lilies, wildflowers and tall grasses. A rock outcropping at 0.8 miles offers nice views to the east. A few switchbacks facilitate the ascent.

At 1.5 miles the trail plunges into a spruce/pine forest. Soon the grade abates and the trail travels on easy grades along the right (east) side of a small creek.

Reach a trail junction at 1.7 miles. Here the Henderson Park trail turns right (east) toward Carter Lake. We continue straight ahead on the Tellurium Lake Trail. Beyond the junction cross to west side of the creek and continue along the trail a short distance to the southwest corner of pretty Henderson Park, a large marshy meadow. Peak 12191 towers above the park to the northeast. Smaller peaks and ridges rise to the east. Our trail will eventually climbs along the ridge extending west from Peak 12191.

The trail now heads north through trees, skirting the west side of Henderson Park. In the early morning you may be lucky enough to spot deer or elk grazing in the meadows.

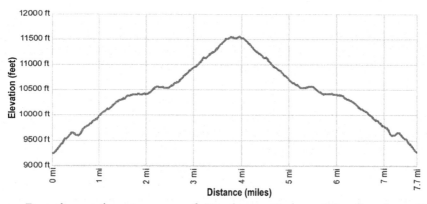

Past the northwest corner of Henderson Park at 2.0 miles the trail climbs steeply for a short distance and then drops down to the southwest corner of Coffeepot Park, a smaller meadow at 2.3 miles. Here we get another view of Peak 12191 to the northeast. The summits of several 12,000-ft. mountains peek above the trees to the north.

Follow the trail as it travels along the western edge of Coffeepot Park to a trail junction just beyond the northwest end of the meadow. To the left (west) is the Last Chance trail. We bear slightly right on the trail toward Josephine Lake.

The trail now climbs on moderate to moderately steep grades through forest and soon curves to the right (northeast). At 3.2 miles the trail turns right (east) near the crest of the ridge. Beyond this point the trail ascends through scattered trees along the south side of the ridge, just below the crest. As you gain elevation the trees thin and terrific views open to the Elk Mountains to the south.

At 3.5 miles the trail briefly travels along the top of the ridge with great views of the jagged 12,000-ft peaks rising to the north. Attain the top of the ridge again at 3.9 miles. Josephine Lake is now visible below the north side of the ridge, tucked in a rocky basin beneath the rugged west face of Peak 12191. A very steep trail drops down from ridge to the little cobalt blue lake at 4.0 miles. Use care when descending the steep trail to the lake.

While the lake is nice, my preference is to have lunch atop the ridge and enjoy the great, albeit distant, panoramic views of the Elk Range to the south stretching from Mount Sopris to the Collegiate Peaks. On a clear day you should be able to pick out Capitol Peak, Snowmass Mountain, the Maroon Bells and Pyramid Peak. Near at hand a rugged ridge of 12,000-ft peaks fills the skyline to the north/northwest of the lake basin.

If time and energy permit, continue up the ridge to the top of Peak 12191. There is no trail but the route is obvious. From the summit enjoy views of Savage Peak (13,191-ft.) rising to the east above the Carter Creek basin. Below you are Carter Lake and Savage Lake. In the distance are the peaks and lakes in the Hunter Fryingpan and Holy Cross Wilderness areas along with the Elk Mountain Range to the south. This side trip will gain over 640-ft in elevation and add 1.4 miles round to the hike.

When you are done enjoying the views, retrace your steps to the trailhead.

Driving Directions

From Aspen: From the corner of Mill Street and Main Street in Aspen, drive west on West Main Street/CO 82 W for 17.5 miles and turn right on 2 Rivers Road in Basalt. Travel on 2 Rivers Road for 0.8 miles and turn right onto Midland Ave which turns into the Fryingpan Road. Follow the scenic Fryingpan Road as it travels along sections of the beautiful Fryingpan River and high above Ruedi Reservoir for 27 miles to an intersection with Road #501 (County Road 4B). There will be a sign for the Elk Wallow Campground at the intersection. Turn left on Road #501. (This turn is right before the Fryingpan Road crosses the Fryingpan River.)

Drive 4.5 miles on Road 501 to a "Y" intersection. Bear left at the intersection to stay on Road 501. (The road to the right is Cunningham Creek Road / CR 4C). In 0.15 miles find a sign for the Henderson Park trailhead on the left side of the road. Parking is on the right side of the road just past the trailhead sign.

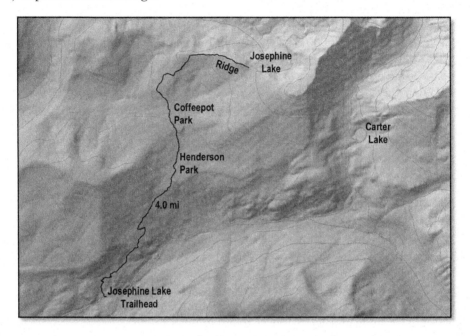

17. Geneva Lake ★★★★★
Distance: 4.2 miles (RT)

This trail, our personal favorite, has waterfalls, wildflowers, a pristine lake and gigantic views of the Lead King Basin and backside of the Maroon Bells. Additionally, you can and should combine this trip with 4WD or ATV circumnavigation of the Lead King Basin road with stops in Crystal City and the Crystal Mill.

Distance: 4.2 miles (RT)
Elevation: 9,678-ft. at Trailhead
Maximum elevation: 10,985-ft.
Elevation Gain: 1,307-ft.
Difficulty: moderate

Basecamp: Marble and Aspen
Area: Maroon Bells-Snowmass Wilderness, White River NF
Best Season: July –September
USGS Map(s): Snowmass Mountain

Why Hike to Geneva Lake

This short hike packs in a lot of scenic delights as it travels to a Geneva Lake (10,985-ft.), an alpine jewel tucked in a pretty basin at the foot of Snowmass Mountain (14,092-ft.) and Hagerman Peak (13,841-ft.). Along the way the climb to the lake passes waterfalls, travels through alpine meadows sprinkled with wildflowers and offers great views of Treasure Mountain and the Maroon Bells.

Trailhead to Geneva Lake

From the North Fork trailhead (see Driving Directions below), hike north through pine forest. At 0.4 miles bear left on the Geneva Lake Trail. The trail wanders through meadows and trees for a mile. At the base of a switchback in a pretty meadow, views open to the waterfall on Geneva Lake's outlet stream and Treasure Mountain (13,528-ft.) to the south.

The trail gets steeper for the next mile as it switchbacks up the hillside, enjoying awesome views of the water tumbling down the stream on your right. Near the top of the switchbacks, look southeast for fine views of the Maroon Bells towering above the head of the North Fork Valley. Behind you are more great views of Treasure Mountain.

The trail then reenters a pine forest before breaking out along the meandering stream. Soon superb views open to Geneva Lake.

Reach Geneva Lake (10,985-ft.) at 1.6 miles after gaining a little over 1,300-ft. This beautiful alpine lake, surrounded by pretty meadows and subalpine firs, sits at the base of Snowmass Mountain (14,092-ft.) and Hagerman Peak (13,841-ft.). Treasure Mountain rises above the Crystal River Valley to the south.

The trail continues along the west side of the lake where it meets a boot beaten path to Little Gem Lake, another 1.25 miles up the valley. At the head of the lake the official trail turns right (southeast), crosses the inlet stream at 2.1 miles and then climbs over a low wooded saddle on Hagerman Peak's southwest ridge. On the climb to the saddle enjoy great views of Meadow Mountain to the west.

Beyond the saddle the trail traverses the hillside beneath Hagerman Peak's southeast ridge to a trail junction at 3.2 miles. Here the Geneva Lake trail branches left and climbs to Trail Rider Pass. To the left is the Cutoff trail descending to the North Fork trail. See the Four Pass Loop trail for more information on the connecting trails.

Use trails circumnavigate the lake providing fishermen access to various point along the shoreline to try their luck catching the cutthroat trout stocked by National Forest Service.

Backpackers wishing to camp at Geneva Lake must camp in designated sites. The lake is within the Maroon Bells-Snowmass Wilderness where bear containers are now required. See the regulations section at the end of the Four Pass Loop trail for more information and/or check out the White River National Forest Wilderness Regulations pdf.

You can and should combine this trip with 4WD or ATV circumnavigation of the Lead King Basin road with stops at Crystal City and the Crystal Mill. We recommend hiking first and stopping in Crystal City after your hike to avoid afternoon thunderstorms. The road before and after Crystal City is rocky and rough, you've been warned.

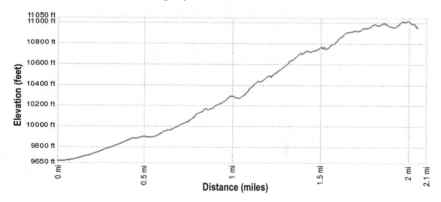

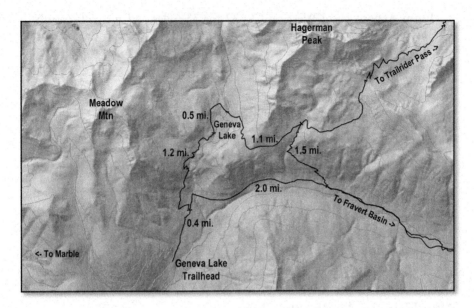

Driving Directions

From Marble: The Geneva Lake Trailhead is 7.5 miles from Beaver Lake in Marble on the Lead King Basin Road. Start in Marble, Colorado by renting an ATV, hiring the local Jeep Tours (Crystal River Jeep Tours) or driving a high clearance 4WD. Combine this trip/hike with a return stop in Crystal City and take some pictures of the Crystal Mill.

If you are driving to the trailhead from Mable: Drive through Marble, following the signs for Crystal City. Proceed past Beaver Lake east, climb Daniel's Hill and go left at the intersection for Lead King Basin (left) and Crystal City (right turn). The road is 4WD only all the way to the trailhead. (Note: The road to Crystal City will also get you to the trailhead. The road to the left for Lead King Basin is more precarious, but the ride is smoother and faster if the road is dry. The right fork, the southern route to Crystal, is rough and the road is very difficult to negotiate beyond Crystal City.)

Follow the rough jeep road for 7.5 miles, bearing left at the first junction and right at the second junction. Beyond the second junction the road climbs over a pass (10,900-ft.) and then descends into the Lead King Basin. The Geneva Lake trailhead is located on the left side of the road, just before the road reaches the valley floor.

While driving to the trailhead we recommend stopping and taking some pictures at the highpoint (10,900 feet) before descending into Lead King Basin. Another short diversion is to hike the Silver Creek Trail to take pictures. The views are great from the start. Silver Creek Trailhead is 0.3 miles from the highpoint (10,900) on the Lead King basin side of the mountain.

From Aspen: Head West on CO-82 for 35 miles and turn left (south) on Colorado Hwy 133. Follow CO-133 for 25 miles, passing Carbondale, and turn left on County Road 3. Travel along CR-3 for 6 miles to the town of Marble. Follow the directions above to find the trailhead.

18. Avalanche Pass ★★★★☆
Distance: 7.4 miles (RT)

This lightly used trail ascends beautiful Buckskin Basin to a stunning pass with wonderful views of Capitol Peak, Snowmass Mountain and Mount Daly.

Distance: 7.4 miles (RT)
Elevation: 9,080-ft. at Trailhead
 12,100-ft. at Avalanche Pass
Elevation Gain: 3,020-ft.
Difficulty: strenuous

Basecamp: Marble and Aspen
Area: Maroon Bells-Snowmass Wilderness, White River NF
Best Season: July –September
USGS Map(s): Redstone and Capitol Peak

Why Hike to Avalanche Pass

The west side of the Maroon Bells-Snowmass Wilderness is as scenic as the east side but more lightly used, providing a degree of solitude not possible on most of the east side trails. One of my favorite hikes from the west is the trail to Avalanche Pass. The route ascends North Fork Creek and beautiful Buckskin Basin (not to be confused with Buckskin Pass in the east) to a 12,100-ft. pass with terrific views of the south face of Capitol Peak, Snowmass Mountain and Mount Daly.

It is a long drive from the Aspen area to the trailhead but worth the time and effort. Hikers with passenger cars will want to hike the final 0.8 miles to the trailhead instead of driving the rough Lead King Basin Road.

Trailhead to Avalanche Pass

From the trailhead the path to Avalanche Pass heads north, ascending along the west side of the North Fork Lost Trail Creek on moderately steep grades through a forest of aspen, spruce and pine trees and intermittent meadows, to a creek crossing at 0.5 miles. Cross the creek. On the east side of the creek the path climbs and then traverses a hillside above the drainage, making a wide arc to the east before dropping down to meet and to cross to the west side of the creek at 1.3 miles. Openings along this section of the trail provide views of Sheep and Treasure Mountain to the south.

Beyond the second crossing the trail follows a low, narrow ridge separating the creek from a small stream. Pretty waterfalls tumble down the hillsides along both sides of the trail. At 1.75 miles the trail arrives at a junction with the Carbonate Creek Trail. Turn left (west) toward Avalanche Pass. Follow the trail for a short distance as it crosses a creek and reaches a second junction in 0.2 miles.

At the second junction turn right (north) toward Avalanche Pass. The trail now climbs a pretty valley on switchbacks and then turns northwest into Buckskin Basin. Buckskin Basin is a real gem. The steep narrow basin is clad in emerald green meadows filled with wildflowers and decorated with rock outcroppings and small copses of stunted evergreens.

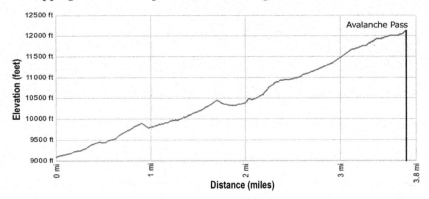

Reach an unnamed pass (11,930-ft.) separating the Carbonate Creek Valley and Buckskin Basin at 3.4 miles. Avalanche Pass is now visible on the long ridge to the northeast. Mount Daly (12,610-ft.) rises to the southwest. Be sure to turnaround for views extending southeast to Treasure Mountain.

Slightly beyond the top of the pass is an unmarked trail junction. Turn right at the junction and follow the trail as it ascends through alpine tundra for 0.3 miles to Avalanche Pass (12,100-ft.) at 3.7 miles. (The trail straight ahead descends Carbonate Creek to Marble.)

As you crest the pass a breathtaking panorama unfolds. To the northeast the impressive south face of Capitol Peak (14,130-ft.) towers above the surrounding mountains. Snowmass Mountain (14,092-ft.) and Hagerman Peak (13,841-ft.) rises to the southeast of Capitol Peak. In between are an impressive sea of peaks and ridges. To the south are wonderful views of Mount Daly (12,610-ft) and the peaks and ridges lining Buckskin Basin and Carbonate Creek.

After soaking in the views and taking a lot of pictures return to the trailhead, enjoying great views of Treasure Mountain on the descent. With a car shuttle the hike can be turned into a 9.0 mile semi-loop with the return leg heading down Carbonate Creek to Marble, losing 3,970-ft in 5.3 miles.

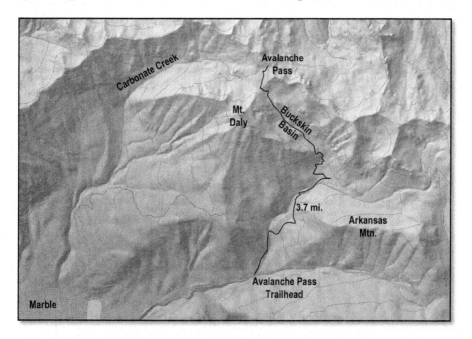

Driving Directions

From Aspen: From Aspen follow CO-82 West for 28 miles to CO-133. Turn left (south) on CO-133 toward Carbondale and follow the road for 22 miles to County Road 3. Turn left (east) on County Road 3 and drive 2.8 miles to the town of Marble. Drive through the town and continue past Beaver Lake on the now unpaved road to an intersection (2 miles past Marble and 1-mile beyond the lake). If you have a 4WD/high clearance vehicle take the left fork, Road #315 / Lead King Basin Road. (The right fork is Road #314 to Crystal.) Follow this steep, rough road, which stays to the left (north) of Lost Trail Creek, for 0.8 miles to the trailhead. The trailhead is located to the west of a stream crossing.

Passenger cars should find a good place to park off the road in the vicinity of the intersection of Road #315 and at #314 and walk the final 0.8 miles to the trailhead.

From Marble: Drive through the Marble on County Road 3 and continue past Beaver Lake on the now unpaved road to an intersection (2 miles past Marble and 1-mile beyond the lake). If you have a 4WD/high clearance vehicle take the left fork, Road #315 / Lead King Basin Road. (The right fork is Road #314 to Crystal.) Follow this steep, rough road, which stays to the left (north) of Lost Trail Creek, for 0.8 miles to the trailhead. The trailhead is located to the west of a stream crossing.

Passenger cars should find a good place to park off the road in the vicinity of the intersection of Road #315 and at #314 and walk the final 0.8 miles to the trailhead.

19. Anthracite Pass ★★★★☆
Distance: 2.5 to 6.8 miles (RT)

The Anthracite Pass trail features excellent views of Treasure Mountain and Marble Peak with Mount Daly in the distance. The trail is a nice 3.5-4.5 hour hike that can be hiked from late June to October (snow dependent).

Distance: 6.8 mile (RT)
Elevation: 8,081 at Trailhead
Maximum elevation: 10,295-ft.
Elevation Gain: 2,214-ft.
Difficulty: moderate

Basecamp: Marble and Aspen
Area: Maroon Bells-Snowmass Wilderness, White River NF
Best Season: July –September
USGS Map(s): Marble

Raspberry Trailhead to Anthracite Pass or Yule Creek

Park at Mill Park in Marble or drive up the Quarry Road to the small parking lot at the trailhead (see driving directions below). The hike starts out steep, but gets more enjoyable after the first mile. You will be hiking up an avalanche chute that runs every winter from No Name Peak to the Crystal River. The force of nature is evident by the sheer number of bent trees and thick undergrowth. Reach a trail junction (9,124-ft,) at 0.85 miles and turn left on the Anthracite Pass trail. The trail to the right is the Raspberry Creek Loop.

Beyond the junction the trail continues its ascent on moderate to moderate-steep grades. At 1.3 miles the trees give way to meadows and the trail becomes quite scenic with views of Treasure Mountain, Ant Mountain, Thompson Peak and Marble Peak. Soon the grade abates as the trail travels along the base of the ridge rimming the west side of the Yule Valley. Along the way the trail travels through numerous aspen groves and lush meadows.

At 2.0 miles the trail crosses the first of several deep ravines/creek beds. Keep your eyes open for rock cairns or slashings to stay on the trail. The final crossing has a large rock cairn to mark the trail.

Beyond the the last ravine, at 2.5 miles, the trail climbs steeply up a hillside through a beautiful mature pine forest and then traverses below Marble Peak to Anthracite Pass. Anthracite Pass (10,295-ft.), at 3.4 miles, is located on a flat bench where several trails meet. Nearby pine trees block most of the views at the pass. For the best view move 300-ft. north of the pass where you can enjoy excellent views of the Raggeds Wilderness including Treasure Mountain and Marble Peak. Mount Daly can be seen in the distance.

Most hikers will turn around at the pass and retrace their steps back to their cars for a 6.8 mile round trip hike. Another great option is to hike up Mt. Justice (bring a map or GPS). This is an off-trail route.

Groups with two cars or who have made prior arrangements for a car shuttle can turn left and descend an obvious trail to the Yule Creek Trailhead for a 4.6 mile hike, or back to Marble via the Quarry Road for a 7.4 mile hike. (See the Yule Creek to Anthracite Pass description below.)

Yule Creek Trailhead to Anthracite Pass

Distance: 2.5 miles (RT)
Elevation: 8,985-ft. at Trailhead
Maximum elevation: 10,295-ft.
Elevation Gain: 1,310-ft.
Difficulty: moderately-strenuous

An alternative start to the hike is 2.8 miles up the 4WD Quarry Road at the Yule Creek trailhead (8,981-ft.). Either walk up the road or drive to the trailhead. (There is very limited parking at the trailhead.) The trailhead is located about a quarter mile from the Yule Quarry. The trail initially travels along the Yule Creek trail for a short distance. Soon you will see a trail branching to the right toward Anthracite Pass. Turn right and follow the steep trail for 1.25 miles as it gains 1,310-ft. to the pass (10,295-ft.).

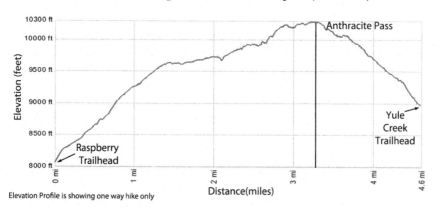

Elevation Profile is showing one way hike only

Driving Directions

From Marble: In Marble turn onto the Quarry Road (Fire Station on corner). Drive 0.25 miles from the bridge over the Crystal River on Quarry Road to a small parking lot on your right. The trailhead is 0.33 miles from the bridge. This is a dirt road but well maintained.

Note: Overflow parking is available at Mill Park. Parking at Mill Park adds 0.25 miles (one way) to the hike.

If starting the hike at the Yule Creek Trailhead, drive 2.8 miles up the 4WD Quarry Road. Parking is VERY limited at the Yule Creek trailhead. The Marble Chamber of Commerce warns drivers to exercise caution on the Quarry Road. You may encounter a large white truck from the marble quarry descending the road. If so, find a wide spot on the road and get out of the way. The truck will take the inside lane, all other vehicles must stop on the outside of the road and give way to the truck. These trucks can carry up to 50-tons of marble.

From Aspen: Head West on CO-82 for 35 miles and turn left (south) on Colorado Hwy 133. Follow CO-133 for 25 miles, passing Carbondale, and turn left on County Road 3. Travel along CR-3 for 6 miles to the town of Marble. In Marble turn onto Quarry Road (Fire Station on corner). Drive 0.25 miles from the bridge over the Crystal River on Quarry Road to a small parking lot on your right. The trailhead is 0.33 miles from the bridge. This is a dirt road but well maintained.

Note: Overflow parking is available at Mill Park. Parking at Mill Park adds 0.25 miles (one way) to the hike.

If starting the hike at the Yule Creek Trailhead, drive 2.8 miles up the 4WD Quarry Road. Parking is VERY limited at the Yule Creek trailhead. The Marble Chamber of Commerce warns drivers to exercise caution on the Quarry Road. You may encounter a large white truck from the marble quarry descending the road. If so, find a wide spot on the road and get out of the way. The truck will take the inside lane, all other vehicles must stop on the outside of the road and give way to the truck. These trucks can carry up to 50-tons of marble.

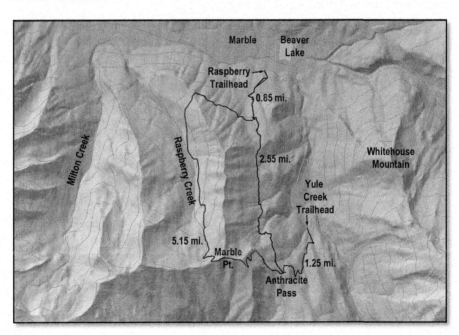

20. Raspberry Creek Loop ★★★★☆
Distance: 9.4 miles (RT)

This great loop hike starts by ascending the pretty Raspberry Creek Valley to Marble Peak (11,314-ft.). The trail then descends to Anthracite Pass and returns via the Raspberry Creek/Anthracite Pass trail. From the peak enjoy panoramic views of Snowmass Mountain, Capital Peak, Treasure Mountain and beyond.

Distance: 9.4 miles (Loop)
Elevation: 8,081-ft. at Trailhead
Maximum elevation - 11,314-ft.
Elevation Gain: 3,233-ft.
Difficulty: strenuous

Basecamp: Marble and Aspen
Area: Raggeds Wilderness, White River NF
Best Season: July –September
USGS Map(s): Marble
See Page 93 for Map

Raspberry Creek Loop

Proceed 0.33 miles up the Quarry Road from Crystal River Bridge. Turn right at the Raspberry Trailhead. The hike starts out steep, but gets more enjoyable after the first mile. You will be hiking up an avalanche chute that runs every winter from No Name Peak to the Crystal River. The force of nature is evident by the sheer number of bent trees and thick undergrowth. Look for fresh Raspberries in the late summer.

At 0.85 miles (9,124 ft) you will come to the trail intersection. Go right on the Raspberry Creek trail. The trail to the left, the Anthracite Pass trail, will be used on the return leg of the loop.

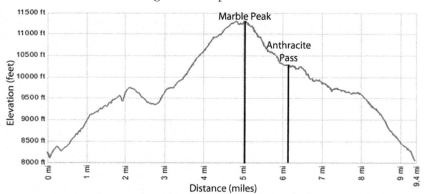

The trail gets steep at 3.5 miles until you top out on a high ridge (11,200 ft.). If the trail gets faint just follow game trails to the ridge. Go left along the ridge to the top of Marble Peak (11,314-ft.) at 5.0 miles. From the top of the peak enjoy panoramic views of the Elk Mountains, including Snowmass Mountain and Capitol Peak to the northeast. Treasure Mountain rises to the east.

Follow the trail that descends steeply from Marble Peak to Anthracite Pass, dropping 1,000 feet in a little over a mile. Turn left at Anthracite Pass and descend the Anthracite Pass trail to the trailhead. Alternatively you can drop down to the Yule Creek Trailhead. (See the Anthracite Pass trail for more information on the options for the return leg of this hike.)

Driving Directions

From Marble: In Marble turn onto the Quarry Road (Fire Station on corner). Drive 0.25 miles from the bridge over the Crystal River on Quarry Road to a small parking lot on your right. The trailhead is 0.33 miles from the bridge. This is a dirt road but well maintained.

Note: Overflow parking is available at Mill Park. Parking at Mill Park adds 0.25 miles (one way) to the hike.

From Aspen: Head West on CO-82 for 35 miles and turn left (south) on Colorado Hwy 133. Follow CO-133 for 25 miles, passing Carbondale, and turn left on County Road 3. Travel along CR-3 for 6 miles to the town of Marble. In Marble turn onto Quarry Road (Fire Station on corner). Drive 0.25 miles from the bridge over the Crystal River on Quarry Road to a small parking lot on your right. The trailhead is 0.33 miles from the bridge. This is a dirt road but well maintained.

21. Frigid Air Pass ★★★★★
Distance: 9.6 miles (RT)

Hikers ascending the beautiful East Fork Valley to Frigid Air pass are rewarded with stunning views of the Maroon Bells, Snowmass Mountain and the nearby peaks of the Elk Mountains. In season the East Fork is famous for its spectacular displays of wildflowers.

Distance: 9.6 miles (RT) to Frigid Air Pass
Elevation: 10,420-ft. at Trailhead 12,415-ft. at Frigid Air Pass
Elevation Gain: 1,995-ft. to Frigid Air Pass
Difficulty: moderate-strenuous

Basecamp: Crested Butte
Area: Maroon Bells-Snowmass Wilderness, White River NF
Best Season: July –September
USGS Map(s): Snowmass Mountain

Why Hike to Frigid Air Pass

This hike offers a totally different perspective on the Maroon Bells, viewing this famous massif from Frigid Air Pass, a high saddle to the southwest side of the peaks. The scenic hike starts from Schofield Park and ascends the beautiful East Fork valley, renowned for its spectacular display of wildflowers during the height of the summer. As the trail gains height, fine views open to the surrounding peaks including Mt. Bellview (12,519-ft.), Treasure Mountain (13,462-ft.) and Galena Mountain (12,580-ft.).

At the head of the valley the trail splits, with the path to the right (east) heading toward West Maroon Pass. We turn left (northwest), following an ascending traverse along an undulating trail through beautiful meadows to the bowl beneath Peak 12648. Here a short, steep climbs leads to Frigid Air Pass (12,415-ft.) with stunning views of Maroon Bells towering above the emerald green meadows of Fravert Basin. Snowmass Mountain (14,092-ft.) and Hagerman Peak (13,841-ft.) dominate the view to the southwest.

Optional extensions to the hike visit West Maroon Pass or the Hasley Basin with more great views of the Elk Mountains and the peaks in the Raggeds Wilderness.

This trail is a favorite of hikers and backpackers. Backpackers use a portion of the trail as part of the popular 26-mile Four Pass Loop, a 3-5 day backpacking trip climbing four 12,000-ft. mountain passes in the Maroon Bells-Snowmass Wilderness. So expect to see plenty of backpackers, along with day hikers, along this terrific trail.

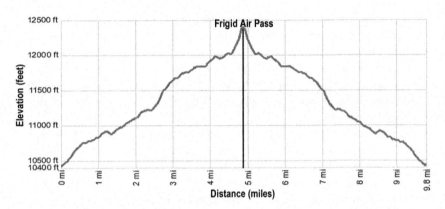

Trailhead to Frigid Air Pass

The trail to Frigid Air Pass starts at the East Fork trailhead. (See driving directions below.) Follow the trail as it heads east through spruce trees along the north side of the East Fork of the Crystal River. Soon the trail curves to the left (northeast) and leaves the river behind as it climbs switchbacks on moderate grades. The trees thin as the trail reaches an old mining cabin at 0.3 miles. A short distance beyond a sign marks the boundary for the Maroon Bells-Snowmass Wilderness.

At 0.4 miles the grade abates as the trail curves to the right (east) and begins an ascending traverse through meadows along the northeast side of the East Fork valley, high above the river. Views open to Mt. Bellview (12,519-ft.) to the southeast, Mount Baldy (12,805-ft.) and Cinnamon Mountain (12,933-ft.) to the southwest and Galena Mountain (12,580-ft.) to the west. Closer at hand, the meadows along the trail sport a spectacular display of wildflowers during late July and early August.

As you progress up the valley the trail crosses a few streams that are typically dry. At 1.2 miles the path crests a small rises and then descends briefly. At the bottom of the descent a faint, unmarked trail branches to the right (south). This trail eventually leads to Schofield Pass. We continue straight ahead, ascending the valley on moderate grades.

As you climb enjoy ever improving views of the peaks and ridges defining the head of the valley. Behind you, to the west/southwest, are fine views of Mt. Baldy, Cinnamon Mountain, Galena Mountain, Treasure Mountain and, in the distance, Purple Mountain and the summits of the Ruby Range.

Reach a "Y" intersection at 2.0 miles. We bear right on the trail signed for West Maroon Pass. The unmarked trail to the left (northwest) climbs to Hasley Pass. Beyond the junction the trail climbs briefly and then curves to the right (east), contouring through lush meadows and clusters of low willows. Along the way cross a stream which is typically dry after the snow melts.

At 2.4 miles start a steep ascent through meadows and willow patches. As you climb the trail curves to the southwest. To the west are great views of Galena and Treasure Mountains.

The grade eases at 2.9 miles and now ascends on moderate grades, reaching a signed trail junction at 3.1 miles. Here the trail to West Maroon Pass continues straight ahead (southeast). We turn left (northwest) on the trail to Frigid Air Pass.

Follow the undulating trail as it ascends northwest through lovely meadows. To the west/southwest are gorgeous views of Galena Mountain, Treasure Mountain, Mount Baldy, Cinnamon Mountain and, in the distance, Purple Mountain and the other peaks of the Ruby Range. Peak 12648, a red, pyramid-shaped mountain, towers above the valley to the northwest.

Reach a junction near a small pond beneath Peak 12648 at 4.5 miles. Turn right (north) on the signed trail to Frigid Air Pass. The unsigned trail to the left (west) leads to Hasley Basin. The trail to the pass skirts the left (west) side of the pond and climbs very steep switchbacks to Frigid Air Pass (12,415-ft.) at 4.8 miles, gaining 365-ft in 0.3 miles. Trekking poles are extremely help, especially when descending this section of the trail.

As you crest the pass stunning views open to the Maroon Bells towering above the emerald green meadows of the Fravert Basin. The white granite of Snowmass Mountain (14,092-ft.) and Hagerman Peak (13,841-ft.), dominating the view to the northwest, stands in sharp contrast to the crimson-brown mudstone of the Maroon Bells massif. Bellview Mountain (13,233-ft.) rises along the ridge at the head of Fravert Basin. Behind you, to the west/southwest, Mt Baldy, Treasure Mountain and Purple Mountain fill the skyline.

Find a perch atop the pass to rest and take in the views. The pass is the turnaround point for most day hikers. Expect to see plenty of backpackers at the pass. Backpackers cross Frigid Air Pass as part of the popular 26-mile Four Pass Loop, a 3-5 day backpacking trip climbing four 12,000-ft. mountain passes in the Maroon Bells-Snowmass Wilderness.

There are several options for the return leg of the hike. The easiest is to turnaround and retrace your steps for a 9.6 miles round trip (RT) hike. If time, energy and the weather permit, a side trip to West Maroon Pass is a great option. Extending the hike to West Maroon Pass will add 1.5 miles and 800-ft. in elevation gain to the hike. Total distance for the combined Frigid Air/West Maroon Pass hike is 11.1 mile RT. (See the West Maroon Pass from Crested Butte hiking description for more information.)

A second option is to follow the trail to the Hasley Basin Overlook for more great views. To reach the overlook descend from Frigid Air pass to the junction and turn right (west) on the unmarked trail toward Hasley Basin. Follow the narrow trail as it ascends on easy grades to a saddle at 5.5 miles, which I call the Hasley Basin Overlook, situated on the ridge between Peak 12648 and Peak 12345 to the west. Walking to the Hasley Basin Overlook and back will add 0.5 miles to the Frigid Air hike.

From the saddle enjoy panoramic views of Snowmass Mountain, Hagerman Peak and the summits rising above the Geneva Lake basin to the north. Below you are the beautiful green meadow of Hasley Basin. Along the ridge on the west side of the basin note the interesting stripped rock formation.

Behind you, to the east, Belleview Mountain towers above West Maroon Pass. To the northeast is Frigid Air Pass, where you will probably see hikers silhouetted against the skyline. When you are done enjoying the views retrace your steps to the trailhead.

Experience hikers comfortable with route finding can loop back from the Hasley Basin overlook to the East Fork trail on one of two routes for an 8.75-mile or 9.6 miles loop. See the Frigid Air and Hasley Pass hiking description for more information on this option.

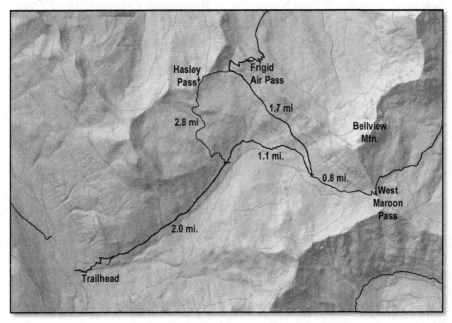

Driving Directions

From Crested Butte: From the intersection of Elk Avenue (main street) and 6th Street in Crested Butte, head north on 6th Street, which turns into the Gothic Road (sometimes referred to as the Schofield Pass Road). Follow the Gothic Road (CO 317) for 13.2 miles to Schofield Pass, passing the ski area and the research facilities at Gothic along the way. The dirt road is suitable for 2WD cars up to the town of Gothic at 7.9 miles. Beyond Gothic the road become rougher and a high clearance/4WD vehicle is recommended. (AWD/4WD is necessary if the road is wet.)

Continue over Schofield pass, descending the north side of the pass on switchbacks and then through meadows for 0.8 miles and turn right (east) into the signed East Fork trailhead. The turn is right before you hit Schofield Park, a large open park at the foot of the switchbacks. As you enter the trailhead, bear right into the parking area. The road branching to the left is for horse trailers.

22. North Pole Basin ★★★★★
Distance: 7.0 miles (RT)

Few hikers know about the gorgeous North Pole Basin. Scenic highlights include pristine meadows, cascading waterfalls, wildflowers and rugged peaks. A short off-trail stint leads to a saddle with breathtaking views of the high peaks of the Elk Mountains.

Distance: 7.0 miles (RT) to North Pole Basin
Elevation: 10,360-ft. at Trailhead 12,190-ft. at North Pole Basin
Elevation Gain: 1,830-ft. to North Pole Basin
Difficulty: moderate-strenuous

Basecamp: Crested Butte
Area: Maroon Bells-Snowmass Wilderness, White River NF
Best Season: July –September
USGS Map(s): Snowmass Mountain

Why Hike to North Pole Basin

Until June of 2013 the stunningly beautiful North Pole Basin was off limits to the public. Thankfully the Rocky Mountain Biological Laboratory (RMBL) and the Crested Butte Land Trust (CBLT) purchased the 160-acre basin, previously used as a private resort, to preserve the land and ensure public access to the property. Since few people know about this beautiful secluded basin hikers can expect a degree of solitude not found on many trails in the area.

The basin, cradled in a long, narrow cirque form by Galena Mountain (12,580-ft.), Treasure Mountain (13,462-ft.) and Crystal Peak (12,632-ft.), features lovely waterfalls cascading through pristine alpine meadows filled with wildflowers during the height of the summer. Small ponds, some man-made, are spread along the valley floor, linked by a sinuous stream.

The terrific hike up the basin follows an old mining road through the RMBL/CBLT property and onto the National Forest land beyond. Views initially encompass the gorgeous basin and its surrounding peaks. As the trail gains height vistas of the Maroon Bells and the peaks at the head of the East Fork valley unfold to the east.

The road ends in the meadows beneath Treasure Mountain. From there it's an easy climb to the saddle on the ridge between Treasure Mountain and Crystal Peak. The saddle enjoys stunning views of the Maroon Bells to the east. The pretty meadows of Bear Basin lie beneath the saddle to the west. Capitol Peak (14,130-ft.), Snowmass Mountain (14,092-ft.) and the peaks surrounding the Geneva Lake basin dominate the view to the north while a sea of summits in the Elk Range fills the skyline to the northwest. Closer at hand is Crystal Peak rising along the ridge to the northeast of the saddle.

The land owned by RMBL/CBLT is used for sensitive research. No dogs or bicycles are allowed and no fishing or hunting is permitted on the property. Hikers walking through the lower basin will likely see areas cordoned off for field research. Please respect these closures.

Trailhead to North Pole Basin

Please note: This hike passes through land owned by the Rocky Mountain Biological Laboratory (RMBL) and the Crested Butte Land Trust (CBLT). No dogs or bicycles are allowed and no fishing or hunting is permitted on the property.

From the intersection of the Gothic/Schofield Pass Road and the unmarked North Pole Basin road (see driving directions below), bear left (northwest) on the North Pole Basin road. Soon the road turns left (west) and crosses the South Fork of the Crystal River. Beyond the crossing the two-track dirt/gravel road turns right (northwest) ascending on moderate grades through spruce/fir forest. Openings in the trees offer occasional views of the 12,000-ft peaks rising along the east side of the South Fork Crystal River valley.

Reach a metal gate at 0.7 miles blocking vehicles from continuing up the road. A short distance beyond pass a red sign posted on a tree indicating that you are now on land owned by the Rocky Mountain Biological Laboratory (RMBL) and the Crested Butte Land Trust (CBLT). The site, once a private resort, was purchased in June of 2013 and is now open to public access. Prior to the resort the valley was home to the North Pole mine, which produced silver and copper ore.

The road now curves to the left (southwest) as it ascends on easy grades, passing an old cabin on the right side of the road. As you climb through the basin you will pass more remnants of the resort and a few mining relics.

At 1.1 miles the trail turns to the right (west) and travels through small meadows beneath the north facing slopes of Galena Mountain (12,580-ft.). Here views open to the Snowmass Peak and the summits rising above Geneva Basin to the north. Looking up the valley the distinctive diagonal stripes of white and gray rock along Crystal Mountain's southwestern ridge provide an excellent example of geologic uplift and tilting.

Soon you will reach a flooded section of the road where the track turns right (northwest) and skirts the east side of a pond. Follow a use trail that continues straight ahead for a short distance to a dam. Turn right and cross the dam. A section of the dam is now broken, submerging the road. When I was last in the basin a piece of wood spanned the gap to facilitate the crossing. If the wood is missing you should have no problem jumping the gap. On the north side of the dam the use trail briefly travels between the pond and a cluster of willows before rejoining the road.

Past the dam follow the road as it ascends through trees and meadows along the north side of the valley, avoiding the boggy meadows and ponds on the valley floor. You may see areas of the valley which are cordoned off for scientific work. Please respect these closures and stay on the road as you pass through the RMBL/CBLT property.

At 1.5 miles views open to a waterfall cascading down a rocky slope. Soon the road turns to the left (south) and travels along a low ridge, passing ponds surrounded by dense willows on the valley floor before turning back to the right (west).

Reach the foot of the largest pond in the basin at 1.8 miles. Treasure Mountain (13,462-ft.) towers above the basin to the west. Crystal Mountain (12,632-ft.) rises to the northwest. During the early morning Crystal Mountain's uplift bands are nicely mirrored in the pond's still waters.

The trail now climbs on moderate grades through meadows and small cluster of trees along the north side of the valley. As you ascend enjoy ever improving views of beautiful North Pole basin. Waterfalls cascades through pristine meadows scattered with willows and stunted conifers. Treasure

Mountain dominates the views at the head of the basin while Galena Mountain rises to the south.

Reach a sign marking the western boundary of the RMBL/CBLT property at 1.9 miles. Past this point you are on National Forest lands. A tenth of a mile beyond the sign the road splits. Take the path to the right that climbs steeply along the southeast facing slopes of Crystal Mountain. As you gain altitude turn around to see Bellview Mountain (13,233-ft.) rising above the East Fork Valley and the summits of Maroon Bells to the east.

The trail begins curving left (south) at 2.25 miles. Soon the grade abates as the trail continues its ascent on easy to moderate grades high above the west side of the basin. Galena Mountain looms above the valley to the east. An old mining road cuts across the peak's talus slopes.

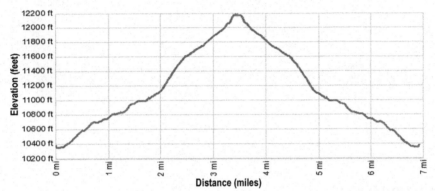

At 2.9 miles the trail curves to the right (southwest/west) as it enters the hanging valley beneath the north face of Treasure Mountain. A small pond lies cradled in a tundra-clad bowl in the center of the basin. Our trail climbs along north side of the basin and soon curves to the right (northwest). The road fades in places but is not difficult to follow.

Reach a junction of sorts at 3.2 miles. Ahead an old two-track road curves to the left (west). A faint trail, branching to the right (northwest) climbs the meadows to the road above. My advice is to bear right and climb to the road with the objective of reaching the saddle on the ridge between Crystal and Treasure Mountains.

Once you reach the upper road look north toward the saddle. Plot a cross-country route that climbs the meadows to the saddle, avoiding the talus. The steep climb, gaining about 200-ft. in 0.2 miles, is accompanied by great views of the upper basin and the peaks rising to the east.

From the saddle (12,190-ft.) enjoy stunning views of the Maroon Bells to the east. The pretty meadows of Bear Basin lie beneath the saddle to the west. Capitol Peak (14,130-ft.), Snowmass Mountain (14,092-ft.) and the peaks surrounding the Geneva Lake basin dominate the view to the north while a sea of summits in the Elk Range fills the skyline to the northwest.

Closer at hand is Crystal Peak rising along the ridge to the northeast of the saddle.

When you are done taking in the amazing views drop down from the saddle to the road and retrace your steps to the trailhead. On the return trip the peaks of the Maroon Bells are now directly in front of you during the descent.

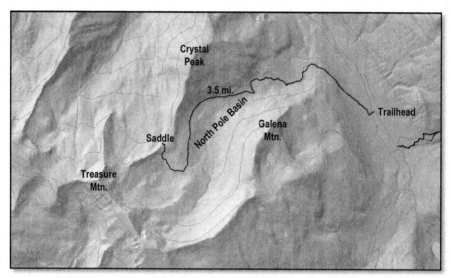

Driving Directions

From Crested Butte: From the intersection of Elk Avenue (main street) and 6th Street in Crested Butte, head north on 6th Street, which turns into Gothic Road (sometimes referred to as the Schofield Pass Road). Follow the Gothic Road (CO 317) for 13.2 miles to Schofield Pass, passing the ski area and the research facilities at Gothic along the way. The dirt road is suitable for 2WD cars up to the town of Gothic at 7.9 miles. Beyond Gothic the road become rougher and a high clearance/4WD vehicle is recommended. (AWD/4WD is necessary if the road is wet.)

Continue on the road over Schofield pass, descending the north side of the pass on switchbacks and then through meadows for 1.2 miles, past the East Fork trailhead on the right (east). Immediately after a sign announcing the "End of County Maintenance" is a road branching to the left (northwest). This is the road to the North Pole basin. Find a place to park off the Gothic/Schofield Pass road in the area near the intersection. You can also park at the East Fork trailhead, 0.4 miles back up the road.

It is possible to drive up the North Pole road for 0.7 miles to a pull off on the right (east) side of the road where there is room for a few cars. Beyond the pull off is the gate marking the beginning of the North Pole Basin parcel owned by Rocky Mountain Biological Laboratory and the

Crested Butte Land Trust. The land between the pull off and the Gothic / Schofield Pass Road is private property. Don't park along this section of the road. I recommend parking at a safe spot off the Gothic /Schofield Pass road and walking up the North Pole Road, a very pleasant walk through a forest with intermittent views of the peaks to the east.

23. West Maroon Pass - Crested Butte ★★★★★
Distance: 7.8 miles (RT)

Starting in Schofield Park near Crested Butte, this lovely hike ascends through the wildflower-filled meadows of the East Fork Valley to West Maroon Pass. From the pass enjoy grand views of the Maroon Bells, Pyramid Peak and Treasure Mountain massifs.

Distance: 7.8 miles (RT) to Pass
Elevation: 10,420-ft. at Trailhead
12,500-ft. at West Maroon Pass
Elevation Gain: 2,080-ft. to Pass
Difficulty: moderate-strenuous
Basecamp: Crested Butte

Area: Maroon Bells-Snowmass Wilderness, White River NF
Best Season: July –September
USGS Map(s): Maroon Bells, Snowmass Mountain
See Page 99 for Map

Why Hike to West Maroon Pass

One of the great hikes in Crested Butte leads up the East Fork of Crystal River valley, renowned for its amazing display of wildflowers, to West Maroon Pass, a high saddle boasting stunning views of the Maroon Bells and Pyramid Peak massifs to the northeast. Treasure Mountain dominates the views to the west.

This trail, starting in Schofield Park near Crested Butte, is about half as long as the alternative route to West Maroon Pass starting at Maroon Lake near Aspen. Both hikes enjoy fabulous views. As an added bonus the day hike from the Crested Butte side of the Elk Mountains offers hikers the option to extend the walk by visiting scenic Frigid Air Pass, a 3.3 mile detour. Alternatively, with properly planning a point to point hike leads over the pass to the Maroon Lakes trailhead near Aspen.

Don't expect solitude on the trail or at the pass. The hike to the pass, either from Schofield Park or Maroon Lake, is very popular. The pass is also part of the famous 26-mile Four Pass Loop, a 3-5 day backpacking trip climbing four 12,000-ft. mountain passes in the Maroon Bells-Snowmass Wilderness.

Trail head to West Maroon Pass

The trail to West Maroon Pass starts at the East Fork trailhead. (See driving directions below.) Follow the trail as it heads east through spruce trees along the north side of the East Fork of the Crystal River. Soon the trail curves to the left (northeast) and leaves the river behind as it climbs switchbacks on moderate grades. The trees thin as the trail reaches an old mining cabin at 0.3 miles. A short distance beyond a sign marks the boundary for the Maroon Bells-Snowmass Wilderness.

At 0.4 miles the grade abates as the trail curves to the right (east) and begins an ascending traverse through meadows along the northeast side of the East Fork valley, high above the river. Views open to Mt. Bellview (12,519-ft.) to the southeast, Mount Baldy (12,805-ft.) and Cinnamon Mountain (12,933-ft.) to the southwest and Galena Mountain (12,580-ft.) to the west. Closer at hand, the meadows along the trail sport a spectacular display of wildflowers during late July and early August.

As you progress up the valley the trail crosses a few streams that are typically dry. At 1.2 miles the path crests a small rises and then descends briefly. At the bottom of the descent a faint, unmarked trail branches to the right (south). This trail eventually leads to Schofield Pass. We continue straight ahead, ascending the valley on moderate grades.

As you climb enjoy ever improving views of the peaks and ridges defining the head of the valley. Behind you, to the west/southwest, are fine views of Mt. Baldy, Cinnamon Mountain, Galena Mountain, Treasure Mountain and, in the distance, Purple Mountain and the summits of the Ruby Range.

Reach a "Y" intersection at 2.0 miles. We bear right on the trail signed for West Maroon Pass. The unmarked trail to the left (northwest) climbs to Hasley Pass. Beyond the junction the trail climbs briefly and then curves to the right (east), contouring through lush meadows and clusters of low willows. Along the way cross a stream which is typically dry after the snow melts.

At 2.4 miles start a steep ascent through meadows and willow patches. As you climb the trail curves to the southwest. To the west are great views of Galena and Treasure Mountains.

The grade eases at 2.9 miles and now ascends on moderate grades, reaching a signed trail junction at 3.1 miles. Here the trail to Frigid Air Pass branches to the left (northwest). We continue straight ahead (southeast/east) toward Maroon Pass on a steep trail climbing through pretty meadows sprinkled with wildflowers.

At 3.75 miles the meadows give way to scree covered slopes. A few switchbacks help ease the final steep haul to West Maroon Pass (12,500-ft.) at 3.9 miles. From the pass views extend west to the Treasure Mountain massif. Below are the vast meadows of Purity Basin at the head of the East Fork valley. To the northeast the Maroon Bells and Pyramid Peak massifs fill the skyline above the West Maroon Valley. Belleview Mountain (13,233-ft.) rises along the rugged ridge extending northwest from the pass.

The pass is the turnaround point for most day hikers. Backpackers cross the pass as part of the popular 26-mile Four Pass Loop, a 3-5 day backpacking trip climbing four 12,000-ft. passes in the Maroon Bells-Snowmass Wilderness.

There are several options for the return leg of the hike. The easiest is to turnaround and retrace your steps for a 7.8 mile round trip (RT) hike. If time, energy and the weather permit, a side trip to Frigid Air Pass is a great option. Extending the hike to Frigid Air will add 3.3 miles to the hike for a 11.1 mile RT hike with an additional gain of about 700-ft. (See the Frigid Air Pass hiking description for more information.)

With proper planning it is possible to cross West Maroon Pass on a day hike and end up at the Maroon Lake trailhead, with bus service to nearby Aspen Highland and Aspen. You will need to spot a car at Aspen Highlands parking area near Aspen or arrange a ride (taxi/shuttle: (970) 349-2620 or (970) 948-9893).

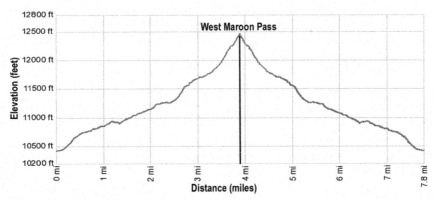

Driving Directions

From Crested Butte: From the intersection of Elk Avenue (main street) and 6th Street in Crested Butte, head north on 6th Street, which turns into the Gothic Road (sometimes referred to as the Schofield Pass Road). Follow the Gothic Road (CO 317) for 13.2 miles to Schofield Pass, passing the ski area and the research facilities at Gothic along the way. The dirt road is suitable for 2WD cars up to the town of Gothic at 7.9 miles. Beyond Gothic the road become rougher and a high clearance/4WD vehicle is recommended. (AWD/4WD is necessary if the road is wet.)

Continue over Schofield pass, descending the north side of the pass on switchbacks and then through meadows for 0.8 miles and turn right (east) into the signed East Fork trailhead. The turn is right before you hit Schofield Park, a large open park at the foot of the switchbacks. As you enter the trailhead, bear right into the parking area. The road branching to the left is for horse trailers.

24. Oh Be Joyful to Blue Lake ★★★★☆
Distance: 13.2 miles (RT)

This hike ascends the beautiful Oh Be Joyful Valley through wildflower-filled meadows to pretty Blue Lake cradled beneath Purple Mountain and Afley Peak. Along the way views unfold to the panorama of 12,000-ft. peaks ringing the head of the valley.

Distance: 13.2 miles (RT)
Elevation: 8,960-ft. at Trailhead
11,075-ft. at Oh Be Joyful/Blue Lake
Elevation Gain: 2,115-ft.
Difficulty: moderate-strenuous

Basecamp: Crested Butte
Area: Raggeds Wilderness, White River NF
Best Season: July –September
USGS Map(s): Oh Be Joyful

Why Hike Oh Be Joyful to Blue Lake

This long, scenic trail climbs the Oh Be Joyful valley to pretty Blue Lake (11,075-ft.), nestled beneath Purple and Afley Peaks in the Ruby Range. Initially the trail ascends an old mining road which gives way to a trail ascending a steep-walled "U" shaped valley clad in timber and beautiful wildflower-filled meadows. Several waterfalls along with views of Mount Emmons and Peeler Peak add interest to the walk.

As the trail ascends the valley views open to Schuylkill Mountain and then the peaks forming the valley's headwall. Richmond Mountain (12,501-ft.) towers above Democrat Basin to the northwest while Hancock Peak (12,410-ft.), Oh Be Joyful Peak (12,420-ft.) and Afley Peak (12,646-ft.) dominate the view to the west. Near the head of the valley Purple Peak (12,820-ft.) joins the scene to the southwest.

Soon the trail climbs the slopes at the head of the valley and turns south toward Blue Lake, traveling along a bench beneath Little Silver Basin. A final short, steep climb leads to the shelf cradling Blue Lake. Purple Mountain and Afley Peak form the backdrop for this pretty lake. The cliffs of the Scarpa Ridge rim the lake basin to the south. Schuylkill Mountain (12,146-ft.) dominates the views to the northeast.

Except for the final short steep climb to the lake this trail travels along easy to moderate grades but is rated as moderately-strenuous due to the length of the hike. For a shorter day simply hike up the valley as far as time and energy allow. During late July and early August the meadows are adorn with wildflowers making this a very scenic walk, no matter your destination.

Trailhead to Oh Be Joyful and Blue Lake

The Oh Be Joyful trail starts from the Oh Be Joyful Camping area off the Slate River Road. (See driving directions below.) From the east side of the campground, drive or wade across the Slate River to a trailhead parking area on the west side of the river and turn left (south), following an old mining road past campsites along the river.

Soon the road curves to the right (west), ascending on moderate grades up the north side of the Oh Be Joyful valley through meadows and wooded areas. To the south views open to Mt Emmons (12,392-ft.) and the Gunsight Pass Jeep road climbing through Redwell Basin.

Pass a beautiful waterfall on the Oh Be Joyful creek, running below the left (south) side of the road, at 0.4 miles. This is the first of several pretty falls along the creek.

After walking a little over a mile the trail reaches the trailhead kiosk. In the past it was possible to drive to this point. A short distance beyond a cascade tumbling down an avalanche slope beneath Redwell Basin is visible on the south side of the valley.

Watch for a trail branching to the right off the road at 1.2 miles. This detour circumvents a flood section of the road and boggy meadows.

At 1.5 miles the road gives way to a trail that curves to the right (northwest) as it travels up the valley on easy grades. Cross the boundary into the Raggeds Wilderness at 1.9 miles and then traverse a pretty meadow with views of Peeler Peak (12,227-ft.) rising to the west. On the valley floor a waterfall is seen spilling down rocky ledges along the creek bed. Past the waterfall the trail briefly travels through a wooded area.

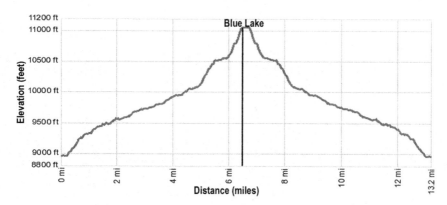

Soon the trail emerges from the trees into pretty meadows sprinkled with wildflowers during the height of the summer season. Views extend up the steep-walled "U" shaped valley to Schuylkill Mountain (12,146-ft.) towering above the northeast side of the valley. Beaver Ponds are seen along the creek meandering down the valley floor.

At 3.0 miles views open to head of the valley where Richmond Mountain (12,501-ft.) rises above Democrat Basin to the northwest. The saddle on the ridge is Oh Be Joyful Pass. Soon Hancock (12,410-ft) and Oh-Be-Joyful Peaks (12,420-ft.) join the scene.

At 3.5 miles the trail starts to curve to the left (west). Turn around here for fine views of Mt. Emmons rising to the south. A nice campsite is found in the trees to the south of the trail.

Pass through a metal gate at 3.9 miles. Ahead Afley (12,646-ft.), Oh Be Joyful and Hancock Peaks fill the skyline at the head of the valley. A short distance beyond Purple Peak (12,820-ft.) comes into focus, bookending the head of the valley to the southwest. Blue Lake, the destination for this hike, lies nestled beneath the peak's northeast face. As you ascend, enjoy ever improving views of the scenic wall of mountains defining the valley's headwall.

Cross a stream draining the north facing slopes beneath Schuylkill Mountain at 4.4 miles. The trail climbs briefly and reaches a confusing section of the trail at 4.8 miles. Here the trail splits with a track heading right (northwest) and another path branching left (southwest) through willows and crossing a creek. The right branch eventually crosses the creek a little high up and rejoins the main trail a short distance beyond. During high water the upper crossing is probably a little easier. Later in the season it doesn't matter.

Beyond the crossing the trail enters the woods and starts climbing on moderately-steep grades up the slopes at the head of the valley to a poorly marked junction at 5.4 miles. At the junction a sign labeled "Slate River" points back down the trail. The unmarked trail to the right (north) heads to Democrat Basin and Oh Be Joyful Pass. We turn left (south) toward Blue Lake.

After a short climb the trail curves to the left (south) and ascends on easy grades along a meadow clad bench beneath Little Silver Basin. Rock-hop across Blue Lake's outlet stream at 5.9 miles and then follow the trail as it climbs steeply through meadows and then trees to a small bench.

After crossing the bench a final steep climb leads to the shelf cradling Blue Lake (11,075-ft.) at 6.6 miles. Purple and Afley Peaks form the backdrop for this beautiful lake, nestled in rocky alpine meadows. The cliffs of the Scarpa Ridge rim the lake basin to the south. Schuylkill Mountain dominates the views to the northeast.

From the lakeshore, look east to see the trail climbing to Star Pass and the Peeler Lake basin beyond. Climbing to the pass is too far for most day hikers. When you are done exploring the lake basin retrace your steps to the trailhead.

Note: The Oh Be Joyful basin is a great option for a short backpack. In addition to Blue Lake, hikers can visit Democratic Basin, Oh Be Joyful Pass and/or Daisy Pass. Good campsites can be found in the trees near the head of Oh Be Joyful valley and in small stands of trees in lovely Democratic Basin.

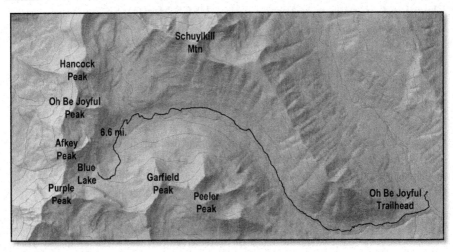

Driving Directions

From Crested Butte: From the intersection of Elk Avenue (main street) and 6th Street in Crested Butte, head north on 6th Street, which turns into the Gothic Road. Follow the Gothic Road (CO 317) for 0.9 miles and turn left (northwest) onto the Slate River Road (CR 734). Drive 4.6 miles and turn left at the Oh Be Joyful Campground. CR 734 is paved for the first 3.6 miles and then turns into a dirt road, which is OK for low clearance, 2WD cars.

Drive down the road to the campground for 0.4 miles to a parking area on the left. The road down to the campground is very rough. Hikers with low clearance vehicles should park off CR 734 near the intersection with the campground road. High clearance vehicle can make it to the parking area near the campground.

During low water it is possible to cross to the west side of the Slate River and park in the trailhead parking lot on the west side of the river. High clearance AWD or 4WD drive is required for the crossing. When in doubt, park on the east side of the river and wade across the river to the start of the hike.

25. Yule Pass ★★★★☆
Distance: 4.9 miles (RT)

Panoramic views accompany every step of this great, easy hike along an old mining road to Yule Pass, where sweeping views extend to the peaks rising beyond Yule Creek, Purple Canyon and the Upper Slater River Valleys. Near at hand Purple and Treasure Mountains tower overhead.

Distance: 4.9 miles (RT) to Pass
Elevation: 11,250-ft. at Trailhead
11,715-ft. at Yule Pass
Elevation Gain: 465-ft. to Pass
Difficulty: easy-moderate

Basecamp: Crested Butte
Area: Gunnison NF
Best Season: July –September
USGS Map(s): Snowmass
Mountain

Why Hike to Yule Pass

It is not often that you find a short, easy trail to a scenic pass that starts above timberline and features nonstop views. But that is the perfect description of the hike to Yule Pass.

Most of the work gaining elevation is done by driving your car to Paradise Divide at 11,250-ft. Here you will find the Yule Pass trail, which follows an old mining road carved into the talus fields along the steep flanks of Cinnamon and Treasure Mountains high above Purple Canyon. Over the length of the hike the trail gains a little over 450-ft. to the pass.

Great views accompany every step of the hike. Purple Mountain (12,958-ft.) and Treasure Mountains (13,462-ft.) tower above steep-walled Purple Canyon channeling the nascent Slate River far below the trail. To the southwest vistas extend down the length of Purple Canyon to the Slate River Valley and the peaks beyond.

At the head of the valley the trail climbs to Yule Pass, situated on the saddle between Purple and Treasure Mountains. Mount Justice, Marble Peak, Rugged Mountain and Chair Mountain form the backdrop for the Yule Creek Valley to the west. Cinnamon Mountain, Gothic Peak and Mount Crested Butte dominate the view to the east. Treasure and Purple Mountains soar overhead while below you the Slate River tumbles down the canyon floor.

Wait for the snow to melt, usually in late July, before attempting this hike. Several steep snowfields that typically cover segments of the road beneath Treasure Mountain are extremely dangerous.

Rock slide have obliterated sections of the road which are now spanned by narrow, boot beaten trails with some exposure. As such this trail is not recommended for anyone with a fear of heights or who are uncomfortable on trails with steep drop-offs.

Trailhead to Yule Pass

The mileage for this hike assumes you park near Paradise Divide. If you park near the Yule Pass trailhead subtract 0.15 miles from the directions below. (See driving directions below for more information.)

Note: Don't attempt this trail if snow is present. Steep snowfields along the trail are extremely dangerous and should not be crossed except by experienced parties equipped with ice axes and crampons. It is best not to try this hike until the end of July. Check with the Crested Butte Visitor Center for current trail conditions.

From Paradise Divide head north/northwest up the Yule Pass road, marked with a sign. At 0.15 miles the trail curves to the left, skirts the north side of a small pond and passes a trailhead sign.

Soon the old wagon road curves to the left (west) and ascends on easy grades along the southern flanks of Cinnamon Mountain (12,293-ft.), crossing rock slides/avalanche chutes along the way. Views open across the valley to a waterfall tumbling down a rocky cleft along the Purple Canyon wall and into the nascent Slate River. Turn around for nice views down the Slate River Valley.

At 0.5 miles the trail curves to the right (northwest) around Cinnamon Mountain's southwest ridge and continues its ascent along the old road, etched into valley's steep talus slopes high above the river. Treasure Mountain (13,462-ft.) dominates the view to the northwest while Purple Mountain (12,958-ft.) fills the skyline to the west. Yule Pass, the saddle on the ridge between the two peaks, is visible at the head of the valley.

After walking a little over a mile the trail curves to the left (west/southwest) and crosses two gullies along the flanks of Treasure Mountain's southeast ridge. Rock slide have obliterated sections of the road which are now spanned by narrow, boot beaten trails. As you progress up the valley long sections of the road are now just a trail. Sections of the path are quite narrow with some exposure and not recommended for people with a fear of heights or uncomfortable with steep drop-offs.

Soon the trail curves to the right (west/northwest) and continues its easy ascending traverse along the flanks of Treasure Mountain's southeastern ridge. This segment of the trail enjoys terrific views of Purple Mountain. Turn around for fine views down the length of Purple Canyon to the Slate River Valley.

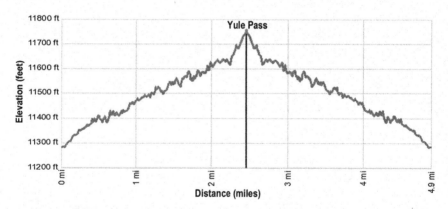

At 1.8 miles a stream cascades down the rugged flanks of the ridge and spills across the trail. A short distance beyond the trail travels through a rock slide and crosses some seeps and another stream tumbling down a gully carved into the steep slopes above the trail.

Follow the trail as it curves to the left (southwest) at 2.3 miles and climbs to Yule Pass (11,715-ft.) at 2.5 miles. As you crest the pass the Yule Creek Valley springs into views. Mount Justice (11,730-ft.) and Marble Peak (11,314-ft.) rise to the west/northwest with Chair Peak (12,721-ft.) and

Ragged Peak (12,094-ft.) in the distance. To the east great views extend down the length of Purple Canyon to Cinnamon Peak, Gothic Mountain (12,625-ft.) and Mount Crested Butte (12,162-ft.).

On the west side of the pass are three trails. The center trail drops down the Yule Creek Valley to the Yule Creek trailhead near Marble, CO in 5.6 miles. A trail to the left leads to a class 3 route climbing to the summit of Purple Mountain while the trail to the right heads toward the summit of Treasure Mountain, another class 3 ascent.

After taking in the views retrace your steps to the trailhead, enjoying the great views of Purple Canyon and the Slate River valley along the way.

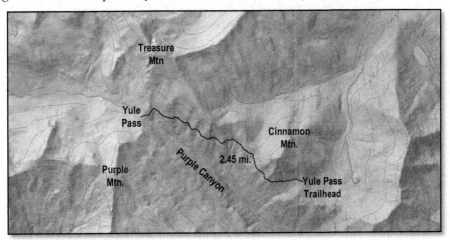

Driving Directions

From Crested Butte (Option 1): From the intersection of Elk Avenue (main street) and 6th Street in Crested Butte, head north on 6th Street, which turns into the Gothic Road. Follow the Gothic Road (CO 317) for 0.9 miles and turn left (northwest) onto the Slate River Road (CR 734). Follow CR 734 for 11.9 miles to Paradise Divide, adjacent to a large pond and marked with a sign. The route will go through the summer cabins at Pittsburg and then climbs steep switchbacks with steep drop-offs. Turn left at Paradise Divide and find a good place to park off the road and out of traffic.

It is possible to drive up the Yule Pass road (the first right turn) for 0.15 miles. A limited number of parking places are located along the side of the road. Make sure you do not block the road. My advice is to park near Paradise Divide and walk up the road.

Note: CR 734 is paved for the first 3.6 miles and then turns into a dirt road, which is OK for 2WD cars under good conditions. Check at the Crested Butte Visitor Center for current road condition.

From Crested Butte (Option 2): From the intersection of Elk Avenue (main street) and 6th Street in Crested Butte, head north on 6th Street,

115

which turns into the Gothic Road (sometimes referred to as the Schofield Pass Road). Follow the Gothic Road (CO 317) for 13.2 miles to Schofield Pass, passing the ski area and the research facilities at Gothic along the way. The dirt road is suitable for 2WD cars up to the town of Gothic at 7.9 miles. Beyond Gothic the road become rougher and a high clearance/4WD vehicle is recommended. (AWD/4WD is necessary if the road is wet.)

Just beyond Schofield Pass turn left on CR 734 to Paradise Divide. Drive 2.4 miles through Elko Park and Paradise Basin to Paradise Divide, adjacent to a pond and marked with a sign, and turn right. Find a good place to park off the road and out of traffic.

It is possible to drive up the Yule Pass road (the first right turn) for 0.15 miles. A limited number of parking places are located along the side of the road. Make sure you do not block the road. My advice is to park near Paradise Divide and walk up the road.

Note: The rough, rocky road to Paradise Divide through Elko Park and Paradise Basin is steep in places and can be wet. AWD/4WD is recommended. Check at the Crested Butte Visitor Center for current road condition.

26. Rustler Gulch ★★★★☆
Distance: 7.4 - 9.2 miles (RT)

This moderately easy hike to a high alpine basin beneath Precarious Peak is recommended during mid-July through August when the meadows of Rustler's Gulch are filled with colorful wildflowers.

Distance: 7.4 miles (RT)
9.2 miles (RT) from the 2WD
parking area west of the East River
Elevation: 10,235-ft. at Trailhead
9,695-ft. at the 2WD parking area
11,500-ft. at the head of the valley
Elevation Gain: 1,265-ft.
1,805-ft. from the 2WD parking area

Difficulty: moderately easy
Basecamp: Crested Butte
Area: Maroon Bells-Snowmass
Wilderness, Gunnison NF
Best Season: July –September
USGS Map(s): Oh Be Joyful,
Maroon Bells

Why Hike Rustler Gulch

Hike as far as you wish along this pretty trail ablaze with wildflowers during the height of the summer. The path ascends a beautiful valley traveling through spruce-fir forest and meadows along Rustler Creek, passing a few waterfalls on Rustler Gulch Creek along the way. As you approach the head of the valley views open to a rugged cirque anchored by Precarious Peak (13,380-ft.), Cassi Peak (13,232-ft and Golden Tops (13,010-ft.).

A high clearance AWD/4WD is required to reach the trailhead. Hikers in passenger vehicles should park on the west side of the East River, wade the river and then walk 0.9 miles up the road to the trailhead. During periods of high water everyone should park before the river and walk. Walking to the trailhead adds 1.8 miles round-trip and 540-ft. in elevation gain to the hike.

Trailhead to the Basin at the head of the Valley

Note: This description assumes you are starting at the 4WD trailhead. If walking from the west side of the East River, add 1.8 miles (round-trip) and 540-ft. in elevation gain to the hiking statistics. The 0.9 mile walk up the access road is moderately steep.

At the trailhead, take the trail branching right (north) up Rustler Gulch. The broad dirt track to the left is the #401 trail, a popular mountain biking route. Mt Avery (12,653-ft.) fills the skyline to the southeast while Gothic Mountain (12,625-ft.) dominates the view behind you to the southwest.

The trail, once an old mining road, travels through wildflower–filled meadows and spruce-fir forest along the west side of Rustler Gulch Creek. Pass a sign marking the boundary of the Maroon Bells-Snowmass Wilderness area a short distance beyond the trailhead. As you climb, enjoy ever-improving views of Mt. Bellview (12,519-ft.) rising above the west side of the valley.

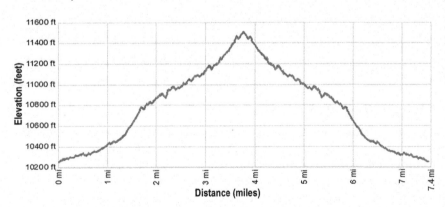

At 0.8 miles wade across the creek to the east side. To keep your feet dry, head downstream a short distance and cross on a downed trees spanning the creek. Pass a trail coming in from the right at 1.0 mile. Cross back to the west side of the stream at 1.3 miles.

The grade now steepens as it climbs the hillside above the river. At 2.7 miles the grade abates as the trail curves to the northeast and the east toward the head of the valley.

After walking about 2.0 miles views open to Precarious Peak (13,380-ft.) towering above the head of the valley. Soon Cassi Peak (13,232-ft.) and Golden Tops (13,010-ft.) join the scene.

At 2.9 miles the trail reaches a junction with an old road branching right and dropping down to the creek near a pretty waterfall. Stay left and continue up the valley. Near the head of the valley pass mining ruins and some rusted equipment. The trail end abruptly at 4.6 miles in a pretty basin beneath the rugged cirque anchored by Precarious, Cassi and Golden Tops peaks.

After taking a break, turn around and retrace your steps to the trailhead.

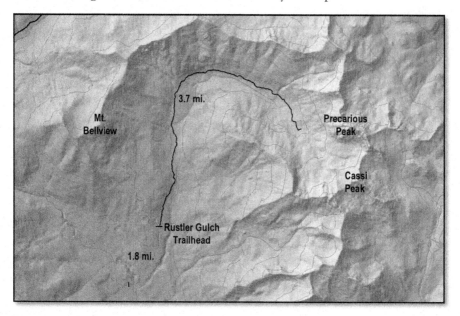

Driving Directions

From Crested Butte: From the intersection of Elk Avenue (main street) and 6th Street in Crested Butte, head north on 6th Street, which turns into the Gothic Road (sometimes referred to as the Schofield Pass Road). Follow the Gothic Road (CO 317) for 10.5 miles and turn right (east) at the Rustler Gulch trailhead. Follow the access road for 0.1 miles to the East River. If driving a passenger car or if the water is high, find a place to park off the road on the west side of the river. Otherwise, cross the river and follow the steep access road for a mile to the small trailhead parking lot. The road is very slippery when wet.

27. Frigid Air and Hasley Pass Loop ★★★★★
Distance: 9.6 miles (loop)

This great loop hike travels up wildflower-filled meadows to two scenic passes with stunning views of the high peaks of the Elk Mountains including the Maroon Bells, Snowmass Mountain and Hagerman Peak. Route finding and off-trail travel is required to complete the loop.

Distance: 9.6 miles (RT) to Frigid Air Pass
9.6 miles (loop) to Hasley Pass Loop
8.8 miles (loop) to Hasley Overlook Loop
Elevation: 10,420-ft. at Trailhead
12,415-ft. at Frigid Air Pass
12,150-ft. at Hasley Pass Loop
12,110-ft. at Hasley Overlook Loop
Elevation Gain: 1,995-ft. to Frigid Air Pass
2,095-ft. to Hasley Pass Loop
2,030-ft. to Hasley Overlook Loop

Difficulty: strenuous
Basecamp: Crested Butte
Area: Maroon Bells-Snowmass Wilderness, White River NF
Best Season: July –September
USGS Map(s): Snowmass Mountain
See Page 99 for Map

Why Hike the Frigid Air and Hasley Pass Loop

Hikers comfortable with route finding will enjoy this hike that visits two scenic passes, Frigid Air and Hasley, with stunning views of the high peaks of the Elk Mountains. The hike starts with a beautiful walk up the East Fork valley through meadows adorn with an amazing display of wildflowers during late July and early August. Along the way enjoy fine views of Mt. Bellview (12,519-ft.), Treasure Mountain (13,462-ft.) and Galena Mountain (12,580-ft.).

At the head of the valley an ascending traverse through beautiful meadows with more great views leads to a bowl beneath Peak 12648 where the trail splits. A short, steep signed trail to the right leads to Frigid Air Pass (12,415-ft.) with stunning views of Maroon Bells towering above the emerald green meadows of Fravert Basin. Snowmass Mountain (14,092-ft.) and Hagerman Peak (13,841-ft.) dominate the view to the southwest.

After visiting Frigid Air Pass return to the junction and follow the unmarked trail to the Hasley Basin Overlook. From the overlook Snowmass Mountain, Hagerman Peak and the summits rising above the Geneva Lake basin fill the skyline to the north. Below you are the beautiful green meadow of Hasley Basin.

The overlook marks the beginning of an off-trail route that traverses the head of Hasley Basin to Hasley Pass (12,110-ft.). The pass boasts panoramic views stretching from Snowmass Mountain and Hagerman Peak in the north to the peaks along the Ruby Range to the south. Belleview Mountain

(13,233-ft.) and West Maroon Pass (12,500-ft.) dominate the view to the southeast.

From Hasley Pass a trail, sometimes difficult to follow, descends steeply through meadows to the East Fork trail, two miles from the trailhead.

The routes to Hasley Pass should only be attempted by hikers with route finding experience and comfortable with off-trail hiking. A good map is essential to stay on track.

Trailhead to Frigid Air Pass

Distance from Trailhead: 9.6 miles (RT)
Ending/Highest Elevation: 12,415-ft.
Elevation Gain: 1,995-ft.

Note: The hike to Frigid Air Pass is along a good, established trail that any hiker should be able to follow. Beyond Frigid Air the hike requires route finding skills.

I am somewhat reluctant to describe hikes that require off-trail travel and route finding skills for fear that hikers who don't know what they are doing will get lost. Don't attempt the route portion of this hike unless you are experienced with route finding and have a good map of the area. A compass and/or GPS are also extremely helpful when traveling off trail and along routes where use trails fade and, at times, disappear.

Finally, it is always good idea to turn around and look back at the way you have walked. In the event of trouble this will help you to find your way back to the last well marked trail.

The trail to Frigid Air pass starts at the East Fork trailhead. (See driving directions below.) Follow the trail as it heads east through spruce trees along the north side of the East Fork of the Crystal River. Soon the trail curves to the left (northeast) and leaves the river behind as it climbs switchbacks on moderate grades. The trees thin as the trail reaches an old mining cabin at

0.3 miles. A short distance beyond a sign marks the boundary for the Maroon Bells-Snowmass Wilderness.

At 0.4 miles the grade abates as the trail curves to the right (east) and begins an ascending traverse through meadows along the northeast side of the East Fork valley, high above the river. Views open to Mt. Bellview (12,519-ft.) to the southeast, Mount Baldy (12,805-ft.) and Cinnamon Mountain (12,933-ft.) to the southwest and Galena Mountain (12,580-ft.) to the west. Closer at hand, the meadows along the trail sport a spectacular display of wildflowers during late July and early August.

As you progress up the valley the trail crosses a few streams that are typically dry. At 1.2 miles the path crests a small rises and then descends briefly. At the bottom of the descent a faint, unmarked trail branches to the right (south). This trail eventually leads to Schofield Pass. We continue straight ahead, ascending the valley on moderate grades.

As you climb enjoy ever improving views of the peaks and ridges defining the head of the valley. Behind you, to the west/southwest, are fine views of Mt. Baldy, Cinnamon Mountain, Galena Mountain, Treasure Mountain and, in the distance, Purple Mountain and the summits of the Ruby Range.

Reach a "Y" intersection at 2.0 miles. We bear right on the trail signed for West Maroon Pass. The unmarked trail to the left (northwest) climbs to Hasley Pass, the return leg of the loop. Beyond the junction the trail climbs briefly and then curves to the right (east), contouring through lush meadows and clusters of low willows. Along the way cross a stream which is typically dry after the snow melts.

At 2.4 miles start a steep ascent through meadows and willow patches. As you climb the trail curves to the southwest. To the west are great views of Galena and Treasure Mountains.

The grade eases at 2.9 miles and now ascends on moderate grades, reaching a signed trail junction at 3.1 miles. Here the trail to West Maroon Pass continues straight ahead (southeast). We turn left (northwest) on the trail to Frigid Air Pass.

Follow the undulating trails as it ascends northwest through lovely meadows. To the west/southwest are gorgeous views of Galena Mountain, Treasure Mountain, Mount Baldy, Cinnamon Mountain and, in the distance, Purple Mountain and the other peaks of the Ruby Range. Peak 12648, a red, pyramid-shaped mountain, towers above the valley to the northwest.

Reach a junction near a small pond beneath Peak 12648 at 4.5 miles. Turn right (north) on the signed trail to Frigid Air Pass. The unsigned trail to the left (west) leads to Hasley Basin. The trail to the pass skirts the left (west) side of the pond and climbs very steep switchbacks to Frigid Air Pass (12,415-ft.) at 4.8 miles, gaining 365-ft in 0.3 miles. Trekking poles are extremely help, especially when descending this section of the trail.

As you crest the pass stunning views open to the Maroon Bells towering above the emerald green meadows of the Fravert Basin. The white granite of

Snowmass Mountain (14,092-ft.) and Hagerman Peak (13,841-ft.), dominating the view to the northwest, stands in sharp contrast to the crimson-brown mudstone of the Maroon Bells massif. Bellview Mountain (13,233-ft.) rises along the ridge at the head of Fravert Basin. Behind you, to the west/southwest, Mt Baldy, Treasure Mountain and Purple Mountain fill the skyline.

Find a perch atop the pass to rest and take in the views. Expect to see plenty of backpackers at the pass or heading toward the pass in both directions. Backpackers cross Frigid Air Pass as part of the popular 26-mile Four Pass Loop, a 3-5 day backpacking trip climbing four 12,000-ft.-plus mountain passes in the Maroon-Snowmass Wilderness.

When you are done enjoying the views, descend from the pass to the junction and turn right (west) on the unmarked trail toward Hasley Basin. Follow the narrow, faint trail as it ascends on easy grades to a saddle at 5.5 miles, which I call the Hasley Basin Overlook (12,085-ft.), situated on the ridge between Peak 12648 and Peak 12345 to the west.

From the saddle enjoy terrific views of Snowmass Mountain, Hagerman Peak and the summits rising above the Geneva Lake basin to the north. Below you to the north/northwest are the beautiful meadows of Hasley Basin. Note the interesting stripped rock formation on the ridge along the west side of the basin.

Behind you, to the east, Belleview Mountain (13,233-ft.) towers above West Maroon Pass (12,500-ft.). To the northeast is Frigid Air Pass, where you will probably see hikers silhouetted against the skyline.

You now have several options, retrace your steps to the trailhead or follow one of two routes back to the unsigned junction along the East Fork trail passed on the trip up valley. Note: Both options require route finding skills. Use trails along sections of both routes fade and disappear at times. There are also numerous cow tracks to further complicate route finding. Make sure you have a good map and understand the route before you try one of these options.

Option1: Hasley Pass Loop

Segment Stats: 5.7 miles (one-way) with a 400-ft. elevation gain / 2,410-ft. elevation loss
Distance from Trailhead: 9.6 miles (loop)
Ending/Highest Elevation: 12,150-ft.
Elevation Gain from Trailhead: 2,395-ft elevation gain / 2,410-ft elevation loss

This is the longer of the two routes, crossing the head of Hasley Basin to Hasley Pass and then dropping down to the East Fork trail. Looking left (west) while standing at the Hasley Basin Overlook you will see a ridge extending north into Hasley Basin. The upper sections of the ridge are covered in talus that give way to meadows and stunted trees.

122

From the overlook, head left (west) across the head of Hasley Basin through alpine meadows. Aim to cross the ridge extending into the basin by climbing up the meadows just below the point where the talus ends. Pass through the vegetation atop the ridge and then look southwest at the talus slopes along the west side of the ridge. Here you should see a faint trail crossing the talus that eventually meets a trail coming up the valley. Follow the faint trail across the talus to the trail coming up the valley. Beyond the junction, the combined trails heads south, climbing steeply to the ridge at the head of the valley.

As the trail crests the ridge it curves to the right and descends along the top of the ridge to Hasley Pass (12,110-ft.) at 6.3 miles. Take a break here to enjoy the panoramic views that stretch from Snowmass Mountain and Hagerman Peak to north to the peaks along the Ruby Range to the south. Belleview Mountain and West Maroon Pass dominate the view to the southeast.

When you are done taking in the views head down the southeast side of Hasley Pass on a trail that soon curves to the southeast, descending through meadows on moderate to moderately steep grades. As the trail reaches a few scatter trees it starts curving to the east, reaching a junction at 7.1 miles. Turn right (southeast) at the junction and follow the trail as it drops down to and crosses a creek. Beyond the crossing the trail descends steep switchbacks to the junction with the East Fork trail at 7.6 miles. Turn right at the junction and follow the East Fork trail back to the trailhead for a 9.6 mile hike.

Note: The trail descending from Hasley Pass to the East Fork is unmaintained and may be faint in places and difficult to follow.

Option 2: Hasley Overlook Loop

Segment Stats: 4.9 miles (one-way) with a 200-ft. elevation gain / -2,210-ft. elevation loss
Distance from Trailhead: 8.8 miles (loop)
Ending/Highest Elevation: 12,110-ft.
Elevation Gain from Trailhead: 2,195-ft. elevation gain / -2,210-ft. loss

The shortest route from the Hasley Overlook back to the East Fork trail follows a use trail on the southeast side of the overlook that descends southwest and then south on easy grades. At times the route fades and is difficult to follow. At 5.7 miles reach the crest of the ridge extend east into the East Fork valley. You should reach the ridge near a copse of trees. Here you will lose the trail.

Below the south side of the ridge is a steep, grassy hillside. If you are lucky you will see a faint trail making a wide arc as it descends the hillside on very steep grades to a narrow bench. If you can't find the trail simply drop down to the bench.

Upon reaching the bench, continue the steep descent by heading southeast along the bench. You may pick-up vestiges of a trail along the way. As you descend the trail curves to the south at 6.0 miles and then turns southwest, dropping down to and crossing a creek. It is very difficult to follow the faint trail. If you get off the trial or can't find it, descend steeply along the bench and then curve to the south/southwest, staying to the north of a cluster of trees growing amid rock outcroppings. The goal is to cross the creek before you hit a deep gully. Descend along the west side of the creek until you hit the trail descending southeast toward the valley floor.

For hikers who have found the trail, on the west side of the creek the trail heads south and reaches a junction at 6.25 miles. Ignore the trail to the left (southwest), instead continue straight ahead following the trail as it curves to the southeast along the west side of the creek. Soon the path crosses the creek and drops down steep switchbacks to the junction with the East Fork trail at 6.75 miles. Turn right at the junction and follow the East Fork trail back to the trailhead for an 8.8 mile round-trip hike.

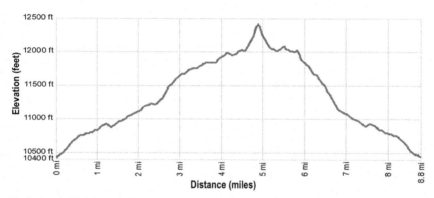

Driving Directions

From Crested Butte: From the intersection of Elk Avenue (main street) and 6th Street in Crested Butte, head north on 6th Street, which turns into the Gothic Road (sometimes referred to as the Schofield Pass Road). Follow the Gothic Road (CO 317) for 13.2 miles to Schofield Pass, passing the ski area and the research facilities at Gothic along the way. The dirt road is suitable for 2WD cars up to the town of Gothic at 7.9 miles. Beyond Gothic the road become rougher and a high clearance/4WD vehicle is recommended. (AWD/4WD is necessary if the road is wet.)

Continue over Schofield pass, descending the north side of the pass on switchbacks and then through meadows for 0.8 miles and turn right (east) at the signed East Fork trailhead. The turn is right before you hit Schofield Park, a large open park at the foot of the switchbacks. As you enter the trailhead, bear right into the parking area. The road branching to the left is for horse trailers.

28. Beckwith Pass ★★★★☆
Distance: 4.7 - 9.4 miles (RT)

This short hike features fine views of the Ruby Range, the Raggeds and East Beckwith Mountain. Extend the hike by walking to a high point with panoramic vistas of the West Elk Wilderness or continue to Beckwith Bench where the Anthracite Range joins the scene.

Distance: 4.7 miles (RT) to Beckwith Pass
Elevation: 8,860-ft. at Trailhead 9,954-ft. at Beckwith Pass
Elevation Gain: 1,094-ft. to Beckwith Pass

Difficulty: moderate
Basecamp: Crested Butte
Area: West Elk Wilderness, Gunnison NF
Best Season: July –September
USGS Map(s): Anthracite Range

Why Hike to Beckwith Pass

The trail to Beckwith Pass, a low saddle on the border of the West Elk Wilderness, ascends through forest and lovely meadows with fine views of Ruby Peak (12,644-ft.) and Mount Owen (13,058-ft.) to the north. At the pass panoramic views stretch north to Marcellina Mountain (11,348-ft.), the Ruby Range and the Raggeds. East Beckwith Mountain (12,432-ft.) dominates the view to the west while Storm Ridge and the Castles rise to the south.

Extend the hike by walking to a high point beyond the pass or to Beckwith Bench, a huge meadow on a high shelf to the south of East Beckwith Mountain. Both destinations feature fabulous vistas of the Anthracite Range and peaks in the West Elk Wilderness.

Trailhead to Beckwith Pass

There are two ways to get to Beckwith Pass, the Beckwith Pass trail #842 that begins at Lost Lake Slough and the Cliff Creek Trail #840, which starts just beyond Horse Ranch Park on the Kebler Pass Road. The Cliff Creek Trail involves more elevation gain but requires less driving and has the better views. Both are nice hikes. The description below is for the Cliff Creek trail to Beckwith Pass.

The Cliff Creek trail is located at the southeast end of the parking area. (See driving directions below.) Follow the trail as it heads southwest on easy grades through aspen. Soon the trail climbs a steep hillside to a crossing of Cliff Creek at 0.6 miles. Beyond the creek the trail ascends on moderate grades through spruce/fir forest and meadows. From the meadows enjoy ever-improving views of Ruby Peak (12,644-ft.) and Mount Owen (13,058-ft.) in the Ruby Range to the northeast. As you climb the views expand to include the peaks and ridges to the north of Mount Owen.

At 1.5 miles the grade abates. Soon views open to East Beckwith Mountain (12,432-ft.) rising to the west. At 1.8 miles the trail enters dense forest and reaches the junction with the Beckwith Pass trail. (Turning right at the junction will take you to Lost Lake Slough.) Continue straight ahead on the Cliff Creek trail, which crosses the creek and then climbs steeply through trees. At 2.0 miles the trail curves to the left (southeast). Soon the grade abates and the trees give way to pretty wildflower-filled meadows. The pass is now in sight.

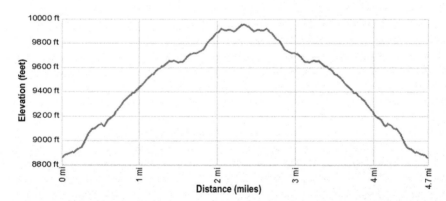

Reach Beckwith Pass (9,954-ft.) at 2.35 miles. Here you will find a sign marking the beginning of the West Elk Wilderness and a gate. Past the gate is a signed trail junction. From the pass the Ruby Range, Ragged Mountains and Marcellina Mountain (11,348-ft.) fill the skyline to the north. East Beckwith Mountain dominates the view to the west. Storm Ridge rises to the south. The interesting rock formation to the left (east) beyond Storm Ridge is the Castles, formed from dark volcanic breccia rock that eroded into spires, towers and stone walls.

At the trail junction a sign points left for the trail heading toward Swampy Pass and right for the trail to Beckwith Bench. Ignore the two minor trails that travel along the fence line. If you have the time and energy you can continue 0.9 miles beyond the pass, ascending through beautiful meadows along the Beckwith Bench trail to a high point with panoramic views of the West Elks and the peaks to the north.

Beyond the high point the trail drops down through aspens to a swampy area. Just before you hit a group of small ponds an unmarked trail turns right (west). (If you reach the ponds turnaround and ascend along the trail until you see the path.) This trail climbs through a rock slide and then aspen groves to emerge at Beckwith Bench, a huge meadow on a shelf below the south face of East Beckwith Mountain, at 4.7 miles. From the bench enjoy grand views of the Anthracite Range to the east and the peaks of the West Elk Wilderness to the south.

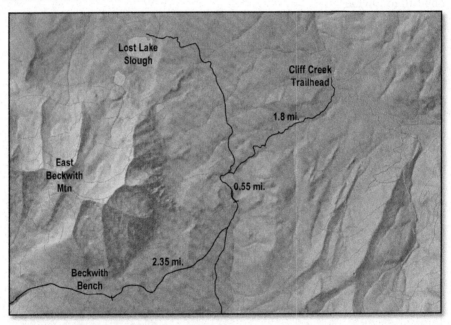

Driving Directions

Driving Directions from Crested Butte: From the intersection of Elk Avenue (main street) and 6th Street in Crested Butte, head south on 6th Street for 0.1 miles and turn right on Whiterock Ave. Follow the road through downtown Crested Butte. At the west end of town Whiterock Ave becomes the Kebler Pass Road (CO 12). Follow Whiterock/Kebler Pass road for 12.1 miles and turn left at the signed Cliff Creek trailhead. Follow the dirt access road for 0.2 miles to the trailhead parking area.

29. Browns Pass ★★★★☆
Distance: 7.6 to 10.2 miles (RT)

The ascent of the Denny Creek valley to Brown's pass features terrific view of the 14ers in the Collegiate Peaks Wilderness. Extend the hike with a high traverse to a saddle overlooking the North Cottonwood Creek with more great views of the high peaks of the Sawatch Range.

Distance: 7.6 miles (RT) to Pass
10.2 miles (RT) to Divide
Elevation: 9,910-ft. at Trailhead
12,020-ft. at Pass
12,550-ft. at Divide
Elevation Gain: 2,110-ft. to Pass
2,640-ft. to Divide

Difficulty: moderate-strenuous
Base camp: Buena Vista
Area: Collegiate Peaks
Wilderness, San Isabel NF
Best Season: July –September
USGS Map(s): Mount Yale

Why Hike to Brown's Pass

Brown's Pass on the Continental Divide in the Collegiate Peaks Wilderness features great views of prominent 14,000-ft. peaks in Sawatch Range. For even better views extend the hike by climbing to a high saddle on the divide between Texas Creek and the North Cottonwood Creek Valleys.

Initially the trail ascends along an old dirt road up the Denny Creek valley. Past the turnoff for the trail to Mt. Yale intermittent views open to Mt. Yale (14,196-ft.) to the east, Mt. Princeton (14,197-ft.) to the south and the peak rising along the west side of the valley.

Beyond the split off for the path to Hartenstein Lake the trail turns north, ascending through trees along the west side of the valley. Near the head of the valley the trail crosses the creek and then climbs through willows and meadows to Brown's Pass (12,020-ft.) on the Continental Divide.

From the pass views stretch north/northwest to the high peaks along the Continental Divide rising above Texas Creek including the Three Apostles. In the distance, Mt. Harvard (14,420-ft.), Mt. Oxford (14,153-ft.), Mt. Belford (14,197-ft.) and Emerald Peak (13,904-ft.) rise beyond the Divide. To the south Mt Antero (14,276-ft.) punctuates the skyline above a sea of peaks in the Sawatch Range. Turner Peak (13,237-ft.) dominates the view to the southwest.

After enjoying the pass I highly recommend extending the hike to the divide separating the Texas Creek and North Cottonwood Creek valleys. This trail heads east from the pass, climbing the ridge along the south side of the Continental Divide. Soon the trail crosses to the north side of the divide and ascends northeast on gentle grades through alpine tundra to the divide between the two valleys.

The traverse enjoys ever expanding views of the peaks seen from Brown's Pass in addition to distant views of the Elk Mountains to the west. From the saddle views extend northeast to Mt. Columbia (14,073-ft.) and southeast to Mt. Yale.

With a car drop or second vehicle, hikers can continue over the east side of the divide on a trail that drops down to Kroenke Lake and then descends to the North Cottonwood Creek trailhead.

Don't attempt to walk to the divide if the weather is threatening. The trail is totally exposed and not a place to be during a lightning storm.

Trailhead to Browns Pass

Distance from Trailhead: 7.6 miles (RT)
Ending/Highest Elevation: 12,020-ft.
Elevation Gain: 2,110-ft.

There are three ways to get to Brown's Pass; from the Denny Creek trailhead, the North Cottonwood Creek trailhead and the Texas Creek trailhead. This description, starting from the Denny Creek trailhead, is the shortest way to the pass and includes an optional extension to a saddle overlook the upper North Cottonwood Creek valley.

From the Denny Creek parking area, the Brown's Pass/Denny Creek trail heads north, climbing steep switchbacks up an old, rocky road through a forest of Lodgepole Pines. Shortly after passing the boundary of the Collegiate Peaks Wilderness at 0.25 miles the grade ease and the old road curves to the northwest, continuing its ascent on moderate grades through mixed forest along the left (west) side of Denny Creek.

Cross to the right (east) side of Denny Creek on a log bridge at 1.0 mile and then cross a smaller stream a short distance beyond. Openings in the trees offer a brief glimpse of Mount Yale (14,196-ft.) towering above the valley to the northeast.

Pass the trail to Mount Yale on the right (east) at 1.3 miles. Soon the trees thin as the trail travels through an old burn. Views open to the peaks rising to the west. Mt. Princeton (14,197-ft.) fills the skyline to the southeast (behind you).

Top a small rise at 1.8 miles and enjoy views of Tuner Peak (13,237-ft.) and the unnamed peaks ringing above the Hartenstein Lake basin to the west. Mt. Yale towers above the valley to the east. To the southeast are more great views of Mt. Princeton.

At 2.0 miles pass the trail to Hartenstein Lake branching to the left (west). Here the old road turns left. Stay right, now on a trail, that travels on easy grades through a meadow and then turns left (northwest) and crosses to the west side of North Fork of Denny Creek on a log bridge. There are some nice campsites in the trees to the west of the crossing.

Beyond the crossing the trail enters the trees and soon turns north, following an undulating course along the low hills on the west side of the valley. The valley bottom, seen through the trees, is choked with willows.

After a short descent the trail climbs two switchbacks and then curves to the northeast, emerging from the trees near the head of the valley at 3.2 miles. The path now travels through shoulder high willows as it rock hops across the nascent North Fork Creek. On the north side of the creek the trail ascends on steep grades through dense willows along the east side of the valley.

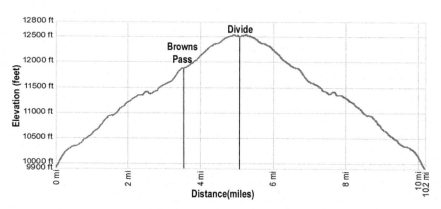

Soon the willows thin and give way to small meadows. Reach at bench at 3.5 miles with fine views of the Mt. Antero (14,276-ft.) and the peaks to the south. Turner Peak (13,237-ft.) rises to the southwest.

The trail now curves to the northwest, ascending on moderately-easy grades through meadows and scatters clumps of low willows. The pass, a low saddle on the ridge, is now in view. Finally the willows give way to alpine tundra as the trail climbs on moderate grades to Brown's Pass (12,020-ft.) on the Continental Divide at 3.8 miles.

From the pass enjoy a stunning panorama to the north/northwest of the peaks and ridges along the Continental Divide rising above the Texas Creek Valley, including the Three Apostles. In the distance, Mt. Harvard (14,420-ft.), Mt. Oxford (14,153-ft.), Mt. Belford (14,197-ft.) and Emerald Peak

(13,904-ft.) rise beyond the Divide. To the south the distinctive shaped Mt. Antero Peak punctuates the skyline above a sea of peak in the Sawatch Range while Turner Peak and several unnamed summits dominate the views to the southwest.

The pass offers an opportunity to trace the Continental Divide as it snakes east from the pass, eventually curving around the head of Texas Creek and back along the ridges and peaks rimming the north of Texas Creek. To the west the divide climbs the ridge beyond the pass before turning southwest to follow the ridge along the west side of the Denny Creek Valley.

History buffs will want to descend 0.3 miles down the north side of the pass to the ruins of Brown's Cabin and the remnants of the nearby mine openings. This side trip loses over 300-ft. on the way to the cabin.

To North Cottonwood Creek Divide

Segment Stats: 1.3 miles (one-way) with a 530-ft. elevation gain
Distance from Trailhead: 10.2 miles (RT)
Ending/Highest Elevation: 12,550-ft.
Elevation Gain: 2,640-ft.

If time, energy and the weather permit, I strongly recommend extending the hike by continuing to the divide separating the Texas Creek and North Cottonwood Creek Valleys, which adds 2.6 miles round trip and 530-ft. of elevation gain to the hike. The extra effort is amply rewarded with terrific views.

At Brown's Pass a signed trail heads east toward Kroenke Lake. Follow the trail as it climbs switchbacks through alpine tundra up the ridge along the south side of the Continental Divide. As you gain elevation, enjoy every improving views of Mt. Princeton and Mt. Antero to the south and the peaks rising along the west side of the Denny Creek valley.

At 4.4 miles the trail crosses to the north side of the divide and then ascends on easy grades along the northeast face of a low, unnamed peak. Views as you cross the tundra encompass the sea of peaks rises above and beyond the north side of Texas Creek Valley. The distinctive profile of the Three Apostles marks the northwest end of the valley. Mt. Columbia (14,073-ft.), Mt. Harvard, Mt. Oxford and Mt. Belford punctuate the skyline to the north/northeast. To the west, distant views extend to the Elk Mountains.

Reach the high point of the hike (12, 550-ft.) at 4.9 miles. From this point the trail gently descends to the divide overlooking the head of the North Cottonwood valley. Mt. Yale dominates the views to the southeast while Mt Columbia rises to the northeast. To the north/northwest are more great views of the high summits of the Collegiate Peaks. The Elk Mountains fill the skyline to the west.

When you are done taking in the views, retrace your steps to the trailhead for a 10.2 mile round-trip hike. With a car drop or second vehicle, hikers can continue over the east side of the divide on a trail that drops down to Kroenke Lake and then descends to the North Cottonwood Creek trailhead.

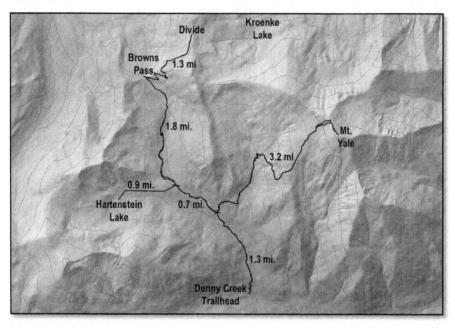

Driving Directions

From Buena Vista: From the traffic light at the intersection of U.S.24 and Country Road 306 in downtown Buena Vista, drive west on CR 306 for 12 miles and turn right (north) into the paved Denny Creek Trailhead parking area. The parking area is about a mile beyond the Collegiate Peaks Campground (located along the left (south) side of CR 306). There is additional parking in a gravel lot just to the east.

Note: This is a very popular trailhead, providing access to Hartenstein Lake, Mount Yale and Brown's Pass. The parking area fills early during the height of the summer hiking season.

30. Lake Ann ★★★★☆
Distance: 6.6 - 12.0 miles (RT)

The hike to Lake Ann, cradled in a pretty alpine basin beneath the Continental Divide, features great views of Huron Peak and the Three Apostles. Continue the hike to a saddle on the divide with stunning views of the Taylor Valley and the peaks riming the Clear Creek valley.

Distance: 6.6 miles (RT) Lake Ann
8.0 miles (RT) to Continental Divide
Add 4.0 miles (RT) if walking from Winfield
Elevation: 10,256-ft. at Winfield
10,600-ft. at Trailhead
11,805-ft. at Lake Ann
12,620-ft. at Continental Divide
Elevation Gain: 1,205-ft. Lake Ann
2,020-ft. to Continental Divide
Add 344-ft. if walking from Winfield

Difficulty: moderate
Basecamp: Buena Vista and Leadville
Area: Collegiate Peaks Wilderness, San Isabel NF
Best Season: July –September
USGS Map(s): Winfield

Why Hike to Lake Ann

This scenic hike ascends through meadows and trees up the South Fork Clear Creek Valley to beautiful Lake Ann, an aquamarine gem cradled in a small cirque of 13,000-ft. peaks along the Continental Divide. As you ascend the trail enjoy fine views of the Three Apostles rising to the southwest and Huron Peak towering above the east side of the valley.

Extend the hike by climbing the trail to a saddle on the Continental Divide with terrific views of the Taylor Valley to the south, the Elk Mountains to the west and Huron Peak (14,003-ft.) and the 13,000-ft. summits lining the north side of the Clear Creek valley to the north.

The road to the Lake Ann trailhead requires a high clearance/4WD vehicle. Hikers with a 2WD/low clearance vehicle can park in the ghost town of Winfield and walk up the 4WD road. The walk adds 4.0 miles round trip to the hike.

Trailhead to Lake Ann

Distance from Trailhead: 6.6 miles (RT)
Ending/Highest Elevation: 11,805-ft.
Elevation Gain: 1,205-ft.
Distance from 2WD Trailhead: 10.6 miles (RT)
Ending/Highest Elevation: 11,805-ft.
Elevation Gain: 1,549-ft.

From the 2WD parking lot near Winfield, walk south up County Road (CR) 390.2B on easy grades for 0.7 miles to an intersection. Take the road branch right to stay on CR 390. (The road to the left climbs the hill towards Browns Peak.)

Continue up the road for 1.3 miles to the 4WD parking area for Lake Ann and Huron Peak. The walk to the trailhead gains about 350-ft. in 2.0 miles, adding 4.0 miles round trip to the hike to Lake Ann. The mileage in the description below assumes you are starting from the 4WD Parking area.

Before beginning the hike to Lake Ann, walk to the pond to the west of the trailhead parking area for fine views of the peaks rising above the head of the Silver Creek basin to the southwest. Granite Mountain (12,848-ft.), a distinctive triangular peak, towers above the ridge separating the Silver Creek and the South Fork valleys.

The trailhead for Lake Ann and Huron Peak (14,003-ft.) is located at the south end of the 4WD parking area. Here the path to Huron Peak branches to the left (southeast). We head south on the Lake Ann/Continental Divide trail, which curves around the large sign at the trailhead.

Follow the trail as it ascends on easy grades through spruce/fir forest and small meadows on the east side of the South Fork valley. Along the way the trail passes the boundary for the Collegiate Peaks Wilderness. At 0.9 miles cross a large meadow with a pond where views open to the Three Apostles (West Apostle (13,568-ft.), Ice Mountain (13,951-ft.) and North Apostle (13,860-ft.)) rising to the southwest. Huron Peak (14,003-ft.) soars overhead to the east.

Beyond the meadow the trail wanders through clusters of trees and brushy meadows. Keep an eye out for the ruins of an old cabin across the creek. Reach a "Y" intersection in a meadow at 1.5 miles. The Three Apostles trail branches left. We bear right (southwest) on the trail to Lake Ann. Ahead are fine views of the Apostles.

Past the junction the trail crosses to the west side of the South Fork of Clear Creek on a make-shift log bridge and briefly travels through willow-clogged meadows before curving to the left (south). Soon the trail enters the forest, climbing south/southwest on moderately-steep grades. Views are limited as the path climbs through the trees although a few nice waterfalls along the creek add interest to this section of the trail.

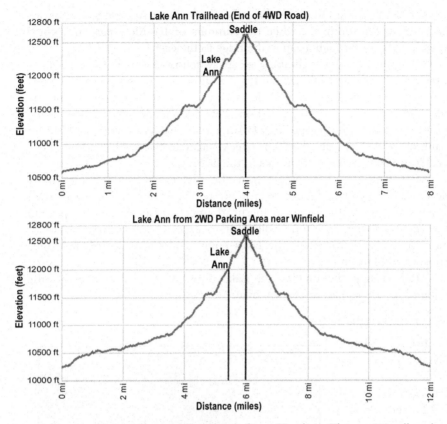

Cross a small cascade tumbling down from Harrison Flats at 2.8 miles. A short distance beyond the trail curves to the left (southeast) as it descends to and crosses a creek. On the east side of the creek the trail climbs steeply through trees which soon give way to meadows.

At 3.2 miles reach the junction with the use trail branching left to Lake Ann (11,805-ft.), an aquamarine jewel nestled in a beautiful basin beneath rugged 13,000-ft peaks. The trail to the right climbs to a saddle on the Continental Divide.

To the Saddle on the Continental Divide

Distance from Trailhead: 8.0 miles (RT)
Ending/Highest Elevation: 12,620-ft.
Elevation Gain: 2,020-ft.
Distance from 2WD Trailhead: 12 miles (RT)
Ending/Highest Elevation: 12,620-ft.
Elevation Gain: 2,364-ft.

A visit to the saddle on the Continental Divide is highly recommended. The trail to the divide ascends steeply along the meadow-clad ridge to the west of the lake. Rock cairns mark the way. As you gain elevation enjoy great views of the lake and the peaks along the divide. West Apostle towers above the basin to the southwest while the summits of Ice Mountain and North Apostle are seen through a gap in the ridge to the east.

Soon the trail starts climbing steep switchbacks up the divide's talus slopes, reaching the saddle on the ridge at 4.0 miles. From the saddle enjoy panoramic views of the Taylor Valley and reservoir to the southwest and the Elk Mountains to the west. Huron Peak dominates the views to the northeast while Mount Hope (13,993-ft.), Ervin Peak (13,531-ft.) and Mount Blaurock (13,616-ft.) rim the Clear Creek Valley to the north. La Plata Peak (14,336-ft.) towers above the peaks to the northwest.

After taking in the views from the divide, descend to the pretty meadows surrounding Lake Ann for impressive views of the steep sided cirque surrounding the lake and the nearby peaks. Backpackers camping in the vicinity of the Lake Ann will want to explore the unnamed lakes of Harrison Flats to the west. The lakes enjoy stunning views of the Three Apostles and Huron Peak.

After visiting the divide and Lake Ann, retrace your steps to the trailhead for a 8.0 miles round-trip hike.

Driving Directions

From Buena Vista: From the traffic light at the intersection of U.S.24 and Country Road 306 in downtown Buena Vista, travel north on U.S. Hwy 24 for 15 miles to County Road (CR) 390 / Clear Creek Reservoir Road. Turn left (west) on Clear Creek Road/CR 390 and follow the gravel road, which turns into Forest Road 120, for 11.7 miles to the ghost town of Winfield.

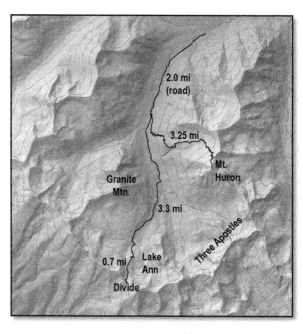

In Winfield turn left (south) on Forest Road (FR) 390.2B. The road crosses Clear Creek on a bridge. Hikers who do not have a high clearance/4WD vehicle should turn left (east) after 0.1 miles into a large parking lot and camping area.

If you have a high clearance/4WD vehicle, continue 0.7 miles on the rough road to an intersection and bear right. (Don't take the road to the left that heads uphill towards Browns Peak.) Continue up FR 390.2b for 1.3 miles to the parking lot at the end of the road. (Total distance from the Clear Creek Road to the trailhead is 2.0 miles.) Note: This road crosses streams and negotiates deep ditches and potholes. Don't try to take a 2WD, low clearance vehicle on this road.

The small 4WD parking area can get quite crowded since it also serves as the parking lot for Huron Peak, a popular 14'er.

From Leadville: Travel south on U.S. Hwy 24 for 19.5 miles to County Road (CR) 390 / Clear Creek Reservoir Road. Turn right (west) on CR 390 and follow the gravel road, which turns into Forest Road 120, for 11.7 miles to the ghost town of Winfield.

In Winfield turn left (south) on Forest Road (FR) 390.2B. The road crosses Clear Creek on a bridge. Hikers who do not have a high clearance/4WD vehicle should turn left (east) after 0.1 miles into a large parking lot and camping area.

If you have a high clearance/4WD vehicle, continue 0.7 miles on the rough road to an intersection and bear right. (Don't take the road to the left that heads uphill towards Browns Peak.) Continue up FR 390.2b for 1.3 miles to the parking lot at the end of the road. (Total distance from the Clear Creek Road to the trailhead is 2.0 miles.) Note: This road crosses streams and negotiates deep ditches and potholes. Don't try to take a 2WD, low clearance vehicle on this road.

The small 4WD parking area can get quite crowded since it also serves as the parking lot for Huron Peak, a popular 14'er.

31. Bear Lake ★★★★☆
Distance: 11.0 miles (RT)

Great views of three Colorado 14ers; Mt. Harvard, Mt. Columbia and Mt. Yale, are the rewards of this hike up the scenic Horn Fork basin to Bear Lake, an alpine jewel nestled in a rugged bowl beneath the Continental Divide in the Collegiate Peaks Wilderness.

Distance: 11.0 miles (RT) to Bear Lake
Elevation: 9,890-ft. at Trailhead 12,410-ft. at Bear Lake
Elevation Gain: 2,520-ft. to Bear Lake
Difficulty: moderate-strenuous

Basecamp: Buena Vista
Area: Collegiate Peaks, San Isabel NF
Best Season: July –September
USGS Map(s): Mount Harvard

Why Hike to Bear Lake

This excellent hike travels up the scenic Horn Fork Valley to beautiful Bear Lake, cradled in a stark, rocky shelf beneath a rugged ridge along the Continental Divide. From the lake enjoy stunning views of the area's 14'ers - - Mt. Harvard (14,420-ft.), Mr. Columbia (14,073-ft.) and Mt. Yale (14,196-ft.).

The trail initially travels through forest up the North Cottonwood Creek Valley before turning north into the Horn Fork. As the trail gains elevation intermittent views open to Mt. Yale to the south and Mt. Columbia towering over the east side of the valley.

Near the head of the valley the trail breaks from the trees and views open to Mt. Harvard and the peak and ridges ringing the head of the valley. Behind you are grand views of Mt. Yale and, in the distance, Mt. Princeton (14,197-ft.).

At the head of the valley the trail crests a high bench and curves to the west, passing the trail climbing to Mt. Harvard, which branches to the north. A short climb leads to Bear Lake (12,374-ft.), a starkly beautiful alpine jewel nestled in a rocky bowl beneath the valley's rugged west ridge. In addition to the panoramic views of the nearby 14,000-ft peaks, the lake features good fishing for cutthroat trout.

This trail is popular with hikers climbing to Mt. Harvard, so don't expect solitude. Parties wishing to overnight near the lake will find the best campsites in the trees a mile and a half below the lake. These campsites are typically crowded with people who spend the night in the Horn Fork basin and then summit Mt Harvard on the second day.

Trailhead to Bear Lake

The Horn Fork Trail to Bear Lake and Mt. Harvard starts at the southwest side of the North Cottonwood Creek trailhead. (See driving directions below.) Follow the trail as it heads west through trees for 0.15 miles and then crosses a good wood bridge to the south side of North Cottonwood Creek. Beyond the bridge the trail ascends on moderate grades through a spruce-fir forest, passing the boundary of the Collegiate Peaks Wilderness at 0.6 miles.

Just past the wilderness border the grade abates and the trail now ascends on easy grades beside the creek. Cross back to the north side of the creek on a wood bridge at 1.6 miles and a short distance beyond reach a trail junction. The trail branching to the left (west) leads to Kroenke Lake and Brown's Pass. We bear right on the Horn Fork Trail toward Horn Fork Basin and Bear Lake.

The trail now heads northwest, climbing the hillside along the north side of the valley on moderately-steep grades. Intermittent openings in the trees offer nice views of Mt Yale to the southwest. The grade eases at 2.25 miles as the trail curves into the Horn Fork valley. A quarter mile beyond logs and rocks facilitate the crossing of a creek draining the south ridge of Mt. Columbia.

Past the crossing follow the trail as it climbs on moderate to easy grades along the east side of the Horn Fork Valley. At 3.0 miles the path skirts the east edge of a small meadow. Here views open to the ridge rimming the western side of the valley. A short distance beyond a second meadow offers views of Mt. Columbia towering above the east side of the valley.

Soon the trail reenters the trees, ascending the valley on moderate grades. At 3.9 miles the trees give way to a large park revealing Mt. Harvard, the high point of the stunning cirque at the head of the valley. The trail now curves to the east to avoid the willow-choke valley floor.

Soon the trail curves back to the north and continues its moderate ascent up the valley beneath Mt. Columbia's west face and the rugged ridge lining the west side of the valley. Along the way enjoy ever improving views of Mt. Harvard and the unnamed jagged peaks ringing the head of the valley. Turn around for great views of Mt. Yale rising to the south.

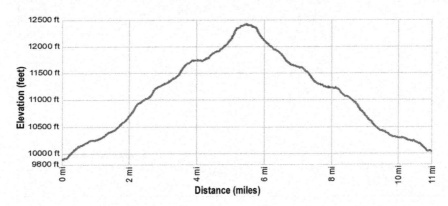

Cross to the west side of Horn Fork Creek at 4.3 miles and then ascend a small rise with scatter Krummholz firs. Soon we pass the last of the stunted firs. The trail now travels up valley through alpine meadows scattered with clusters of low willows. As you gain elevation, Mt. Princeton is now visible in the distance to the south.

At 5.2 miles the trail curves to the left (west) as it crests the top of a bench and reaches the unmarked junction with the trail to Mt. Harvard branching to the right (north). We continue heading west toward Bear Lake, crossing the nascent Horn Fork. Look right (north) to see hikers climbing a rocky trail to a saddle on the way to Mt. Harvard. Ahead jagged unnamed peaks tower above the west side of the valley.

A short climbs leads to Bear Lake (12,374-ft.) at 5.5 miles. This starkly beautiful jewel lies nestled on a rocky shelf beneath the Continental Divide, which runs along the valley's rugged west ridge. From the lake enjoy great views of Mt. Harvard, Mt Columbia, Mt Yale and in the distance Mt. Princeton, along with the unnamed peaks and ridges surround the head of the valley. Fishermen may want to try their luck catching the lake's cutthroat trout.

Parties wishing to overnight will find exposed and windy campsites around the lake. The best campsites are located in the trees a mile and a half below the lake. These sites are often crowded with hikers who spend the night in the Horn Fork basin and then summit Mt Harvard on the second day.

When you are done enjoying Bear Lake, retrace your steps to the trailhead for an 11.0 mile round trip hike.

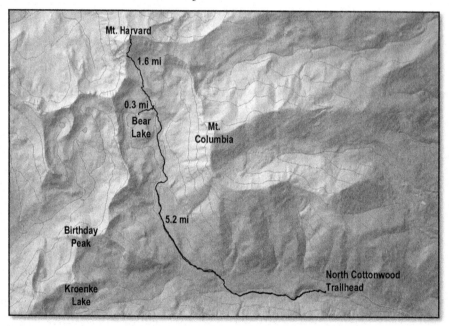

Driving Directions

Driving Directions from Buena Vista: From the traffic light at the intersection of U.S.24 and Country Road 306 in downtown Buena Vista, drive north on U.S. 24 W for three blocks (0.7 miles) and turn left on Crossman Avenue (CR 350). The turn is just beyond the Super 8 in Buena Vista.

Follow CR 350 for 1.8 miles to a "T" intersection and turn right on CR 361. Drive on CR 361 for 0.9 miles to a 2nd "T" intersection and turn left on

CR 365. Follow CR 365 for 5.1 miles to the North Cottonwood Creek trailhead at the end of the road. The road gets noticeable rougher after the first 2.0 miles. Beyond this point normal passenger cars can make it to the trailhead if driven carefully. High clearance is better.

This is a very popular trailhead providing access to Mt. Harvard. As such it fills early in the morning during the summer. Additional parking is available along the road leading to the parking lot. Be sure to pick a spot that is well off the road.

32. Missouri Gulch / Elkhead Pass ★★★★☆
Distance: 9.0 miles (RT)

The strenuous hike to Elkhead Pass, one of the highest passes in Colorado, steeply ascends scenic Missouri Gulch to a 13,220-ft. pass with panoramic views of the 13,000 and 14,000-ft. peaks looming above the expansive meadows of Missouri Basin.

Distance: 9.0 miles (RT)
Elevation: 9,660-ft. at Trailhead
Maximum elevation: 13,220-ft.
Elevation Gain: 3,560-ft.
Difficulty: strenuous

Basecamp: Buena Vista and Leadville
Area: Collegiate Peaks, San Isabel NF
Best Season: July –September
USGS Map(s): Mount Harvard, Winfield

Why Hike to Missouri Gulch / Elkhead Pass

The Elkhead Pass/Missouri Gulch hike is a great illustration of why I like hiking to a pass. Upon arriving at Elkhead Pass a dramatic panorama unfolds all at once. Mt. Harvard (14,414-ft.), to the southeast, and Mt. Belford (14,197-ft.), to the northeast, anchor a jagged cirque of 13,000 and 14,000-ft. peaks that tower above the expansive meadows of beautiful Missouri Basin. Mt. Yale (14,194-ft.) rises to the south beyond the cirque. To the north, vistas extend to Mount Hope (13,933-ft.), Quail Mountain and, in the distance, Mt. Elbert (14,433-ft.).

The hike starts with a stiff climb up the timbered southern slopes of the Clear Creek Valley and then enters Missouri Gulch. Soon the trees give way to scenic meadows and for the last 3 miles the hike traverse a gorgeous basin with wonderful views of Mt. Belford (14,197-ft.) and Missouri Mountain (14,076-ft.).

From the pass hikers with the time and energy can climb Mt. Belford. Beyond the pass the trail drops into the Missouri Basin and links with the Pine Creek trail, creating interesting options for backpacking trips.

Trailhead to Elkhead Pass

The Missouri Gulch/Elkhead Pass trail is located at the western end of the large trailhead parking area (see driving directions below). Follow the path as it descends to and crosses Clear Creek on a good bridge. On the other side of the creek steep switchbacks ascend the south side of the valley through aspen, pine and spruce-fir forest to the foot of Missouri Gulch, gaining 670-ft. in 0.7 miles.

Once in the gulch the steep ascent continues along the west side of Missouri creek for 0.5 miles to a crossing at 1.2 miles. Cross the creek and climb steeply up switchbacks on the east side of the gulch that soon enter a section of dense timber. Right before exiting the trees pass the remains of an old log cabin at 1.5 miles.

The trail emerges from the trees into a pretty basin decorated with rocky meadows scatter with copses of trees and small thickets of scrub willows. Ahead Mount Belford (14,197-ft.), rising to the southeast, dominates the scene while a granite ridge extending from Missouri Mountain forms the gulch's western wall.

Follow the trail as it stays to the east of the creek and ascends the beautiful basin on moderately steep grades. Reach the junction with the trail leading to Mount Belford at the 2.1 miles. Here the Belford trail heads left (southeast). Our trail curves southwest and continues climbing the basin.

Cross to the west side of the creek shortly after the junction and follow the trail as it curves to the southeast and then climbs steeply up a small rise. Atop the rise the grade abates a bit as the path curves southwest through meadows and scrub willows. Along the way enjoy wonderful views of the basin's western wall.

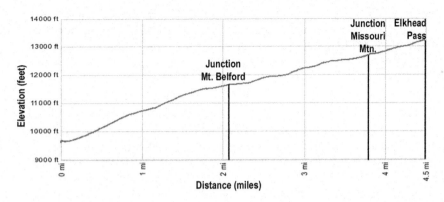

At 2.9 miles the path crosses back to the east side of the creek through scrub willows and steeply ascends another small rise. The trail now traverses on moderately steep grades a rolling landscape clad in tundra, crossing back to the west side of the creek at 3.4 miles. As you climb be sure to turn around for nice views down the gulch to the peaks rising above the north side of the Clear Creek Valley. Ahead, Missouri Mountain (14,067-ft.) towers above the basin.

Reach the junction with a trail heading right (west) to Missouri Mountain at 3.7 miles. Our trail curves left (southeast), climbing a steep, rocky hillside with the aid of a few switchbacks beneath the south face of Mount Belford.

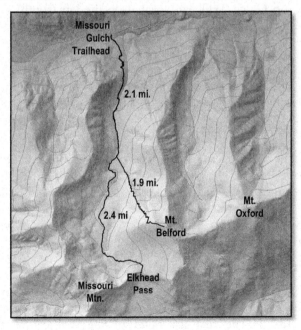

At the top of the hill the grade abates as bit as the trail ascends rocky meadows sprinkled with wildflowers and then swings south for the final stiff climb to Elkhead Pass, reached after gaining 3,560-ft. in 4.5 miles.

The broad pass, located at a low point on the ridge between Missouri Mountain and Mt. Belford, enjoys stunning views to the south of the huge granite cirque towering above the emerald green meadows of Missouri Basin. Mt. Harvard (14,414-ft.), rising to the southeast, anchors a jagged ridge of

13,000-ft. peaks running west to an unnamed 13,694-ft. summit rising above Silver King Lake. From the unnamed summit the ridge heads north to Emerald Peak (13,904-ft.), Iowa Peak (13,831-ft.) and Missouri Mountain and then turns northeast to Mt. Belford. Mt. Yale (14,194-ft.) rises to the south beyond the cirque. To the north, vistas extend to Mount Hope (13,933-ft.), Quail Mountain and, in the distance, Mt. Elbert (14,433-ft.).

From the pass the Missouri Gulch trail descends to the wildflower-filled meadows of Missouri Basin and then switchbacks down to Pine Creek to meet the Pine Creek trail in 3.3 miles, losing 1,670-ft. along the way.

A trail also leads east from the pass to the top of Mt. Belford. This steep climb gains 977-ft. in 1.1 miles. Hikers reaching the top of Belford along this trail typically descend the Mt. Belford trail to Missouri Gulch and back to the trailhead, a total distance of 9.6 miles.

Driving Directions

From Leadville: Travel south on U.S. Hwy 24 for 19.5 miles to County Road 390 / Clear Creek Reservoir Road. Turn right (west) and follow the gravel road, which turns into Forest Road 120, for 8 miles to the Missouri Gulch Trailhead, located on the left (south) side of the road and park.

From Buena Vista: Travel north on U.S. Hwy 24 for 15 miles to County Road 390 / Clear Creek Reservoir Road. Turn left (west) and follow the gravel road, which turns into Forest Road 120, for 8 miles to the Missouri Gulch Trailhead, located on the left (south) side of the road and park.

33. Ptarmigan Lake ★★★★☆
Distance: 6.2 - 6.8 miles (RT)

This family-friendly scenic hike climbs on moderate grades to a lovely lake with terrific views of Mount Yale (14,196-ft.) and Turner Peak to the north, the Gladstone Ridge to the east and Jones Mountains to the West.

Distance: 6.8 miles (RT) to Ptarmigan Lake	**Difficulty:** moderate
	Basecamp: Buena Vista
Elevation: 10,680-ft. at Trailhead	**Area:** San Isabel NF
12,300-ft. at Ptarmigan Lake	**Best Season:** July –September
Elevation Gain: 1,620-ft. to Ptarmigan Lake	**USGS Map(s):** Tin Cup, Mt. Yale

Why Hike to Ptarmigan Lake

This popular, scenic half day hike ascends on moderate grades to beautiful Ptarmigan Lake (12,150-ft.), cradled at the base of Jones Mountain (13,218-ft.). The first 2.4 miles of the trail climbs through trees with intermittent views of the Turner Peak (13,237-ft.) and the Gladstone Ridge (13,208-ft.).

As the trees thin the trail passes a pretty lake and pond with good campsites nearby. Soon the trees give way to beautiful meadows renowned for their spectacular wildflower displays. Great views, which improve as you gain elevation, open to the Jones Mountains (13,218-ft.) and Mount Yale (14,196-ft.).

At 3.1 miles pretty Ptarmigan Lake Spring into view. Continue along the trail as it skirts the lake's eastern shore. At the south end of the lake a panorama of high peaks, including Turner Peak and Mount Yale, fills the skyline to the north.

Extend the hike by climbing the short, steep trail to a saddle between Gladstone Ridge and Jones Mountain with stunning views of the peaks to the north and bird's-eye view of Ptarmigan Lake below. To the south the high peaks along the South Cottonwood drainage dominate the view.

Don't expect solitude along the trail. This hike is a favorite of locals and families looking for a moderately-easy hike. The lake's healthy popular of cutthroat trout also makes it a popular destination for fishermen.

The trail, with nice camping spots near the lower lake, is a great backpacking destination for families with young children. The hike is also a good option for flatlanders trying to acclimatizing before tackling the area's 14'ers.

Trailhead to Ptarmigan Lake and the Saddle

The signed trail to Ptarmigan Lake starts from the south end of the trailhead parking lot. Follow the trail as it heads south through spruce/fir forest and soon crosses a bridge over Middle Cottonwood Creek. Beyond the bridge the trail curves to the left (east) and ascends on easy to moderate grades. The trail briefly breaks out of the trees to reveal views of Turner Peak (12,327-ft.) and Peak 12739 rising along the north side of the Middle Cottonwood Creek Valley.

At 0.5 miles the trail crests a minor ridge and curves to the right (south) into the Ptarmigan Creek Valley. The path now ascends on moderate grades through forest along the right (west) side of Ptarmigan Creek. The creek is heard but seldom seen as you climb the valley. As the trail crosses an old rock slide views open to the Gladstone Ridge (13,208-ft.) rimming the east side of the valley.

Past the slide the trail plunges back into the trees and continues its ascent. The path curves right (west) at 1.25 miles and climbs switchbacks up a hillside. En route pass an old Forest Service Road at 1.4 mile. Soon the trail curves to the left (southwest) and resumes its ascent up the valley.

At 2.4 miles the trees thin as the trail passes between an unnamed lake to the left (east) and a small pond to the right (west). Views open to the Jones Mountain massif lining the west side of the valley. The rugged Gladstone Ridge forms a backdrop for the lake to the east. Several nice campsites are situated among the trees on both sides of the trail.

Beyond the lake the grade steepens as the trail climbs through meadows with scattered willows and trees. Turn around for great views of Mount Yale (14,196-ft.) towering above the north side of the Middle Cottonwood Valley.

Leave the last of the trees behind at 2.7 miles. The path now ascends through meadows and clusters of willows toward the head of the valley, crossing the outlet stream of a small pond to the west of the trail. Views open to a saddle at the head of the valley between Gladstone Ridge and the Jones Mountains. Behind you, to the north, are more great views of Turner Peak and Mount Yale.

At 2.9 miles the trail turns east and climbs on moderately-steep grades to a bench. As you crest the bench Ptarmigan Lake (12,150-ft.) springs into view at 3.1 miles. The beautiful lake lies nestled beneath the north face of Jones Mountain and is surrounded by pretty meadows and willow thickets. Fishermen are often seen on the surrounding shores casting for the lake's native cutthroat trout.

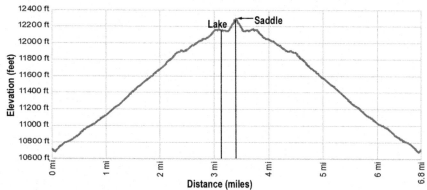

For even better views follow trail around the eastern shoreline to the head of the lake. From this vantage point Turner Peak and Mount Yale form a stunning backdrop for this pretty alpine lake. Early in the day, before the wind picks up, you may be lucky enough to see the peaks reflected in the lake's still waters.

If time and energy permit, extend the hike by climbing the short, steep trail to the saddle (12,300-ft.) at the head of the valley at 3.4 miles. From the saddle enjoy lovely bird's-eye views of Ptarmigan Lake. To the north panoramic views encompass Turner Peak, Brown's Pass, Mount Yale and the summits rising to the north of Texas Creek. To the south the saddle overlooks the South Cottonwood Valley rimmed by 13,000-ft. peaks extending west from Mount Princeton and the 12,000-ft peaks lining Morgan's Gulch.

When you are done enjoying the views, retrace your steps to the trailhead. The return hike is filled with more great views of Mount Yale and Turner Peak, which are now front and center as you descend the valley.

Driving Directions

From Buena Vista: From the traffic light at the intersection of U.S.24 and Country Road 306 in downtown Buena Vista, drive west on CR 306 for 14.4 miles and turn left (south) on to the signed road for the Ptarmigan Lake trailhead. Follow the short paved road as it curves southwest to a small parking area with an outhouse. The signed trailhead is located along the south end of the parking lot.

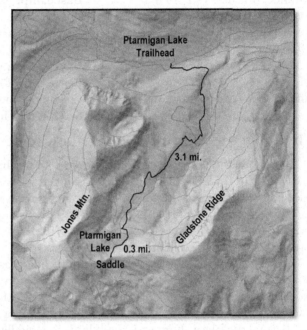

If the parking lot if full, there are a few spaces along the access road. There are also some places to park along CR 306 near the trailhead. Make sure you select a spot that is well off the highway and does not block the entrance to the spur road.

34. North Fork Lake Creek ★★★★★
Distance: 8.1 miles (RT)

This trail travels up a beautiful, secluded valley to wind swept tarn and then a saddle on the Continental Divide overlooking the Fryingpan Lakes. The quiet valley offers good opportunities to spot wildlife and features fine views of the surrounding high peaks.

Distance: 8.1 miles (RT) to the Saddle
Elevation: 10,790-ft. at Trailhead 12,460-ft. at the Saddle
Elevation Gain: 1,670-ft. to the Saddle
Difficulty: moderate-strenuous

Basecamp: Aspen, Buena Vista and Leadville
Area: Mt. Massive Wilderness, San Isabel NF
Best Season: July –September
USGS Map(s): Mount Champion, Independence Pass
See Page 57 for Map

Why Hike the North Fork of Lake Creek

Get off the beaten track with this scenic hike up the North Fork Lake Creek valley in the Mt. Massive Wilderness. The trail, located to the east of Independence Pass, ascends the meadows along the valley floor enjoying fine views of Mt. Champion (13,464-ft.) and Lackawanna Peak (13,823-ft.) rising to the east and several unnamed 12,000-ft. peaks towering above the head of the valley to the north.

At the head of the valley vistas open to two huge basins, to the east and the west, ringed by 13,000-ft peaks. Here the trail turns east and ascends through alpine meadows to the basin beneath Deer Mountain (13,761-ft.) and then climbs steep switchbacks to a bench cradling a small, unnamed lake. Beyond the lake a short, easy climb leads to a saddle on the Continental Divide with panoramic views down the Fryingpan Valley to the Fryingpan Lakes. In the distance are the summits in the Hunter Fryingpan and Holy Cross Wilderness areas.

On the return journey the descent down the Deer Mountain basin to the trailhead features stunning views of the basin to the west and Twining Peak (13,711-ft.) rising along the west side of the valley. To the south Star Mountain (12,941-ft.) and nearby summits in the Collegiate Peaks Wilderness fill the skyline.

The lightly traveled valley provides good opportunities to spot wildlife and offers a degree of solitude not found on many of the hiking trails in the area. Fishermen will want to take a detour up the very steep use trail to Blue Lake nestled beneath Twining Peak.

North Fork Lake Creek to the Saddle

The North Fork Lake Creek trail initially follows an old jeep road heading north and ascending the west side of the valley floor on easy to moderate grades through meadows scattered with willows and trees. Mt. Champion (13,646-ft.) soars above the valley to the northeast.

At 0.4 miles the grade steepens as the trail climbs to the top of a small bench where the road turns into a trail. Beyond the bench the trail climbs steeply for a short distance and then reverts to more moderate grades at 0.6 miles. Here views open to the peaks towering above the head of the valley.

Reach the boundary of the Mt. Massive Wilderness area at 0.7 miles. The border coincides with a self-permitting station. The Forest Service asks everyone hiking the trail to fill out a free permit.

Beyond the permit station the trail crosses the outlet stream for Blue Lake and then passes a route branching left (northwest) to Blue Lake. The lake, which is not well known, is reported to have great fishing. (More information on Blue Lake route is found at the end of this trail description.)

Our trail continues ascending along the west side of the valley on easy grades, skirting the edge of the timbered slopes. Willow thickets choke the valley floor along the creek.

At 1.4 miles the trees give way to meadows and clusters of willows. Views toward the head of the valley expand to include Peak 13202 to the northwest. Turn around for good views of Lackawanna Peak (13,823-ft.) rising above the southeast end of the valley.

Reach the edge of the western tributary of the North Fork Lake Creek and a confusing section of the trail at 2.3 miles. A good trail appears to continue along the left (west) side of the creek. Look across the creek to see

149

the continuation of the trail on the other side. Late in the season you should be able to rock-hop across the creek without getting your feet wet. Earlier in the season you may need to wade the stream.

Note: If you miss the crossing, the trail/route along the left (west) side of the stream weaves through thick willow thickets and, at times, becomes quite faint. After 0.2 miles the route comes to a second crossing that is easier when the water is high. If you take this route look across the stream and up the hill, at approximately one o-clock you will see a rock cairn. Climb up the hill to the cairn to get back on the main trail.

Beyond the crossing the grade steepens as the trails climbs toward the head of the valley, defined by two large basins to the west and the east. As you ascend, views open the stunning basin surrounded by high peaks to the west. Deer Mountain towers above the basin to the east.

At 2.8 miles the trail curves to the right (northeast) and crosses a ridge through a stand of trees. Beyond the ridge the trail descends slightly before continuing its ascent on easy grades through meadows to the scenic basin beneath Deer Mountain. Turn around for great views of the basin to the west along with Twining Peak (13,711-ft.) and the unnamed summits lining the western side of the North Fork Lake Creek Valley. Star Mountain (12,941-ft.) and summits in the Collegiate Peak Wilderness are visible to the south.

Reach the eastern tributary of North Fork Lake Creek at 3.2 mile. Here the creek braids into multiple channels. There are two trails through this area. The best option is to follow the trail that stays to the left (north) of the creek for 0.1 mile. Watch for rock cairns in the meadows to the right (south) marking where you should cross the main channel and rejoin the trail heading up the center of the basin. The other option is to immediately cross the main channel and then follow a faint trail up the center of the basin through boggy meadows. The two trails converge at 3.3 miles.

Toward the head of the basin the trail curves to the left (northeast) and climbs steep switchbacks up a hillside to the west of Deer Mountain, staying to the right (east) of a creek tumbling down the hill. Near the top of the climb the trail crosses the creek.

The trail crests the hill at 3.8 miles, reaching a high bench clad in alpine tundra where a cobalt blue lake (12,400-ft.) lies nestled beneath the northwest ridge of Deer Mountain. Our objective, the saddle to the north of the lake, is now in sight.

Follow the trail are it curves around the west side of the wind-swept lake and then climbs through rocky meadows to the pass at 12,460-ft. From the pass fine views extend north down the Fryingpan Lakes Valley to the Fryingpan Lakes. The high peaks of the Hunter-Fryingpan and Holy Cross Wilderness areas rise beyond the valley. To the south, an unnamed 13,736-ft. peak rises above a small basin. The summits of the Collegiate Peaks Wilderness fill the skyline to the southeast.

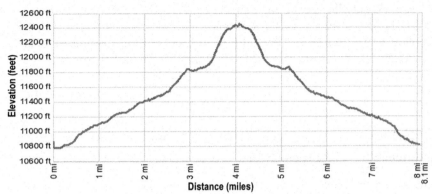

When you are done enjoying the views retrace your steps to the trailhead. The descent down the Deer Mountain basin features excellent views of the beautiful west basin, Twining Peak (13,711-ft.) and the summit rimming the west side of the valley.

Blue Lake Trail

The Blue Lake trail, branching left (northwest) from the North Fork Lake Creek trail, climbs on very steep grades through trees along the right (north) side of Blue Lake's outlet stream. At 0.5 miles the trees give way to pretty alpine meadows and the grade eases a bit. Continue along the trail as it continues ascending on steep to moderately-steep grades through meadows.

The trail becomes difficult to follow as it travels through boggy areas and soon disappears. Rock cairns now mark several routes to the lake. The best route will vary depending on the time of year. The route closest to the stream is the shortest but is quite boggy early in the season.

Reach Blue Lake (12,495-ft.), nestled beneath Twining Peak (13,711-ft.), after gaining over 1,400 feet in 1.5 miles. Total distance from the North Fork Lake Creek trailhead to Blue Lake is 2.2 miles one-way.

Driving Directions

From Aspen: From the intersection of Main Street and South Galena in downtown Aspen, drive east on CO 82 E for 24.2 miles and turn left at the North Fork Lake Creek trailhead. The turn is 4.5 miles down the east side of Independence Pass, just past the third hairpin curve on the road. Follow the dirt road for 0.1 miles to the parking area. A trailhead bulletin board marks the start of the trail.

From Buena Vista: From the traffic light at the intersection of U.S.24 and Country Road 306 in downtown Buena Vista, head north on US 24 W for 19.2 miles and turn left (west) on CO 82 W. Follow CO 82 for 19.1 miles and then turn right at the North Fork Lake Creek trailhead. The turn is just past mile marker 66 and before the first hairpin curve on the switchbacks climbing to Independence Pass. Follow the dirt road for 0.1 miles to the parking area. A trailhead bulletin board marks the start of the trail.

From Leadville: From the intersection at 6th Street and Harrison (U.S.24), head east on US 24 E for 15 miles and turn right (west) on CO 82 W. Follow CO 82 for 19.1 miles and then turn right at the North Fork Lake Creek trailhead. The turn is just past mile marker 66 and before the first hairpin curve on the switchbacks climbing to Independence Pass. Follow the dirt road for 0.1 miles to the parking area. A trailhead bulletin board marks the start of the trail.

35. Browns Falls and Browns Lake ★★★★☆
Distance: 5.8 - 12.0 miles (RT)

Pretty streams, an amazing waterfall and a lovely lake set amid a beautiful basin are some of the scenic rewards of the hike to Brown's Lake in the San Isabel National Forest.

Distance: 5.8 miles (RT) to Falls
12.0 miles (RT) to Browns Lake
Elevation: 8,920-ft. at Trailhead
9,870-ft. at Browns Falls
11,320-ft. at Browns Lake
Elevation Gain: 950-ft. to Falls
2,400-ft. to Browns Lake

Difficulty: moderate-strenuous
Basecamp: Buena Vista
Area: San Isabel NF
Best Season: July –September
USGS Map(s): Mt. Antero

Why Hike to Browns Falls and Browns Lake

This scenic trail travels along pretty streams, visits a stunning waterfall and leads to a gorgeous basin where lovely Browns Lake lies nestled beneath the rugged ridges of Jones Peak and Mount White. A profusion of wildflowers grow amid the meadows around the lake basin during the height of the summer.

Initially the trail ascends through a forest of Ponderosa Pine that gradually gives way to the spruce/fir forest sprinkled with Aspen. A section of the trail traverses a blowdown along the valley floor where high winds have uprooted and toppled trees. One can only image the force of the wind required to cause this level of destruction.

Expect a lot of traffic on the trail to the falls, a popular destination for families and parties looking for a nice half day hike. Beyond the falls the traffic is moderate. Nice campsites are found in the area above and to the west of the lake. Fishermen report good luck catching cutthroats along the lakes south shore.

Trailhead to Browns Falls

Distance from Trailhead: 5.8 miles (RT)
Ending/Highest Elevation: 9,870-ft.
Elevation Gain: 950-ft.

The trail to Brown's Lake begins at the northwest end of the Brown's Creek trailhead parking area. (See driving directions below.) Follow the trail as it ascends west through ponderosa pine for a quarter mile and then briefly turns north, climbing moderately-steep switchbacks up an old moraine to the north of Little Brown's Creek. As the trail crests the moraine it turns left (west) and resumes its moderate ascent through trees along the top of the moraine. Views open to Mount White (13,667-ft.) and the north face of Jones Peak (13,604-ft.) to the west/southwest.

After 0.9 miles the grade eases and soon the trail curves to the southwest, reaching the signed junction with the Colorado Trail at 1.4 miles. Turn left (southwest) on the Colorado Trail in the direction of Browns Creek Falls (1.5 miles) and Brown Lake (4.5) miles. The trail to the right leads to the Little Browns Creek trail in 0.3 miles.

Cross Little Browns Creek on a wood bridge at 1.6 miles. Just beyond the creek reach a "Y" intersection. Bear right on the trail bound for Browns Creek Falls (1.3 miles) and Brown Lake (4.3) miles. The Colorado Trail continues south on the trail branching to the left.

At 1.7 miles the trail crosses a tributary stream on logs and then heads south on easy grades along a good trail. Soon the trail curves to the southwest and heads up the north side of the Browns Creek drainage.

At 2.4 miles the trail travels through a large meadow with nice views of the north face of Jones Peak. Beyond the park the path plunges back into the trees and reaches Browns Creek at a wide ford. Hikers should backtrack a short distance to find a trail branching northwest. This trail leads to log bridge facilitating the crossing to the south side of the creek at 2.6 miles. Cross back to the north side of the creek on a second log bridge at 2.7 miles.

A small wood sign on a pile of rocks at 2.8 miles points left (south) to Browns Creek Falls. I highly recommend taking the short detour that climbs about 50-ft. up a hillside to the falls at 2.9 miles. This stunning cascade gushes over a long drop and then a shorter drop into a pretty pool. Rock ledges around the pool beacon hikers to take a break and enjoy the spectacle.

The falls is a popular destination for families and parties looking for a nice half day hike. Total hiking distance to the falls and back is 5.8 miles with an elevation gain of 950-ft.

Browns Falls to Browns Lake

Segment Stats: 3.1 miles (one-way) with a 1,450-ft. elevation gain
Distance from Trailhead: 12.0 miles (RT)
Ending/Highest Elevation: 11,320-ft.
Elevation Gain from Trailhead: 2,400-ft.

To hike to Browns Lake return to the main trail and follow the rocky path as it climbs up a hillside on moderately-steep grades. Soon the trail curves around a minor ridge extending from the north side of the valley. At 3.6 miles the path resumes its westerly course, ascending above the north side of Brown's Creek, which tumbles down a rocky gully below the trail.

The grade briefly eases at 4.0 miles as the trail travels alongside the creek. Soon a short, steep climb leads to the next level of the valley. Here the trail ascends on easy to moderate grades through a large blowdown, an area along the valley floor where high winds have uprooted, toppled and snapped trees like matchsticks. One can only image the force of the wind required to cause this level of destruction.

For the next 0.8 miles you will travel through areas affected by the windstorm. It is obvious that an enormous effort was required to clear downed trees from the trail.

On the bright side, openings caused by the toppled trees offer fine views of the craggy north face of the Jones Peak massif to the south and Mount White to the north. Young aspen and conifers are now repopulating the area. During the height of the season, a profusion of wildflowers grow amid the downed trees.

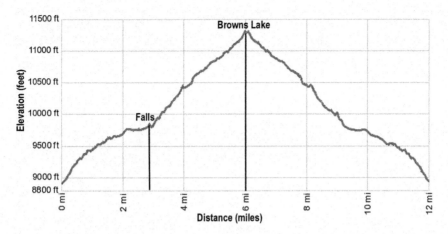

Pass an interesting teepee-shaped rock formation along the lower slopes of Mt. White at 5.2 miles. Beyond the formation we soon leave the last of the down trees behind and now ascend through healthy forest on moderate grades.

At 5.9 miles the trees give way to meadows and views open to a waterfall along Browns Creek to the south. The rugged slopes of Jones Peak massif tower overhead.

Follow the trail as it climbs steeply through rocky meadows scattered with trees and low willows to lovely Browns Lake (11,286-ft) at 6.0 miles. At the east end of the lake water spills over a beaver dam into Browns Creek. The long narrow lake stretches along the valley floor between the west ridge of Jones Peak to the south and White Mountain to the north. Carbondale Mountain (13,663-ft.), Cyclone Mountain (13,596-ft.) and Cronin Peak (13,870-ft.), along with a few unnamed peaks, ring the head of the valley. Tabeguache Peak (14,155-ft.) rises to the southwest. During the height of the summer the lake basin's meadows are filled with wildflowers.

The foot of the lake is the turnaround point for day hikers. Backpackers will find nice campsites to the west of the lake. Fishermen report good luck catching cutthroats along the lake's south shore.

The trail continues heading west along the north side of the lake and its inlet stream for half a mile to a jeep road. The jeep road, which starts in the Chalk Creek valley, heads up the Baldwin Valley, climbs the west facing slopes of Mt. Antero and then descend into Browns Creek. Along the way the road links up with the trail climbing Mt Antero (14,269-ft.).

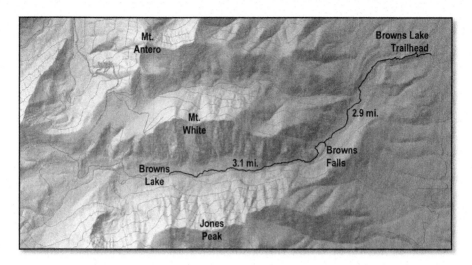

Driving Directions

From Buena Vista: From the traffic light at the intersection of U.S.24 and Country Road (CR) 306 in downtown Buena Vista, drive south on US 24 E for 2.4 miles to an intersection. Here US 24 turn east. We continue straight ahead on U.S. 285 S for 8.8 miles and turn right (west) on County Road (CR) 270 W.

Follow CR 270 for 1.5 miles to the 4-way intersection. CR 270 turns right. We continue heading west (straight ahead) on Forest Road (FR) 272 for 2.0 miles to an intersection. Turn left (south) to stay on FR 272.

Follow FR 272 for 1.6 miles to the Brown's Creek trailhead on the right (west) side of the road. Additional parking is found on the east side of the road. The trail starts at the northwest end of the parking area.

36. Interlaken ★★★★☆
Distance: 4.7 miles (RT)

This easy hike traversing the south shore of Twin Lakes leads to Interlaken, an interesting historic site once home to a popular luxury resort during the late 1800's. From the resort and trail along the lake enjoy fine views of Twin Lakes, Mt. Elbert (14,433-ft.) and the surrounding peaks.

Distance: 4.7 miles (RT)
Elevation: 9,230-ft. at Trailhead
 Maximum elevation - 9,272-ft.
Elevation Gain: 42-ft.
Difficulty: easy

Basecamp: Buena Vista and Leadville
Area: San Isabel NF
Best Season: July –September
USGS Map(s): Granite

Why Hike to Interlaken

During its heyday in the late 1800's, the Interlaken Hotel complex was a popular resort for the wealthy. Visitor's rode the train to a nearby station and then took a short carriage ride to the luxury summer retreat on the south side of Twin Lakes.

Today a section of the Colorado Trail, starting at the southeast end of the larger of the Twin Lakes, leads to the resort's restored buildings, offering an opportunity for hikers to explore an interesting chapter of the area's local history.

James Dexter, who purchased the hotel and grounds in 1883, enlarged and upgraded the facility to include a log tavern, pool hall, a dance hall, guest rooms with panoramic views, stables, a barn, an ice house and a six-sided privy that accommodated 6 guests in separate rooms. Dexter's cabin, constructed in the mid-1890's, is the most interesting structure on the property. The house, surrounded by open verandas, features imported wood trim, gabled dormer windows, a mansard roof and is topped with a glass enclosed cupola with views in all directions.

The resort operated for 25 year before it fell out of favor and closed in the early twentieth century. Contributing to the downfall was the transformation of Twin Lakes, a pair of glacial lakes, into a large reservoir. The reservoir's dam, built in 1896, raised the level of the lakes, flooding the only road to the facility.

In 1970 plans to expand the reservoir and build a higher dam threatened to submerge some of resort's structures. Thankfully the site had been placed on the National Register of Historic Places. After the completion of the dam several of the structures, including the hotel and Dexter's cabin, were saved from the rising waters by moving them 150-ft. to higher ground.

In 2004, local volunteers started a four-year effort to stabilize and restore the resort's structures. Today visitors are allowed to explore the site and wander by the preserved buildings, including the hotel, cabin, granaries and six-sided privy. Dexter's Cabin is open, permitting hikers to see the restored interior and view the lake from the cupola. The stable, which contain the remains of some old carriages and other relics, is also open.

Trailhead to Interlaken

The hike to Interlaken starts at the southeast end of the largest of the Twin Lakes. (See driving directions below.) From the parking area the Colorado Trail heads west on easy grades through trees on an undulating path along the south side of the largest (lower) Twin Lake. Openings in the trees offer fine views of the lake, Mt. Elbert (14,433-ft.) towering above the north side of the valley and the peaks rising to the east.

At 1.3 miles reach a junction. Here the Colorado Trail East, which travels along the eastern side of the Collegiate Peaks, branches to the left (south/southeast). We continue straight ahead on the Colorado Trail West.

At 1.5 miles the trail briefly turns to the right (north) as it climbs a hill. Here nice views open to the peaks rising to the east. Soon the trail turns left (west), crests the hill and then drops down to cross a stream on a wood bridge at 1.9 miles.

Beyond the bridge the trail travels on mostly level grades, reaching Dexter's Cabin at 2.2 miles. The log structure with a mansard roof, dormer windows and a cupola, sits in a meadow with wonderful views of the lake and surrounding peaks. An information board outside the cabin offers a brief history of the site.

Enter the cabin through the front door facing the lake. (Be sure to latch the door when you leave.) The restored interior features walnut woodwork and beautiful wood floors. In its day the house was outfitted with beautiful bird's-eye maple furniture, lavish rugs and high-end decorations. Climb the steps to see the second floor rooms and then ascend the steep, narrow stairs to the cupola (watch your head) for birds-eye views of the lake.

The stable are also open for exploration. Go around the back of the structure and enter through the sliding door. A few old carriages and other relics are now stored in the stable.

When you are done visiting Dexter's Cabin and the stables explore the rest of the site. It is amazing how many buildings still stand. One of my favorites is the privy with doors on each of the structures six sides leading to private rooms.

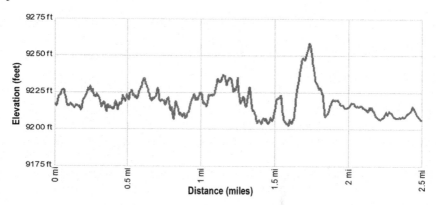

As you wander around the resort be sure to walk to the meadows to the west resort for great views of Mt. Hope (13,953-ft.) and Rinker Peak (13,783-ft.) to the southwest. The Colorado Trail west continues beyond the resort along the south side of the second lake and eventually climbs Hope Pass.

When you are done exploring the historic resort retrace your steps to the trailhead. Total round trip hiking distance, including roaming around the site, is 4.7 miles. Even though the trail is relatively flat, there are quite a few ups and downs that add up to almost 760-ft. of elevation gain (RT).

This is a good hike for families and parties looking for an easy half day walk. It is also a good option when bad weather precludes walking in the high country.

Driving Directions

From Buena Vista: From the traffic light at the intersection of US 24 and Country Road 306 in downtown Buena Vista, head north on US 24 W for 19.2 miles and turn left (west) on CO 82 W. Drive 0.8 miles on CO 82, past Lost Canyon Road and turn left (south) on CR 25, a dirt road across from a log structure. Follow CR 25 for 0.5 miles to an intersection south of the Twin

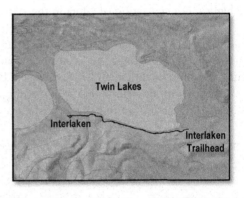

Lakes dam. Turn left at the intersection and continue along CR 25. Follow CR 25 for 0.1 miles and turn right at the second dirt road. Follow this road for 0.3 miles to the Colorado Trail parking area on the left side of the road. (Beyond the parking area the road drops down to the lakeshore.)

Note: Passenger cars, under good conditions, can make it all the way to the trailhead. Otherwise, park at the wide area on the road just south of the dam and then walk to the trailhead.

From Leadville: From the intersection at 6th Street and Harrison (US 24), head east on US 24 E for 15 miles and turn right (west) on CO 82 W. Drive 0.8 miles on CO 82, past Lost Canyon Road and turn left (south) on CR 25, a dirt road across from a log structure. Follow CR 25 for 0.5 miles to an intersection south of the Twin Lakes dam. Turn left at the intersection and continue along CR 25. Follow CR 25 for 0.1 miles and turn right at the second dirt road. Follow this road for 0.3 miles to the Colorado Trail parking area on the left side of the road. (Beyond the parking area the road drops down to the lakeshore.)

Note: Passenger cars, under good conditions, can make it all the way to the trailhead. Otherwise, park at the wide area on the road just south of the dam and then walk to the trailhead.

37. The 14ers – Huron Peak, Mt. Belford, Mt. Yale and Mt. Harvard
Distance: 6.5 - 13.6 miles (RT)

Preparing to Hike a 14er

Many hikers and climbers come to Buena Vista to summit one of the area's 14,000-ft. peaks, known as 14ers. There are 58 14ers in Colorado ranging from hiking trails involving a minor amount of scrambling to technical climbing routes requiring ropes and related equipment. The Sawatch Mountains near Buena Vista, with 14 peaks over 14,000-ft., boasts the highest concentration of 14ers in the state.

Novice and casual hikers will be tempted by the challenge of summiting a 14er. It's a great goal but you need to take the challenge seriously. To summit a 14er you must be in good physical shape and well acclimated. Flatlanders should not plan on arriving in Buena Vista and setting out to next day to summit a peak. The best strategy is to spend a week day hiking the many great trails around Buena Vista, pushing yourself to go higher each day.

Make sure you know the signs of altitude sickness and descend immediately to a lower altitude if symptoms develop. Seek medical help if the symptoms persist at lower altitude.

Get an early start. It is not unusual to see people starting a climb in the wee hours of the morning or at dawn. You will be hiking much slower than you expect. Allocate at least an hour for every 1,000-ft. of elevation gain. Your pace will slow to a crawl once you reach the rarefied air about 12,000-ft. Plan your time accordingly. It is best to be off the summit and below exposed terrain before the early afternoon to avoid thunderstorms, a frequent occurrence in the Rockies during the summer.

Some of the 14ers can be reached by a long day hike. These days will be much harder than you expect. I strongly recommend backpacking to a basecamp and then getting up early the next morning to summit a peak. This will cut down the distance and elevation gain required in a single day. Spending the night at a high altitude will also help you to acclimate.

Check the weather forecast and don't try to summit if bad weather is imminent. Getting caught in a storm is not fun and can be dangerous. Make sure you take plenty of warm clothing, including a hat and gloves. Rain gear including pants is a must. A map, compass and safety equipment, such as matches, a first aid kits, knife and headlamp, are strongly recommended. The Gearlist on the 14ers.com website includes an excellent packing list.

Be sure to take plenty of food and water to maintain your energy level and stay hydrated. Carry two to three quarts of water per person, tons of energy bars or other sources of protein and a substantial lunch.

Pick a 14er that matches your experience level. Plan the route and know what to expect. Read trip reports to learn about the terrain. The 14ers.com website includes an amazing trove of great information on climbing Colorado's 14,000-ft. peaks. Be sure to leave an itinerary with friend or a relative.

Once you set out, don't be afraid to turn around if in doubt. It always disappointing to turn around but if the weather is threatening, the trail is covered in slick snow/ice, you're are feeling unwell or just uncomfortable on the trail, it is the right decision. Be smart, the mountain will be there for another attempt at some later date.

Here are descriptions of some of the easier 14,000-ft. summits in the area. Other peaks to consider include Mt. Elbert and Mt. Princeton.

Note: All the hikes listed below are rated as Class 2 climbs. Grades are assigned to climbs based on their difficulty. A Class 1 climb is really just a hike. A Class 2 climb is a more difficult hike up steep slopes, over boulder fields and/or ascending loose scree slopes. The route may involve some scrambling, with the possible use of the hands. There may be some exposure along the route.

Huron Peak (14,003-ft.). Class 2 ★★★★★

Distance: 6.5 miles (RT)
Add 4.0 miles (RT) if walking from
Winfield
Elevation: 10,256-ft. at Winfield
10,600-ft. at Trailhead
14,003-ft. at Huron Peak
Elevation Gain: 3,403-ft.
Add 344-ft. if walking from Winfield
Difficulty: very strenuous

Base camp: Buena Vista,
Leadville
Area: Collegiate Peaks
Wilderness, San Isabel NF
Best Season: July –September
USGS Map(s): Winfield
See Page 136 for map
See the Lake Ann hike for more
information.

Huron Peak is a good 14ers for beginners since it follows a good trail all the way to the summit. That being said the trail is very steep all the way to the top.

The trail to Huron Peak starts from the same trailhead as Lake Ann. A high clearance AWD/4WD is required to reach the trailhead. Otherwise, park at the lot in Winfield and walk up the jeep road to the trailhead. The walk will add 4.0 miles (RT) and 350-ft. in additional elevation gain. See the Lake Ann driving directions for more information.

At the trailhead, turn left (south/southeast) on the trail to Huron Peaks. (The path branching right is the Continental Divide/Lake Ann trail.) Follow the path as it ascends through trees on moderate grades. At 0.4 miles the trail turns east and climbs steep switchbacks. After a little over a mile the trail again turns to the south/southeast and soon passes through a small meadow offering the first views of the Three Apostles to the south. Beyond the meadow the trail curves to the left (southeast) and climbs a few more switchbacks before emerging from the trees at 1.6 miles.

The trail now turns right (east), climbing steeply through meadows to a basin cradled beneath Browns Peak (to the left) and Huron Peak. Along the way enjoy fine views of both peaks. The grade abates briefly as the trail crosses the heart of the basin. The respite is short lived, soon the trail climbs steeply out of the basin. At 2.25 miles the path turns right (southeast) and begins a very steep ascent, facilitated by switchbacks, up Huron Peak's north facing slope.

Reach Huron's north ridge (13,526-ft.) at 3.0 miles. Take a moment at the ridge to enjoy the great views of Mt Missouri, Mt. Belford and Mt. Harvard to the east/southeast. Here the trail turns south and ascends talus slopes on very steep grades, initially along the west side of the ridge. Soon the trail turns left and climbs to the ridge crest. (There are several different trails ascending very steeply up to the ridge, pick the one that works best for you.) Once atop the ridge, follow the trail along the rocky ridge to the summit (14,003-ft.) at 3.25 miles. (Trekking poles are very helpful along the final steep assault of the summit.)

From the top of Huron Peak enjoy panoramic views of the Collegiate Peaks. The Three Apostles dominate the views to the south while the vast expanse of Taylor Park and its namesake reservoir is seen to the southwest. Missouri Mountain, Mt. Belford and Mt. Oxford fill the skyline to the east. La Plata Peak and the peaks rimming the north side of the Clear Creek valley rise to the north.

Mount Belford (14,197-ft.), Class 2 ★★★★★

Distance: 8.0 miles (RT)
Elevation: 9,660-ft. at Trailhead
14,197-ft. at Mt. Belford
Elevation Gain: 4,537-ft.
Difficulty: very strenuous
Base camp: Buena Vista, Leadville

Area: Collegiate Peaks
Wilderness, San Isabel NF
Best Season: July –September
USGS Map(s): Mount Harvard,
Winfield
See Page 143 for map
See the Missouri Gulch/Elhead
Pass hike for more information.

The route to the summit of Mt. Belford is reached via the Missouri Gulch/Elkhead Pass trail. Follow the trail directions for 2.1 miles to a junction with the trail to Mt. Belford. Turn left (southeast) on the signed trail to Mt. Belford. The trail branching right leads to Elkhead Pass and an alternative route to the summit. (See the Missouri Gulch/Elkhead Pass hike for more information on the alternative route.)

Beyond the junction the trail travels through willows and meadows for 0.3 miles to a stream crossing. At 2.4 miles the trail starts climbing steep switchbacks up the grassy slopes of Mt. Belford's northwest ridge. As you climb the meadows give way to talus slopes. Along the way enjoy great views of Missouri Gulch. The peaks rimming the north side of the Clear Creek valley fill the skyline to the north.

At 3.6 miles the trail turns right (south) for a short distance as it climbs to the crest of the ridge extending west from Mt. Belford. Here the grade abates briefly. Take a break to enjoy the great views of Missouri Mountain to the south. Turn left (east) and follow the trail as it climbs talus slopes along the south side of the ridge. Soon the grade eases at bit. Our destination is now in sight. Continue along the trail to the base of the summit block and then climb the yellowish colored slopes to the summit.

From the summit Missouri Mountain, Missouri Basin, Mt. Harvard and Mt. Yale dominate the views to the south. Mount Elbert forms the backdrop for the peaks rimming the Clear Creek valley to the north. La Plata Peak towers above the peaks to the northwest while Mount Oxford rises to the east.

Some hikers extend the trip to Mt. Belford by continuing east for 1.5 miles to Mt. Oxford. This adds an additional 1,300-ft. in elevation gain to the hike. Only the most fit, well acclimated hikers should try the combined route. I recommend backpacking into Missouri Gulch and then climbing the summits the next day. The combined route spends a lot of time above the tree line on exposed slopes, not the place to be during a storm. Be sure to get a very early start if you want to summit both peaks!

Mount Yale (14,196-ft.), Class 2 ★★★★☆

Distance: 9.0 miles (RT)
Elevation: 9,910-ft. at Trailhead
14,196-ft. at Mt. Yale
Elevation Gain: 4,286-ft.
Difficulty: very strenuous
Base camp: Buena Vista

Area: Collegiate Peaks
Wilderness, San Isabel NF
Best Season: July –September
USGS Map(s): Mount Yale
See Page 132 for map
See the Browns Pass hike for
more information.

The easiest route up Mt. Yale is accessible via the Browns Pass via Denny Creek trail. Follow the trail directions for 1.3 miles and turn right (east) on the signed trail to Mt. Yale. The trail heads east and then northeast ascending through trees up the west side of Denny Gulch. At 2.25 miles (11,240-ft.) the trail crosses a log bridge to the east side of the creek. Beyond the creek the trail heads north, climbing through forest and meadows along the west facing slopes of Mt. Yale.

At 2.6 miles the trail turns southeast and continues its ascent. The grade eases briefly as the trail breaks from the trees at 2.9 miles and then travels along a good path through meadows with a few scattered trees. Soon we leave the last of the trees behind. At 3.0 miles the trail reaches a bench where it curves to the left (northeast) and starts the very steep climb up rocky meadows that soon give way to talus.

Reach the saddle on the ridge extending northwest from the summit of Mt. Yale at 4.2 miles. Turn right (southeast) and follow the trail as it heads toward the summit. The trail is short-lived. Here is where you hit the Class 2 part of the climb. For the rest of the way to the summit follow rock cairns marking the route along the rocky ridge. From the summit of Mt. Yale (14,196-ft.) enjoy expansive views of the Elk Mountains to the west/southwest. Nearer at hand are the high peaks of the Sawatch Range including Huron Peak, Mt. Belford, Mt. Oxford and La Plata Peak to the north, Mt. Harvard and Mt. Columbia to the northeast and Mt. Princeton to the south.

Mount Harvard (14,420-ft.), Class 2 ★★★★★

Distance: 13.6 miles (RT)
Elevation: 9,890-ft. at Trailhead
14,420-ft. at Mt. Harvard
Elevation Gain: 4,530-ft.
Difficulty: very strenuous
Base camp: Buena Vista

Area: Collegiate Peaks
Wilderness, San Isabel NF
Best Season: July –September
USGS Map(s): Mount Harvard
See Page 140 for map
See the Bear Lake hike for more
information.

Note: Given the length and difficulty, the climb to Mt. Harvard is best done as a backpack. I recommend backpacking into the Horn Fork valley and then climbing the peak the next day. See the description of the Bear Lake trail for information on camping along the trail to the lake.

The easiest trail up Mt. Harvard, the third highest peak in Colorado, is accessed by the scenic trail climbing the Horn Fork Valley to Bear Lake. Follow the first 5.2 miles of the Bear Lake trail to the junction with Mt. Harvard. At the junction turn right (north/northwest) toward Mt. Harvard. The trail to the left (west) leads to Bear Lake. (Note: The last time I hiked this trail the sign was missing from the junction.)

Follow the trail as it climbs steeply through rocky meadows and then talus slopes to a ridge extending east from Peak 13598 at 5.7 miles. Switchbacks help ease the climb to the ridge crest. Atop the ridge turn around for fine views of Bear Lake, Mt. Columbia, Mt. Yale and, in the distance, Mt. Princeton to the south. The grade now abates as the trail travels through alpine tundra along a bench. Large rock cairns mark the trail.

At 5.9 miles the climb resumes, ascending steeply up the south facing slopes of Mt. Harvard toward the peak's south ridge. Reach the ridge crest (13,590-ft.) at 6.3 miles. Turn right (north) and climb through rocky meadows along the east side of the ridge. As you climb the meadows give way to scree covered slopes. At 6.7 miles reach the base of the summit block and the hardest part of the hike. From this point it is a Class 2 scramble up a steep slope covered with huge rocks to the summit (14,420-ft.) (Some people argue that the climb to the summit is really a Class 3 scramble.) Take your time and make sure you are climbing stable rock. There are several routes to the summit.

From the summit enjoy great views of the Sawatch Mountains and Collegiate Peaks Wilderness. Mt Yale forms the backdrop for the Horn Fork valley to the south. Mt Princeton and Antero Peak rise in the distance to the south. Mount Columbia towers above the valley to the southeast. The Buffalo Peaks dominate the view to the east while Mount Belford and Oxford rise above the Pine Creek valley to the north. A sea of peaks, including Missouri Mountain and La Plata Peak, fill the skyline to the northwest. To the west is the distinctive profile of the Three Apostles.

38. Fancy Pass - Missouri Pass Loop ★★★★★
Distance: 8.1 mile (loop)

This great loop hike climbs to two scenic passes and visits a pair of gorgeous lake basins surrounded by 13,000-ft. granite peaks and ridges in the Holy Cross Wilderness.

Distance: 8.1 miles (loop)	**Base camp:** Leadville and Vail
Elevation: 10,000-ft. at Trailhead	**Area:** Holy Cross Wilderness,
Maximum elevation: 12,380-ft.	White River NF
Elevation Gain: 2,700-ft.	**Best Season:** July –September
Difficulty: moderate-strenuous	**USGS Map(s):** Mount of the
	Holy Cross, Mount Jackson

Why Hike the Fancy Pass - Missouri Pass Loop

This is one of my favorite loop hikes in the Holy Cross Wilderness. The trail visits two scenic passes, traverses a beautiful alpine valley and wanders through the gorgeous Missouri Lakes basin. There are some steep sections of the loop, but overall the hike features moderate grades on good trails.

If you desire a degree of solitude the hike is best done during the week or in the fall. The Missouri Lakes basin is a very popular camping area that can become quite crowded on weekends and holidays.

If you like ghost towns and mining ruins a 3.0 mile (RT) detour near Fancy Lake contours northeast to Holy Cross City, a mining town occupied during the 1880's and 1890's. There is quite a bit of mining equipment scattered about the site as well as the remains of several cabins.

Trailhead to Fancy Pass

Distance from Trailhead: 6.0 miles (RT)
Ending/Highest Elevation: 12,380-ft.
Elevation Gain: 2,380-ft.

I recommend hiking this loop trail in a counter-clockwise direction, ascending the Fancy Creek drainage and returning via Missouri Creek.

From the Fancy Creek trailhead (see driving directions below) the trail climbs moderate to steep switchbacks up a forested hillside, winding its way to the Fancy Creek drainage at 0.8 miles. The trail then crosses the Zen Bridge to the northeast side of Fancy Creek. Beyond the bridge the grade abates as the trail travels through spruce-fir forests, staying well above the creek.

At 2.0 miles the path traverses a pretty meadow then climbs steeply to Fancy Lake, gaining 400-ft in 0.3 miles. Fancy Creek cascades down a rocky gorge below the trail. The pretty lake, located at timberline, is ringed by granite peaks and crags.

At the lake the trail turns right (northeast) and climbs a steep gully up the hillside running along the north side of the lake. At the top of the hill reach a trail junction. The trail to Holy Cross heads right (northeast), our trail turns left (northwest), following an old road grade that climbs steeply up a rocky ravine to Fancy Pass (12,380-ft.), gaining over 700-ft. in 0.6 miles. Just below the pass some old mining ruins are scattered around the ravine.

From the pass views to the southwest encompass the head of the Cross Creek valley, clad in beautiful meadows dotted with lakes and surrounded by granite peaks. The large lake in the distance is Blodgett Lake while the nearby lake, just below Missouri Pass, is Treasure Vault Lake.

Completing the Loop - Missouri Pass and Back to the Trailhead

Segment Stats: 5.1 miles (one-way) with a 336-ft. elevation gain and 2,700-ft. elevation loss
Distance from Trailhead: 8.1 miles (loop)
Ending/Highest Elevation: 12,380-ft.
Elevation Gain from Trailhead: 2,700-ft.

To complete the loop follow the trail as it descends from the pass to the valley. In the valley the path turns southwest, passing small tarns as it wanders through rocky meadows filled with wildflowers. To the northwest views open to the jagged granite peaks and ridges lining the western wall of the upper Cross Creek valley.

At 3.7 miles reach the junction with the Cross Creek trail, heading right (west). Our path bears left (south) toward Missouri Pass. A short distance after the junction the trail passes to the left (east) of Treasure Vault Lake, an azure gem nestled in pretty meadows at the head of the basin. Past the lake the path starts a short steep climb to Missouri Pass.

Reach Missouri Pass(11,986-ft.) at 4.0 miles. From the pass enjoy expansive views of the upper Cross Creek valley and the beautiful Missouri Lakes basin to the southeast. The basin, covered in rocky knobs and emerald green meadows, lies just below the timberline in an oblong cirque of granite ridges and peaks anchored to the southwest by Savage Peak (13,139-ft.).

After taking in the views descend from the pass to the basin. The steep trail arrives at the first of the Missouri Lake after losing 440-ft. in 0.4 miles. The second and largest lake is 0.2 miles further. The trail then passes between two smaller lakes before arriving at fifth lake located 1.0 mile from the pass. Another large lake, reached by a spur trail heading right (southwest) just beyond the fifth lake, is situated directly beneath the northeastern flanks of Savage Peak.

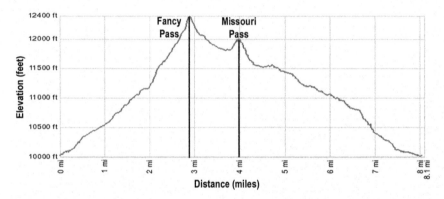

Pockets of trees scatter throughout the meadows in the basin harbor nice campsites. Please remember to camp at least 100-ft. from streams and lakes.

Past the fifth lake the trail follows Missouri Creek, descending on moderate grades through conifers to a large meadow at 6.6 miles (2.6 miles from Missouri Pass). Beyond the meadow the grade steepens and the trail crosses the creek several times, passing pretty cascades and waterfalls along the way. The final creek crossing is at the mouth of a small scenic canyon.

The final leg of the trail passes diversion dams and water pipes that are part of the Homestake Water project. The project, built in the 1960's, transfers water to the Cities of Aurora and Colorado Springs.

Shortly after passing the diversion dam and just before reaching the road look for a trail heading left. The trail leads through the woods and back to your car. Alternatively you can walk down to the road, turn left and walk back to the Fancy Pass trailhead on the road, a distance of 0.7 miles.

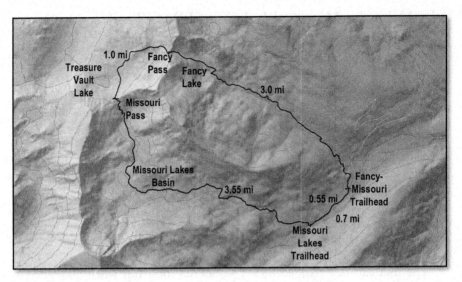

Driving Directions

From Leadville: Travel north on Highway 24 for 19.5 miles to Homestake Road #703. Turn left and follow the road for 8.5 miles, passing the Gold Park Campground along the way. Turn right onto Homestake Road #704 and continue 3 miles on this dirt road to a "T" intersection at 10,200 ft. Turn right and trailhead will be on the left.

From Vail: Travel west on I-70 to Exit #171 for Minturn, Leadville, and Hwy 24. Exit here and turn right onto Hwy 24. Proceed south for 13 miles to Homestake Road #703. Turn right and follow the road for 8.5 miles, passing the Gold Park Campground along the way. Turn right onto Homestake Road #704 and continue 3 miles on this dirt road to a T intersection at 10,200 ft. Turn right and trailhead will be on the left.

39. Missouri Lakes and Pass ★★★★★
Distance: 7.1 miles (RT)

This great hike travels to a beautiful lake basin and scenic pass in the Holy Cross Wilderness.

Distance: 7.1 miles (RT) to Pass
Elevation: 10,130-ft. at Trailhead
11,986-ft. at Missouri Pass
Elevation Gain: 1,856-ft. Pass
Difficulty: moderate-strenuous
Base camp: Leadville and Vail

Area: Holy Cross Wilderness, White River NF
Best Season: July –September
USGS Map(s): Mount of the Holy Cross, Mount Jackson
See Page 169 for Map

Why Hike the Missouri Lakes and Pass Trail

It isn't often that you can walk just 3.5 miles to a beautiful lake basin and scenic pass. The Missouri Lakes trail offers just such an opportunity.

The first leg of the trail is not very picturesque, passing water pipes and a diversion dam. Beyond the water project the scenery improves markedly as the trail climbs through conifers, passing small waterfalls, pretty cascades and interesting cliffs along Missouri Creek on its way to the lakes basin.

The basin, located just below the timberline, is carpeted with emerald green meadows littered with rocky knobs and clusters of trees. For the next 1.2 miles the path wanders through the pretty basin, passing five of the lakes, before the final short, steep ascent to the pass.

Missouri Lakes is a popular destination for hikers and fisherman. Legal camping spots can be in short supply on busy weekends and holidays. If you wish to spend a night in the basin it is best to travel on the weekdays or in the early fall.

The trail can be extended into a wonderful loop trip when combined with the Fancy Pass trail. See the Fancy Pass - Missouri Pass trail for more information.

Trailhead to Missouri Pass

From the parking area (see driving directions below) follow the Missouri Lake trail through a forest of mixed conifers past water pipes and a diversion dam, which are part of the Homestake Water project, to the Holy Cross Wilderness boundary. The water project, built in the 1960's, transfers water to the cities of Aurora and Colorado Springs.

Soon after entering the wilderness the trail crosses Missouri Creek at the mouth of a small scenic canyon. From here the moderately steep trail crosses the creek several times as it ascends alongside the creek to a large meadow. Along the way pretty cascades and small waterfalls add interest to the hike.

Beyond the meadow the grade moderates a bit as the path continues climbing though conifers, never wandering far from the creek. About 2.3 miles from the trailhead the trees give way to open meadows as you enter the Missouri Lakes basin.

The basin, clad in rocky knobs and emerald green meadows, lies just below the timberline in an oblong cirque of granite ridges and peaks anchored to the southwest by Savage Peak (13,139-ft.). Pockets of trees scatter throughout the meadows harbor nice campsites.

For the next mile the trail ascends the basin on gentle grades, wandering by two large and three smaller lakes. A spur trail heading left (southwest), reached soon after entering the basin, leads to the sixth lake located beneath the northeast flanks of Savage Peak. Past the last lake the trail makes a short, steep ascent to Missouri pass, gaining 400-ft. in 0.4 miles.

Missouri Pass (11,986-ft.), reached after hiking 3.55 miles, enjoys expansive views of the Missouri Lakes basin. To the north the granite peaks and ridges of the Middle Mountains rimming the western side of the scenic Cross Creek valley fill the skyline. Treasure Vault Lake, an azure gem, lies nestled in pretty meadows at the head of the valley just beneath the pass.

After enjoying the view retrace your steps to the trailhead or extend the trip into a great loop hike by crossing Missouri Pass into the Cross Creek valley and then following the Fancy Pass trail to Fancy Pass, Fancy Lake and back to your car. (See the Fancy Pass - Missouri Pass Loop hike for more information.)

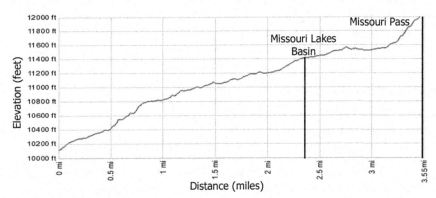

Driving Directions

From Leadville: Travel north on Highway 24 for 19.5 miles to Homestake Road #703. Turn left and follow the road for 8.5 miles, passing the Gold Park Campground along the way. Turn right onto Homestake

Road #704 and continue 3 miles on this dirt road to a "T" intersection at 10,200 ft. Turn right and trailhead will be on the left.

From Vail: Travel west on I-70 to Exit #171 for Minturn, Leadville, and Hwy 24. Exit here and turn right onto Hwy 24. Proceed south for 13 miles to Homestake Road #703. Turn right and follow the road for 8.5 miles, passing the Gold Park Campground along the way. Turn right onto Homestake Road #704 and continue 3 miles on this dirt road to a T intersection at 10,200 ft. Turn right and trailhead will be on the left.

40. Native Lake / Highline Trail ★★★★☆
Distance: 4.6 - 11.2 miles (RT)

A pretty lake along with terrific views of the Continental Divide and Mt. Massive are a few of the scenic delights along this beautiful trail paralleling the eastern flanks of the Continental Divide west of Leadville.

Distance: 4.6 miles (RT) to Divide
7.8 miles (RT) to Native Lake
11.2 miles (RT) to Small Lakes
Elevation: 10,780-ft. at Trailhead
1,860-ft. at Divide
11,240-ft. at Native Lake
11,615-ft. at Small Lakes
Elevation Gain: 1,080-ft. to Divide
-620-ft. to Native Lake
375-ft. to Small Lakes

Difficulty: moderate-strenuous
Base camp: Leadville
Area: Mount Massive Wilderness, San Isabel NF
Best Season: July –September
USGS Map(s): Mount Massive

Why Hike the Native Lake / Highline Trail

The Native Lake / Highline trail traverses the eastern flank of the Continental Divide near Leadville. Along the way the route crosses a broad tundra clad plateau featuring wonderful views of the Continental Divide and Mt. Massive (14,421-ft.), visits scenic Native Lake and then wanders through woods and meadows to two small lakes along the base of Mt. Massive.

Trailhead to the Divide

Distance from Trailhead: 4.6 miles (RT)
Ending/Highest Elevation: 11,860-ft.
Elevation Gain: 1,080-ft.

From the parking area (see driving directions below) the Native Lake trail immediately enters a thick forest of conifers and starts climbing the ridge defining the south side of the Busk Creek drainage. The trail crosses a stream several times as it ascend a series of long switchbacks on moderate grades up the forested hillside. Well-watered meadows around the stream crossings support dense displays of wildflowers. Openings in the trees provide nice views of the Continental Divide to the west.

As you near the top of the ridge the trees thin and views unfold to the west of the peaks and ridges along the Continental Divide. Two miles from the trailhead the trees give way to sprawling meadows with patches of scrub willows and small copses of stunted firs.

Soon the grade abates and the trail wanders across a high tundra clad plateau with wonderful views of Mt. Massive and the peaks and ridges along the Continental Divide. To the east are expansive views of Leadville framed by a wall of 13,000 and 14,000-ft peaks. Shortly after reaching the high point of the plateau, the divide between the Busk Creek and Rock Creek drainages, the trail passes to the left of some small picturesque tarns.

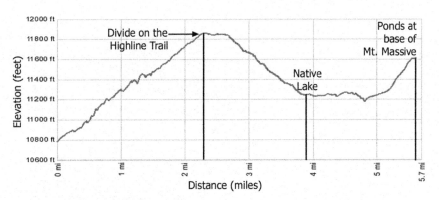

Divide to Native Lake

Segment Stats: 1.6 miles (one-way) with a 620-ft. elevation loss
Distance from Trailhead: 7.8 miles (RT)
Ending/Highest Elevation: 11,240-ft.
Elevation Gain from Trailhead: 1,080-ft.

At 2.6 miles the trail swings to the west and starts descending to Native Lake. The upper reaches of the decent feature great views of Mt. Massive towering above the valley to the southwest.

The trail drops on moderately steep switchbacks through a rocky basin scattered with trees and then curves south. As you descend the trees thicken. At the bottom of the descent a spur trail leads to pretty Native Lake at 3.9 miles. The lake sits in a marshy basin surrounded by forest. Mt. Massive dominates the scene to the southwest.

Native Lake to the Turnaround Point on the Highline

Segment Stats: 1.7 miles (one-way) with a 375-ft. elevation gain
Distance from Trailhead: 11.2 miles (RT)
Ending/Highest Elevation: 11,615-ft.
Elevation Gain from Trailhead: 1,455-ft.

For many hikers Native lake is a good turnaround point. If you wish to continue along the Highline Trail follow the spur back to the main trail and turn left (southeast). The trail, which is difficult to follow at times, leads through the marshy area to the west of Native Lake, crosses the lake's inlet stream in a willow thicket and then heads back into the trees.

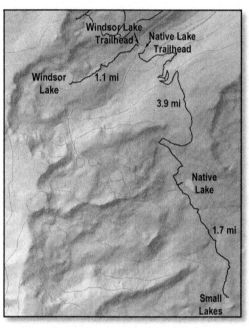

For the next mile the path makes a fairly level traverse through woodlands and pretty meadows, occasionally crossing streams emanating from the aptly named Hidden Lakes, located to the west of the trail. From the meadows enjoy nice views of Mt. Massive and distant views of Leadville and the peaks to the northeast.

At the end of this segment the trail enters a large meadow choked with scrub willows, crosses a stream and then starts to ascend a hillside through meadows. To your right you will see ponds created by the area's industrious beavers.

Soon the meadows give way to trees and the grade steepens. Near the top of the ascent the trail climbs beside a small stream. At the top of the hill views open to Mt. Massive rising above two small tree-lined lakes (11,615-ft.) at 5.6 miles.

This is the turnaround point for the out-and-back hike. A car shuttle is required to hike beyond this point. From the lakes the Highline Trail turns east and drops through forest to the Evergreen Lakes and the Leadville Fish Hatchery, 9.4 miles from the trailhead.

Driving Directions

From Leadville: From US 24 in Leadville, turn west on County Road 4/McWethy Drive and drive 3 miles to a three way "Y" intersection. (Paved to left, dirt in the center, paved to right.) Take the paved road to the right at the intersection to stay on County Road 4, following the signs to Turquoise Lake. Further on the road will travel along the south side of the lake.

Toward the head of the lake reach a "Y" intersection (7.4 miles from US 24) and bear left on the Hagerman Pass Road (Forest Service Road 105) and drive 3.6 miles to the trailhead parking lot, located on the south side of the road.

41. Windsor Lake ★★★★☆
Distance: 2.2 miles (RT)

This short, strenuous hike visits picturesque Windsor Lake, an alpine jewel cradled beneath the peaks and ridges along the Continental Divide in the Mount Massive Wilderness Area.

Distance: 2.2 miles (RT) to Lake
Elevation: 10,800-ft. at Trailhead
11,640-ft. at Windsor Lake
Elevation Gain: 840-ft. to Lake
Difficulty: strenuous

Base camp: Leadville
Area: Mount Massive Wilderness, San Isabel NF
Best Season: July –September
USGS Map(s): Mount Massive
See Page 174 for Map

Why Hike to Windsor Lake

The short hike to pretty Windsor Lake is very steep but well worth the effort. The trail heads straight uphill, gaining almost 800-ft in the first 0.8 miles. The final 0.3 miles traverses pretty alpine meadows on a gentle gradient to the rocky shores of Windsor Lake, nestled in a scenic granite basin along the eastern flank of the Continental Divide. The lake is a popular destination for fishermen and hikers looking for a nice half day hike in the Leadville area.

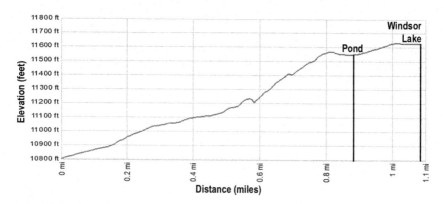

Trailhead to Windsor Lake

The Windsor Lake trailhead, located on the west side of the road across from the parking area (see driving directions), immediately crosses an aqueduct on a small dam. The aqueduct is channeled through the Busk Ivanhoe Tunnel, located 100-yards northwest of the trailhead. The tunnel, part of the Fryingpan-Arkansas project, carries water across the Continental Divide from Ivanhoe Lake, on the west side of the divide, to Busk Creek.

Reach the trail register a short distance past the crossing. The open hillside around the register provides nice views of the Continental Divide to the northwest and Galena Mountain to the northeast.

Beyond the register the trail starts its uphill assault, climbing a dry hillside along the north bank of the creek draining Windsor Lake. Soon the path enters the trees and the Mount Massive Wilderness. As you ascend, openings in the trees provide views of the rocky ridge defining the eastern flank of the Continental Divide.

The grade abates a bit as the trail crosses the creek draining Windsor Lake on logs and then quickly resumes the stiff climb on the other side. At 0.5 miles the path begins a very steep ascent of the hillside, gaining 440-ft. in just over 0.3 miles. Slightly before reaching the top of the hill the trail passes an old mine shaft.

At the top of the hill the trail emerges on a large meadow with a picturesque pond. Views extend west to the granite peaks and ridges along the Continental Divide. The trail stays to the left (south) of the pond, skirting the edge of the forest, and then gently climbs a rocky meadow scattered with conifers to Windsor Lake.

Windsor Lake lies cradled in a large granite basin clad in meadows littered with rock outcroppings and trees. To the west the high peaks and ridges of the Continental Divide command you attention. The rocky shoreline is a favorite with fishermen and the surrounding landscape harbors many nice campsites.

After relaxing by the lake retrace your steps down the steep trail to the trailhead.

Driving Directions

From Leadville: From US 24 in Leadville, turn west on County Road 4/McWethy Drive and drive 3 miles to a three way "Y" intersection. (Paved to left, dirt in the center, paved to right.) Take the paved road to the right at the intersection to stay on County Road 4, following the signs to Turquoise Lake. Further on the road will travel along the south side of the lake.

Toward the head of the lake reach a "Y" intersection (7.4 miles from US 24) and bear left on the Hagerman Pass Road (Forest Service Road 105) and drive 3.7 miles to the large trailhead parking lot, located on the right (east) side of the road. The parking area is at the head of a hairpin curve, right before the road turns right (northeast).

42. Colorado Midland ★★★★☆
Distance: 6.0 - 7.0 miles (RT)

This hike follows the railroad bed of the first standard gauge line to cross the Continental Divide and ends at the Hagerman Tunnel (11,528-ft.), the highest railroad tunnel in the world at the time it was built in 1887.

Distance: 6.0-7.0 miles (RT) to Hagerman Tunnel
Elevation: 10,940-ft. at Trailhead 11,528-ft. at Hagerman Tunnel
Elevation Gain: 550-ft. to Hagerman Tunnel

Difficulty: easy-moderate
Base camp: Leadville
Area: White River NF
Best Season: July –September
USGS Map(s): Homestake Reservoir

Why Hike the Colorado Midland Trail

This easy, interesting hike walks along sections of the Colorado Midland railroad bed to Hagerman Tunnel (11,528-ft.), the highest railroad tunnel in the world at the time it was built in 1887. Construction of the line, the first standard gauge line to cross the Continental Divide, is considered by some to be one of the greatest feats in railroad history. Along the way the trail  traverses pretty meadows, visits two small lakes and passes the remains of trestles, snow sheds, cuts through solid rock and the ruins of Douglass City, which housed immigrants that built the line.

Trailhead to the Hagerman Tunnel

On the drive to the Colorado Midland/Hagerman Tunnel trailhead (see driving directions below) be sure to stop at Busk-Ivanhoe Tunnel (10,953-ft.), located 3.7-miles up the Hagerman Pass road (one mile before the Colorado Midland trailhead). The tunnel, completed in 1893, is 9,393-ft. long and was built to replace the Hagerman Tunnel, which was too expensive to maintain due to its high elevation.

The Busk-Ivanhoe was converted to auto traffic in 1922 after the railroad abandoned it and renamed the Carlton Tunnel. The tunnel remained open to automobile traffic until 1943. Today it is part of the Fryingpan-Arkansas water diversion project, which brings water from Colorado's Western Slope to the Front Range.

The Colorado Midland-Hagerman Tunnel trail starts on the west side of the Hagerman Pass Road, across from the trailhead parking area (see Driving Directions below). Follow the trail as it heading northwest and then makes a wide arc to the south/southwest. At 1.5 miles reach a ravine, where the trail takes a sharp right. This is the site of the former Hagerman Trestle. This curved trestle, 1,100-ft. in length and 84-ft. high, made a wide arc to the northeast to a higher grade that you will reach shortly on the trail.

The trail, which does not follow the route of the trestle, turns right (northeast) onto an old road and climbs to meet the railroad bed at the higher grade. Where the trail meets the grade you have two choices. The first option follows a shortcut trail that crosses the grade and continues on the old road to the ruins of Douglass City, home of the Italian railroad workers who built this part of the line. This city once boasted eight drinking establishments and a dance hall full of "jaded women." It is now one of the more spectacular wildflower areas in this part of the Sawatch Range. Beyond Douglass City the trail climbs to the right (east) of Opal Lake and reaches another segment of the railroad bed just before the Hagerman Tunnel in 0.6 miles.

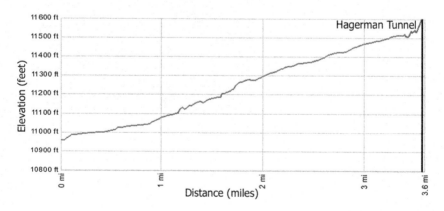

Alternatively, and my preferred route, is to turn right when you reach the railroad grade and follow the grade to the site of a second trestle that spans a deep cut at 2.5 miles. Slightly before reaching the second trestle site there is a trail that goes left (northwest), bypassing the cut. I recommend continuing along the grade as it curves around to the northwest to meet the bypass trail and then traverses the south side of pretty Hagerman Lake.

Beyond Hagerman Lake the trail passes the sites of 13 snow sheds that protected the rails from snow slides. Scattered pieces of lumber are all that is left of the sheds.

It is only a short distance from the shed sites to the east portal of Hagerman Tunnel (11,528-ft.). As you approach the tunnel views open to Opal Lake, located in a bowl below the trail. Just before the tunnel you will see the spur trail dropping down to the east side of Opal Lake to meet a road. This is the other end of the shortcut trail which passes the Douglass City and ends at a lower segment of the railroad grade.

The Hagerman Tunnel, completed in 1887, is 2,161-ft. long, 16-ft. high and 18-ft. wide and cost $200,000 to build. It was replaced by the Busk Ivanhoe tunnel in 1891, which you passed on the way to the trailhead. Today the entrance to the Hagerman Tunnel is partially blocked by a rockslide and floor of the tunnel is usually covered by thick ice. It is not safe to enter the tunnel.

For the return trip either retrace your steps (7 miles RT) or take the shortcut trail that lead past Opal Lake and the Douglass site. This semi-loop is 6.0 miles RT.

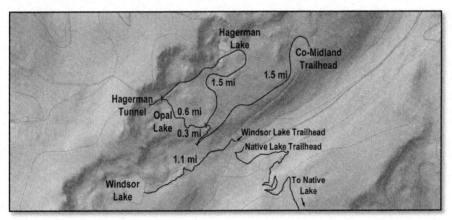

Driving Directions

From Leadville: From US 24 in Leadville, turn west on County Road 4/McWethy Drive and drive 3 miles to a three way "Y" intersection. (Paved to left, dirt in the center, paved to right.) Take the paved road to the right at the intersection to stay on County Road 4, following the signs to Turquoise Lake. Further on the road will travel along the south side of the lake.

Toward the head of the lake reach a "Y" intersection (7.4 miles from US 24) and bear left on the Hagerman Pass Road (which becomes Forest Service Road 105) and drive 4.7 miles to the trailhead parking lot, located on the east side of the road. The trail starts on the west side of the road.

Appendix: Hiking Tips
Staying healthy and safe in the backcountry.

Hiking in the backcountry is a wonderful experience but can also be hazardous if you are not properly prepared. Here are some tips to help you to stay healthy and safe. For more backcountry hiking safety information check out the Hiking Safety tips from the American Hiking Society.

Trip Preparation

Your trip will be more enjoyable and safer if you take the time to plan it at home. Use forest recreation maps, topographic maps and trail guides to create an itinerary, calculate mileage and elevation gains, understand the terrain and learn about any potential hazards.

Take someone with you. Traveling with at least one hiking companion adds to your safety margin.

Before leaving home always leave your itinerary with a relative or friend. Write a full account of who is going, where you are going and when you will be back. For overnight trips include where you plan to stay each night.

Check current conditions posted on the forest service website to find out if there are any know hazards such as slippery roads, high fire danger and flash flood warnings. If possible, stop by the nearest Ranger Station before your trip to get the latest information.

Get in shape before the trip. Do not attempt a trip that is beyond your physical capabilities. Fatigue often leads to injuries.

What to Pack

Sudden shifts in weather are one of the backcountry's greatest dangers. Dress in layers and take the gear needed to keep you warm and dry if the weather turns for the worse. It may seem silly to carry a hat, gloves, rain gear (including pants) and a Polartec when starting your hike on a beautiful sunny day. But you will be glad you have carried all this gear if you get caught in high country during a ferocious afternoon thunderstorm with gale force wind, plummeting temperatures, hail and heavy rains.

I recommend that you bring a warm fleece or wool pullover, a waterproof jacket and pants, a hat, sunglasses, sunscreen, lip balm, insect repellant, first-aid kit, pocket knife, flashlight or headlamp, waterproof matches, maps, compass, a mirror and whistle for signaling if you are lost, plenty of water, and extra food. Wear sturdy boots that are broken in and are comfortable and know how they respond to wet slippery surfaces. A trekking pole or walking stick can be very helpful in maintaining your balance in hazardous conditions Take plenty of water and food. It's very important to drink water! See the section on dehydration under hazards.

Weather

Before you leave check the current weather forecast and change your plans if necessary.

Weather in the mountains is unpredictable. A beautiful sunny day can turn nasty in a blink of an eye. Keep an eye on the weather. High passes, exposed ridges, areas above the timberline, open meadows and isolated trees are dangerous places to be during a lightning storm. Respect Mother Nature and head downhill when you see storms approaching.

During July and August thunderstorms are most common in the afternoons. Your best bet is to get your butt out of bed early and plan your day so you are down from the high passes and ridges by early afternoon to avoid any potential bad weather.

Heavy rains can cause rivers and streams to rise rapidly. The stream you rock-hopped across on the way up the trail can become a raging torrent that becomes hazardous to cross. When in doubt, wait out the storm and let the rivers go down before trying to cross. Move to higher ground and avoid gullies and drainages.

Hazards

Giardia: Don't Drink the Water!!! Giardia, a microscopic organism that can cause severe diarrhea for up to two weeks, is widespread. You should assume all waterways are infected. The most effective treatment to make water safe to drink is to boil it. A good filter can also remove most harmful organisms present in mountain water. Choose a filter with a pore size less than 0.5 microns or a Steripen. These filters will effectively remove most harmful bacteria and protozoa (including Giardia) or, in the case of a Steripen, sterilize the water. Another option is to use iodine tablets to disinfect water collected on the hike. For short trips take a supply of water from home or other domestic sources.

Dehydration and Heat: Heat exhaustion and heat stroke can result from continued exposure to high temperatures and inadequate or unbalanced replacement of fluids. Adults require two quarts of water per day and four quarts or more for strenuous activity at high elevations. To maintain a high energy level and avoid dehydration by:

- Drink 8 to 16 ounces of water before hiking.
- Drink frequently when on the trail.
- Drink as much water as possible during lunch and throughout the evening.
- Limit caffeine drinks such as coffee or cola.
- Avoid alcoholic drinks.
- Plan ahead for drinking water. Don't allow water to run out before resupplying.
- Take breaks in the shade.

Prevent sunburn by wearing lightweight, light colored, and loose fitting clothing that allows air to circulate and sweat to evaporate while offering protection from direct sun. Bare skin absorbs the sun's radiant heat and raises body temperature. Understand the signs and symptoms of heat disorders including heat cramps, heat exhaustion and heat stroke.

Hypothermia: Hypothermia, caused by rapid loss of body heat, is the most dangerous illness of backcountry travel. Hypothermia can occur even in the warm summer months. Symptoms of hypothermia include: apathy, confusion, drowsiness, loss of coordination, pale or cold skin, uncontrollable shivering, shock, slurred speech, and weakness.

To prevent hypothermia, wear non-cotton clothing in layers, including a waterproof outer layer, that allow you to adjust to changing weather and temperatures. To treat hypothermia get the victim out of the wind and any wet clothing they may be wearing. Because skin-to-skin contact can quickly warm somebody back up again, place the victim in a dry sleeping bag then have one or two heat donors surround the victim. When fit for travel, carry or help the victim walk out and get medical attention as soon as possible.

Lightning: During a lightning storm avoid mountaintops, ridgelines, trees, rocks, and boulder fields. Go to a low-lying area and move away from others in your group. Turn off your electronic devices and remove any metal objects you are carrying including jewelry, watches, keys, knife, etc. Make your body a single point ground by putting your ankles and knees together and then crouching down. This posture lessens your chances of being a lightning rod or of a charge entering one foot from the ground, traveling through your vital organs, and exiting through your other foot. Do not lie flat on the ground because electrical current from a strike can easily travel through your vital organs this way, too. If your hair stands on end, immediately take the above safety precautions. A lightning strike could be eminent.

Altitude Sickness: Altitude sickness may occur if you overexert at high elevations (above 5,000 feet) where oxygen supply is reduced. Symptoms of high altitude sickness include nausea, dizziness, confusion, and fatigue. Before hiking at high altitudes it is best to acclimatize yourself by sleeping at these elevations a night or two. If you or someone in your party experiences high altitude sickness symptoms on a hike, do not go any higher! Descend as quickly as possible and, if symptoms get worse, get medical attention.

Fatigue: Exhaustion and fatigue occur because the person may be pushing too hard and is embarrassed to ask the group to slow down. A good principle of backcountry travel is take it slow, rest often, drink and eat snacks frequently to restore body energy and stay warm.

Fatigue slows your awareness and preparedness to hike safely. Watch out for other members of your party getting fatigued and take appropriate action and care.

Leave No Trace

Always practice Leave No Trace technique with hiking and backpacking. Please visit the Leave No Trace website to learn about the 7 Leave No Trace Principles.

Other Useful Tips

Hiking on Variable Terrain: Identify safe routes and local conditions. Test and use secure footing and never run down slopes. Step over logs, not on them. Know how to fall; protect your head and back and roll with the fall. Take extra precautions when encountering steep, loose, or wet trails.

Horses and Pack Stock: When you encounter travelers who have horses or pack stock, move off the trail on the downhill side and let them pass. Horses are easily frightened and have the right-of-way on trails.

Fall Hunting Season: We recommend that you don't hike alone during hunting season and that you stay on established trails. All hikers, as well their dogs, should wear at least one piece of florescent orange clothing during hunting season.

Bears: Bears are generally shy and will avoid people. If you should encounter a bear on the trail, back away slowly while facing the bear. Before you hike in Bear Country be sure to read Be Bear Aware, published by the Sierra National Forest.

CPSIA information can be obtained
at www.ICGtesting.com
Printed in the USA
LVOW13s1731050218
565344LV00045B/2220/P

9 780997 478013